1986

IN
WHOSE
BEST
INTEREST?

———————————————

IN
WHOSE
BEST
INTEREST?

CHILD
WELFARE REFORM
IN THE
PROGRESSIVE ERA

SUSAN TIFFIN

CONTRIBUTIONS TO THE STUDY OF CHILDHOOD AND YOUTH,
NUMBER 1

Greenwood Press
Westport, Connecticut • London, England

Library of Congress Cataloging in Publication Data

Tiffin, Susan.
    In whose best interest?

    (Contributions to the study of childhood and youth,
ISSN 0273-124X ; no. 1)
        Bibliography: p.
        Includes index.
        1. Child welfare--United States.   I. Title.
II. Series.
HV741.T53   362.7'95'0973   81-908
ISBN 0-313-22944-9 (lib. bdg.)   AACR2

Library of Congress Catalog Card Number: 81-908
ISBN: 0-313-22944-9
ISSN: 0273-124X

First published in 1982

Greenwood Press
A division of Congressional Information Service, Inc.
88 Post Road West
Westport, Connecticut 06881

Printed in the United States of America

10 9 8 7 6 5 4 3 2 1

FOR ANDREW

CONTENTS

ACKNOWLEDGMENTS

I should like to express my thanks to Ian Bickerton and Kathleen Woodroofe for their supervision and criticism of this research. The American Council of Learned Societies made the completion of this project possible by awarding me a scholarship to pursue my studies in the United States, where I received an enormous amount of assistance from library staff, particularly at the Joseph Regenstein Library at the University of Chicago, the library of the University of Illinois at Chicago Circle, and the Social Welfare Archives, University of Minnesota, Minneapolis. Final thanks should be given also to Robert Bremner for his advice and hospitality.

IN
WHOSE
BEST
INTEREST?

INTRODUCTION

We have frequently heard the United States described as a "child-centered" society, as a nation that, if anything, has erred on the side of excessive indulgence and sentimentality. Undoubtedly, the concept of youth is central to American culture; the nation's very beginnings, for instance, were seen in stark contrast to an old and corrupt Europe. Today "youth" is prized; it is big business. The necessity to look, feel, act, and think young infiltrates all aspects of employment, consumerism, and entertainment. The preoccupation with youth contributes to a neglect of old age and a denial of death.

It seems surprising, therefore, that until recently students interested in the place of childhood and youth in American history would have discovered a virtual void of information and analysis. Attracted by more vociferous groups and grander conflicts, historians tended to relegate the experience of children to the collectors of factual snippets.[1] There have been exceptions,[2] but in general it has been the behavioral sciences that have made the family and its members a focus of attention. Little was done by historians until the mid-1960s when they began to recognize this area as both viable and valuable. No doubt, interest in the child and the family was stimulated by the growing fields of urban and

women's history. It also received an impetus from current contro-
versies on intergenerational conflict and the future of the family
unit. The result was a number of seminal works that fell into two
broad categories: those dealing with the actual life experiences of
families and the socialization of children and those investigating
reform movements for child welfare.[3] The latter are an obvious off-
shoot of a wider inquiry into humanitarian reform that has occupied historians for some years. A wide variety of studies have
been carried out since 1957, when Merle Curti called the attention
of historians to philanthropy as a field of research.[4] They comprise
individual biographies and organizational analyses, studies of the
professionalization of social work, and accounts of legislative campaigns. They encompass all areas of disease, delinquency, and
dependency. (A discussion of the meaning of "dependency" is
found at the beginning of Chapter 2.)

The current interest in children and reform has also been encouraged by recent debate on the rights of children and their
experiences under the present welfare system. Although America
celebrates "youth," this has not led to just treatment by the state
of those Americans who are classified as minors. Nor does it
follow that the growth of the child's autonomy and potential for
individual fulfillment are furthered by a parental love of "cute-
ness" and a susceptibility to the advertising campaigns of multi-
million-dollar industries. Of late the myth of America's love of
children has been seriously questioned. It has been queried whether
adults have, in fact, consigned juveniles to a self-contained and
less-than-adult world, possibly to protect their own position. Does
making children more comfortable on their side of the barrier
really mitigate the fact that the segregation is made more complete
by prolonging adolescence on the grounds of preparing youth for
the complexities of the modern world? In their contact with authority, children have been largely viewed as an adjunct to the adult
world. Consequently their rights have been subordinated to those
of their parents and of other social agencies.

A number of professionals in law, psychology, and social work
have embarked upon a fairly comprehensive reassessment of the
efficiency of the U.S. welfare system. They have tackled both the
quantitative inadequacy and the qualitative deficiencies of the

services. Their investigations have revealed a system riddled with discretionary authority and class bias, which frequently does no more than perpetuate the status quo and often forces children into a life of desperation and lovelessness.[5]

This wide-ranging debate has given an added impetus both to an interest in the origin and development of the child welfare system and to a reevaluation of the standpoints of the groups involved. Several works have recently been produced. Robert H. Bremner's three-volume documentary history of childhood and youth from colonial times to the present stands out as a major reference on this subject. This massive collection of source materials is the result of a project undertaken by the American Public Health Association to update the work done by the former federal Children's Bureau chief, Grace Abbott. Although it broadens the area of concern to include, for example, health, education, and minority groups, the new study's emphasis has remained on public policy. It does not purport to comprise a history of childhood and youth as such, although it does illuminate many corners of child life, while tracing the development of legislation, institutional care, and the organizational structure of the welfare system.[6]

Of the significant monographs on child welfare published in the 1970s, most have devoted themselves to juvenile delinquency. An exception is Walter I. Trattner's interesting account of the National Child Labor Committee and its fight for regulatory legislation. In *Crusade for the Children* Trattner discusses the economic forces that generated and later undermined the practice of child labor and the conditions that provoked a varied coalition of concerned people to form a national organization devoted to its abolition. Led by professional social workers, the committee waged a prolonged battle not completed until the middle of the twentieth century.[7] Other historians have been more interested in America's attempts to come to terms with juvenile crime and antisocial behavior. Written from different critical vantage points, books by Joseph M. Hawes, Robert Mennel, Anthony M. Platt, Stephen Schlossman, and Jack M. Holl have traced the development of the institutions and court system devised to process and treat juvenile delinquents. They offer a comprehensive picture of the achievements and failures of nineteenth- and early-twentieth-century reform in this area of child welfare.[8]

This study is concerned with another important group of children, the orphaned, destitute, deserted, illegitimate, and ill-treated.
This group was a particular concern of reformers and philanthropists in the late nineteenth and early twentieth centuries. Surprisingly, dependent and neglected children have received very
little historical attention, despite the fact that they provoke as much
anxiety as the more problematic delinquents or the more obviously
distressed physically and mentally handicapped. Where they have
been discussed, it has been largely in connection with delinquency.
Reformers in the Progressive era were somewhat prone to treat
dependency and neglect as the first stages in the development of
adolescent troublemakers. Historians have considered these
children in the same vein. It is hoped that this study will go some
way toward correcting the imbalance.

Its purpose is to investigate the reasons for the accelerated
interest between 1890 and 1920 in dependent and neglected children
and to examine the various changes that were designed to alter and
improve their environment. The study is not exclusively an account
of the legislative innovations, nor is it a history of developing
social work techniques. Rather, it covers a spectrum of activity
including campaigns for new laws, changes in the structure of the
welfare system, and the adoption of new methods of care and standards of treatment. These activities were inextricably intertwined.
The desire to rescue these unfortunate and supposedly dangerous
youngsters brought reform in diverse areas. For example, the
same concern for the survival of the family unit that generated a
campaign for widows' pensions also encouraged the growth of
foster care at the expense of institutional care and transformed
the treatment methods of child-care agencies. A further link
between the different developments relating to dependent and
neglected children is provided by the men and women responsible
for these changes. Campaigns to reduce dependency and neglect
involved shifting coalitions of reformers from many walks of life,
but social workers were in the vanguard. Leading social workers
such as Homer Folks strove untiringly to protect children. At the
same time, they were among the foremost spokespersons for the
new methods of treating cases of dependency and neglect.

In view of the considerable differences in the child welfare systems of the individual states, a complete account of the changes involved is impractical. However, from proceedings of national conferences of charities and from widely-circulated journals and contemporary monographs, general trends in thought and action can be traced. For more specific information I have turned largely to the states of Illinois, New York, and Massachusetts. The annual reports and publications of major children's agencies provide missing details. It may be objected that these three states do not give a comprehensive picture of child-saving activities in the period, that more attention might have been given to the South and West. In the future local studies may illuminate conditions and changes in these areas.[9] Since this study attempts to cover broad developments, it concentrates on three states that were in the vanguard of the child welfare movement. The urgent urban problems of Chicago, New York City, and Boston forced reformers into an early search for the best solution to their problems of disease, destitution, and delinquency. In addition, these three states offer valuable contrasts and comparisons. They varied in the type of care and protection given and in the relative importance placed on public and private welfare.

Why, then, did children, and specifically dependent and neglected children, become the subject of widespread and intensive concern toward the end of the nineteenth century? The increased visibiltiy rested on more than the pressing nature of their deprivation and ill-treatment; it also depended on a pervasive consciousness of childhood as a sociological phenomenon. The United States, like many other nations, was becoming increasingly aware of children as a distinct group with particular characteristics. The new concern was further influenced by a reassessment of the consequences of nineteenth-century economic, political, and social developments for the quality and stability of American life. Those who saw America threatened by internal weaknesses and dissension looked to the child for the nation's salvation. Successful socialization and education of the American child was central to the Progressive vision. By providing the child with a healthy, moral, and secure home environment, adequate schooling, and humane working conditions, reformers envisaged a future American society largely untroubled by vice, crime, and poverty. Class antagonisms, ethnic divisions, and racial tensions would be replaced by cooperation, harmony, and a common adherence to the ideals of American industrial capitalism.

The period 1890 to 1920 saw a host of reform campaigns aimed to improve the child's environment. Compulsory education laws were extended; new schools and vocational institutions were created; and curricula were restructured, while a complementary movement tried to restrict and control the conditions of child labor. New legislation and welfare agencies were designed to cope with juvenile problems. The creation of the first juvenile court in 1899 and the federal Children's Bureau in 1912; the establishment of new agencies and programs to deal with the physically and mentally handicapped, the destitute, and the neglected; the campaign to reduce maternal and infant mortality; public pensions for mothers with dependent children; legislation to improve the child's legal status with respect to his parents—these far from exhaust the list of reforms designed to produce healthy, industrious U.S. citizens. In addition, more wide-ranging reforms to combat disease, improve sanitation and housing, and provide workers with economic security were all undertaken with a recognition of their necessity for the proper development of America's youth.

The problems of youth were thus not merely humanitarian concerns; they were also important problems of social order. The issue of social order has received considerable attention of late. Certain historians of the U.S. welfare system and reform movements have taken a closer look at the background and material interests of the body of reformers who instigated changes. In doing so they have queried the earlier belief in a consensus among the American people and stressed the conflict between groups. They have brought to light the possibility that so-called humanitarian reforms may have actually done more to control underprivileged groups than to benefit them.

Platt's work, *The Child Savers*, is a clear example of this approach. As a lawyer with a strong grasp of current failings in the juvenile justice system, Platt cast a disillusioned eye over the humanitarian impulse that was supposedly the guiding force behind the establishment of the juvenile court in 1899. Juvenile delinquency, according to Platt, is an ascriptive label given by the controlling groups in society. He finds that, in the late nineteenth century, the label was given by upper- and middle-class reformers to the behavior of lower-class, predominantly immigrant, children. The child-saving movement in Illinois, in his opinion, was more concerned with restriction than with liberation and resulted in a system that, by discarding procedural formality and encouraging dependency on extralegal resources, worked against the children's interests. According to this approach the apparent idealism underlying reform for juvenile delinquents was little more than sweet-talking self-interest. Reforms were designed to control these "dangerous" youngsters rather than to liberate them.[10]

Some historians have used the concept of "social control" to describe the process by which ruling groups try to maintain social relationships conducive to their own dominance. This is a controversial term. The ways in which it has been applied have varied considerably, and the term has been used to cover broad changes in the functioning of whole societies as well as marginal adjustments in apparently stable societies. Some historians have defined it so broadly that it is virtually identical with socialization; others have reduced it to specifically conscious attempts by ruling groups to manipulate the lower classes in their own interests. "Social control" has been used by writers who accept a consensus view of society and, despite recent criticism,[11] by adherents to a class conflict model.

Problems have arisen essentially from the simplistic application of the concept, from the assumption that it is "a philosopher's stone whose discovery will resolve the problems of social history."[12] Historians should rightly beware of a term that may reduce the complex conflicts between classes and groups to a simple formula or may imply that such control is necessarily or inevitably successful. Nevertheless, the focus on "social control" has pointed historians of social welfare in the right direction, towards the dominant social and economic forces that determine the existing basis of social relationships. The process of maintaining this basis is a continuous and dynamic one. However, there are times when the question of social order is perceived as more urgent. The late nineteenth century was such a period: the masses, and particular groups within the "lower orders," were defined as a problem; the nature of class and ethnic antagonism was a crucial issue; and the urban scene was considered a source of instability. Social order was sought through a wide variety of economic, political, and ideological means. The barrage of welfare reforms for children was part of this process. That is not to say that the changes put forward under the banner of humanitarianism were necessarily conscious efforts to maintain existing social relationships, nor that the controlling element was the only meaning or even the main characteristic of such reforms. Calls for social justice cannot be seen as merely a hypocritical or self-delusive front for class interest. The visible zeal with which reformers acted on behalf of destitute and handicapped children cannot be dismissed as a cynical use of religion or humanitarianism to defend their own economic and political power. Ideals must be given real weight. Nevertheless, we cannot return to a bland acceptance that pure altruism guided the footsteps of all those who claimed to be "doing good." The values and aims of the predominantly middle-class, professional reformers not surprisingly separated them in many ways from the largely working-class beneficiaries of reform. The stable society they promoted was one in which they took predominant roles, and there was little acknowledgment that what was good for "society" was not necessarily good for those who suffered in the system.

The inherent contradictions in the desire for social order and social justice meant that many of the reforms were limited in scope. For example, the public pensions for mothers with dependent children that were introduced in the second decade of the twentieth century were, in many states, originally limited to widows. Provisions for unwed mothers, divorcees, and even deserted wives were often specifically denied because they might sanction or encourage immorality and family irresponsibility. These women, despite their need, could not be guaranteed economic security to raise their children. Similarly, many welfare benefits were conditional upon the recipient's adherence to middle-class behavioral norms. If they refused to accept restrictions on their sexual behavior, drinking, cleanliness, and other habits, the mothers might be removed from the pension roll.

The following study will, among other things, explore these contradictions at greater length. In addition to the attempt to prevent separation of families by offering public pensions, it will examine the gradual replacement of institutions by foster care as the most desirable method of rearing children outside their natural home, the tightening of desertion and illegitimacy laws, the development of public welfare facilities, and changes in the standards of casework for dependent and neglected children. By these various channels the urban middle-class professionals who concerned themselves with child welfare tried to achieve both social order and social justice. The results frequently demonstrated the complex tensions between these aims.

NOTES

1. For example, Alice Earle's study, *Child Life in Colonial Days* (New York: Macmillan, 1899), while a fascinating storehouse of detail, makes no attempt to place these customs of child-rearing and educational practices in any wider social context.

2. Arthur W. Calhoun, *A Social History of the American Family from Colonial Times to the Present*, 3 vols. (New York: Barnes & Noble, 1960). This traces the changes in family life brought about by the frontier experience, slavery, industrialization, urbanization, and immigration. It still retains its usefulness for those concerned with general trends. Edmund S. Morgan's dissertation, *The Puritan Family: Essays on Religion and Domestic Relations in Seventeenth Century New England* (Boston: Trustees of the Public Library, 1944), discusses the mutual obligations between parent and child and relates these to Puritan ideas of sanctification, salvation, and the order of creation. Bernard Bailyn in his *Education in the Forming of American Society* (Chapel Hill: University of North Carolina Press, 1960), points out the effects of economic changes in the removal of the educational function of the family to external agencies.

3. The impact of sociology, psychology, cultural anthropology, and demography has been profound, as evidenced in the emergence of such periodicals as the *Journal of Family History* and the *History of Childhood Quarterly*. For an early discussion of the boundaries and problems of family history see Tamara K. Hareven, "The History of the Family as an Interdisciplinary Field," *Journal of Interdisciplinary History* 1 (1971): 399-414. Among the notable attempts to utilize concepts from the other social sciences are Philip Greven, *Four Generations: Population, Land*

and Family in Colonial Andover, Massachusetts (Ithaca, N.Y.: Cornell University Press, 1970); John Demos, *A Little Commonwealth: Family Life in Plymouth Colony* (New York: Oxford University Press, 1970); Richard Sennett, *Families against the City: Middle Class Homes of Industrial Chicago, 1872-1890* (Cambridge, Mass.: Harvard University Press, 1970). For recent studies of child welfare reform, see notes 7 and 8 below.

4. Merle Curti, "The History of American Philanthropy as a Field of Research," *American Historical Review* 62 (1957): 352-63. For example, see: Clarke C. Chambers, *Seedtime of Reform: American Social Service and Social Action 1918-1933* (Minneapolis: University of Minnesota Press, 1963); Roy Lubove, *The Professional Altruist: The Emergence of Social Work as a Career 1880-1930* (Cambridge, Mass.: Harvard University Press, 1965); Walker I. Trattner: *Homer Folks: Pioneer in Social Welfare* (Chicago: Quadrangle Books, 1970).

5. A devastating account of the hazards juveniles face in the justice system has been given by Patrick Murphy, *Our Kindly Parent the State: The Juvenile System and How it Works* (New York: Viking Press, 1974). See also Sanford Katz, ed., *The Youngest Minority: Lawyers in Defense of Children* (Chicago: American Bar Association, 1974). A more child-centered analysis has also been made of institutional and foster care, criticizing these agencies for being based on expectations of mediocrity, for maintaining class distinctions, and for being insensitive to the children's individual needs. See, for example, Alvin Schorr, ed., *Children and Decent People* (New York: Basic Books, 1974).

6. Robert H. Bremner, ed., *Children and Youth in America: A Documentary History*, 3 vols. (Cambridge, Mass.: Harvard University Press, 1970-1974). Grace Abbott, *The Child and the State*, 2 vols. (Chicago: University of Chicago Press, 1938).

7. Walter I. Trattner, *Crusade for the Children* (Chicago: Quadrangle Books, 1970).

8. Joseph M. Hawes, *Children in Urban Society: Juvenile Delinquency in Nineteenth Century America* (New York: Oxford University Press, 1971); Robert Mennel, *Thorns and Thistles: Juvenile Delinquency in the United States 1825-1940* (Hanover, N.H.: University Press of New England, 1973); Anthony M. Platt, *The Child Savers: The Invention of Delinquency* (Chicago: University of Chicago Press, 1969); Stephen L. Schlossman, *Love and the American Delinquent: The Theory and Practice of "Progressive" Juvenile Justice* (Chicago: University of Chicago Press, 1977); Jack M. Holl, *Juvenile Reform in the Progressive Era: William R. George and the Junior Republic Movement* (Ithaca, N.Y.: Cornell University Press, 1971).

9. See, for example, Thomas E. Williams, "The Dependent Child in Mississippi 1900-1970" (Ph.D. diss., Ohio State University, 1976).

10. Platt, *The Child Savers*, pp. 1-14.

11. Gareth Stedman Jones, "Class Expression versus Social Control," *History Workshop* 4 (1977): 163-70. Jones criticizes the use by Marxists of a term derived from consensus writers. He says it is not possible to merely add it to a Marxist interpretation, that its use necessarily involves adopting elements of the ideology from which it came.

12. A. P. Donajgrodzi, ed., *Social Control in Nineteenth Century Britain* (London: Rowman & Littlefield, 1978), p. 15.

1

THE
CHILD
AND THE
SOCIAL ORDER

In 1902 Swedish feminist Ellen K. S. Key wrote a controversial treatise on family relations in which she argued that the transformation of the twentieth century would only come about if society's central concern were the new generation. She entitled it *The Century of the Child*.[1] The phrase "the century of the child" became a commonplace in the United States. The expression was part of the vocabulary of various groups espousing humanitarian reforms under the banner of Progressivism. Arguments for improvements in health, the law, education, and working and living conditions all contained a line of logic that led to the child. Local, state, and national organizations promoted legislative and institutional changes designed specifically to alter the child's environment.

In part this concern was provoked by the obviously detrimental effect of industrialization and urbanization on the lives of many American children. It was not difficult to observe. Each tenement spilled out its collection of undernourished and ill-clothed children into the street that was their playground. More terribly, slum areas produced a steady flow of small coffins. The unfortunate physical and mental effects of uncontrolled labor were becoming more and more evident in homes and sweatshops, in factories and mines. These effects were captured in the prose and photography of men such as Jacob Riis and Lewis Hine.[2]

This alone, however, hardly explains the child's central position. The child was not only seen as the victim of American society but also as its savior. Salvation from current social problems seemed to lie in the innocence of children and their amenability to education. Social order and national greatness were thought to depend on their care and protection. "Here was a dream utterly alien to the late nineteenth century. Instead of molding youth in a slightly improved pattern of their fathers, like cyclically producing like, the new reformers thought in terms of fluid progress, a process of growth that demanded constant vigilance."[3]

To explain Americans' sensitivity and faith in this area, and to understand why dependent and neglected children became a focus of concern, it is necessary to look at two developments. The first is the changing status and image of the child, a change that took place largely in the nineteenth century; the second is the economic, social, and political trends of the post-Civil War period, which produced a demand for changes in the social fabric. The confluence of these developments dictated the importance of children in reform and the methods by which improvements were sought.

THE CHANGING STATUS AND IMAGE OF THE CHILD

From the eighteenth century, America, like other Western nations, became increasingly aware of the phenomenon of childhood.[4] It would hardly be an exaggeration to say that, in colonial America, childhood as a distinct period with particular needs, capacities, and consequences was unknown. A child's development was not seen in stages; the term "youth" applied variously to children, adolescents, and young men. In addition, the importance of early experience for adult behavior was hardly recognized. While the Puritans acknowledged that there might be indications of the course a person's life would take, they in no way saw it greatly determined by childhood. Thus biographies and autobiographies, where indeed they touched on the subject of childhood, gave more attention to remarkable and fortuitous events than to the organic growth of a personality. If anything, children were miniature adults, only differing from their elders in their lesser physical and mental capacity. This attitude extended even to children's clothing, which was merely a scaled-down version of their parents' dress.[5]

In a society where the emphasis lay on the function of the group and its relationship to the larger community, the individual child assumed a distinctly subordinate position. In part this was determined by economic necessity. Survival in the New World demanded a cooperative effort based on a division of labor according to age and sex. Large numbers of children were therefore welcomed, but their importance lay in their contribution to the welfare and interests of adults.[6] This position was further reinforced by a belief that family relationships were to be maintained according to the divine order of things. God had ordained that the parent should be superior to the child. Since "parents in regard to their children doe beare a singular image to God, as Hee is the Creator, Sustainer and Governour," their authority was to be unchallenged.[7] Innumerable treatises on manners set down the correct response of children in any situation. Reading them, it seems amazing that children ever expressed an opinion at all. Disobedience, being not only an offense against one's parents but also against the basic values of that society, was punished severely by fines, whipping and incarceration. The death sentence was provided by statute. In 1679 "Edward Bumpus, for stricking and abusing his parents, was whipt att the post; his punishment was alleviated in regard hee was crasey brained otherwise hee had bine put to death or otherwise sharply punished."[8] It seems unlikely, however, that this extreme sentence was ever carried out. Complete subordination was not only required by children's own fathers, but also demanded by the masters of youths under apprenticeship. The masters' duties and responsibilities were virtually identical to the fathers', and servants' obligations were as total as the obligations of children.[9]

Methods of child rearing were comprehensively spelled out. They rested on Calvinist suppositions that tended to deny the child the opportunity to develop a sense of autonomy. According to this view, children were born naturally sinful and might be redeemed only by repentance, baptism, and God's election of them to eternal life. Childhood was a state to be dispensed with as soon as possible and a period in which discipline, labor, and religious training were central concerns. If there was a key concept underlying child-rearing techniques, it was that the child's will should be completely broken. Most Puritan parents agreed with John Robinson that "there is in all children...a stubbornness, a stoutness of mind rising from natural pride, which must, in the first place, be broken and beaten down; that so the foundation of their education being laid in humility and tractableness, other virtues may, in their time, be built thereon....Children should not know, if it could be kept from them, that they have a will of their own, but in their parents' keeping.[10]

Although there is no evidence that parents in colonial America beat their children more often than their twentieth-century counterparts, corporal punishment was more accepted in principle, going hand in hand with the necessity of conquering the will. "When turned a year old...[children] were taught to fear the rod and to cry softly; by which means they escaped the abundance of correction they might otherwise have had."[11] Labor was another means of character formation, discouraging the dreadful sin of idleness. Most important of all in this process of training was religious instruction. This involved an early participation in adult services and a heavy load of reading and rote learning. There seems to have been little escape from the religious influence. Studies by Monica Kiefer and Bert Roller on children's literature during this period show that it was wholly designed to remind them of their precarious spiritual situation. The *New England Primer* was perhaps the epitome of the works available. The text was largely a discussion by children of the nearness of death, the necessity of conversion, and the value of obedience to parents and teachers as an aid to salvation. Arithmetic and spelling books were permeated with the same morbid pietism. General reading, whether narratives or the graceless, unadorned poetry written in America at the time, was overflowing with deathbed scenes in which children left this world either for damnation or for eternal life.[12]

ECONOMIC, SOCIAL, AND POLITICAL TRENDS

While this picture of the child's status is static, in actuality that status was gradually being undermined. The frontier way of life offered opportunities for independence. If land was available and labor at a premium, then it became easier to establish one's own household than it might have been in Europe.[13]

Rapid industrialization and urbanization after 1800 promoted further discontinuity of age groups. Previously, most farming families had a certain solidarity of interest. Their members performed similar tasks, enjoyed the same entertainment, and had the same circle of acquaintances. The children, for the most part, were training to be their parents' replacements. Life in a nineteenth-century city diversified the family members' interests and occupations. The child either no longer worked and therefore came under the control of external institutions or took a job unlike that of the parents. Under different influences, the desires and opinions of parents and children diverged. This was particularly evident in immigrant families, where the cultural gap between generations caused even more friction. Here, as in native American families, peer group contact began to oust intergeneration activities. The seeds of a youth culture were becoming visible.[14]

Despite the tenacity of parental, particularly paternal, authority during the nineteenth century, it was gradually undermined by the rapid economic changes taking place. Evidence for this may be found in the changing legal status of children. The father, particularly in cases of custody, was no longer automatically assumed to have the right of control.[15] It is harder to assess the degrees to which parental authority was also affected by ideas of equality and democracy. Alexis de Toqueville certainly saw a connection between democratic social tendencies and the family structure. He felt that "when the condition of the society becomes democratic and men adopt as their general principle that it is good and lawful to judge of all things for one's self, using former points of belief not as a rule of faith, but simply as a means of information, the power which the opinions of a father exercise over those of his sons diminishes, as well as the legal power."[16] Not all foreign visitors were so laudatory. The English, in particular, tended to find American children precocious, impertinent, and excessively indulged. According to one, there was "seldom any very great restraint imposed upon the youth of America whose precocious intellect brought forth and exercised at an early...age...has generally made them impatient of parental authority.[17]

Whatever the extent and cause of the changes in family relations, by the early nineteenth century, there was undeniably a significant amount of tension. This was reflected in the sudden appearance of large numbers of books on child rearing. In the 1820s American parents could secure, for the first time, a substantial body of information ranging from practical advice to theories on moral training.[18] They no longer had to use books written for English children and adopted by Americans; now books on child rearing were written specifically for American parents by their countrymen.

This upsurge of literature mirrored an increasing awareness of children as a distinct group whose interests were no longer identical with those of their parents or the greater community. It also attested to new ideas on the nature of childhood. Calvinist techniques were being replaced by techniques based on European romanticism. Romantic thought, a reaction against the materialistic, rationalistic, secularistic eighteenth century, was perhaps the most important influence on the changing image of childhood. Rousseau's *Emile* began this radical reappraisal, advancing the belief that everything was good as it left God and only degenerated in the hands of men. Thus the newborn child, being nearest to the divine, was naturally good, as opposed to the artificial, corrupt society in which that child would have to develop. Increasingly it was acknowledged that children have their own particular ways of feeling and thinking and are by no means miniature adults.

A cult of childhood had begun. In English literature childhood became an important and constant theme, symbolizing Nature, the Imagination, and Sensibility against a mechanistic, dehumanizing world. First appearing in the poetry of Blake and Wordsworth, the Romantic view of the child permeated the novel from the 1830s. It provided the inspiration for Eliot's *Silas Marner* and the acidic social criticisms in the novels of Dickens.[19] America followed suit. The decade before the Civil War saw the beginning of a spate of anti-Calvinist novels emphasizing the goodness of children and their amenability to a beneficial environment. In the hands of such writers as Timothy Shay Arthur and Harriet Beecher Stowe, the child became a saintly redeemer, bringing harmony to the family, comfort to the miserable, a sense of purpose to the aimless, religion to the doubter, and love to the misanthropist.[20] As American society grew more industrial and urban, the child as innocent was subsumed and transformed, emerging in the heroes of Horatio

Alger's stories and in Mark Twain's protagonists. Ragged Dick, finding that "in the boot-blacking business, as well as in higher avocations, the same rule prevails, that energy and industry are rewarded," achieves (with the requisite amount of sheer luck) the pinnacle of middle-class, capitalist aspirations.[21] He is a bourgeois savior who illuminates the myth of America as the land of golden opportunity. Tom Sawyer and Huckleberry Finn, reflecting a trend toward a more realistic depiction of boyhood, are, in their own way, innocents who function powerfully as moral commentators on "civilized" society.[22] Particularly after the Civil War, major American literary figures explored the various facets of childhood with a new interest. Some even turned to writing for children, and wrote for children's edification and entertainment rather than for their conversion. The days of the child as sinner had finally disappeared.

Just as important as this image transformation was the impetus Romantic thought, particularly on education, gave to an awareness of human development and of the consequences of child life for adult behavior. This sensitivity increased as the century progressed. When, in the last two decades, Romantic beliefs were amalgamated with concepts of evolution and the fruits of the rapidly developing social sciences, a full-fledged movement for child study emerged. While the movement declined after the first world war and much of its work was forgotten, for approximately thirty years it managed to hold together diverse educational, psychological, and medical elements in a common inquiry into the physical and mental characteristics of children. It advertised the significance of children for the future of America.

THE CHILD STUDY MOVEMENT

This catalytic movement was largely created by one man, G. Stanley Hall. Originally a student and teacher of philosophy, Hall forsook this discipline to become one of the leading figures in the early history of American psychology. Having obtained a doctorate from Harvard under William James and furthered his psychology studies in Germany, Hall pursued a successful career, first at Johns Hopkins University and later at the newly established Clark University in Worcester, Massachusetts.

According to Hall's biographer, Dorothy Ross, children occupied his attention from the early 1880s. Like many American educators, Hall had by that time absorbed the theories of such European pedagogues as Rousseau, Pestalozzi, and Froebel. He fully accepted the Romantic idea that "the guardians of the young should strive first of all to stay out of nature's way. They should feel profoundly that childhood, as it comes fresh from the hands of God is not corrupt, but illustrates the survival of the most consummate thing in the world.[23] Civilization had its claims, but the child's guidance and education should be in total harmony with the subject's natural impulses. To ensure this, it was thought necessary to acquire a thorough understanding of the normal pattern of development. Hall believed that he could expand current knowledge of perception and learning by basing pedagogy on the authority of science. In addition, he felt that child study would provide a foundation for the reconstruction of psychology. Hall was convinced that to understand the deeper springs of activity in adult life, it was necessary first to understand the psychic life of the child. He saw the need to counterbalance the then current concentration of American psychologists on experimentation with the adult mind. Beyond this, there was the light that child study might throw on the evolution of civilization itself. Having accepted the idea, derived from Darwin, that the development of the individual psyche recapitulated the evolution of the race, Hall hoped to correlate with exactness the sequences in each process.[24]

The field for research was wide open. Little scientific investigation had been accomplished up to that point. Early in the century a few systematic observations of juvenile behavior had been made in Germany. With the publication of Darwin's *Origin of Species*, the interest increased, resulting in such seminal works as Wilhelm Preyer's *Mind of the Child* (1881).[25] Calls for a scientific pedagogy were also being made at the University of Jena by Theodor Hebart and his disciples. It was clearly an area to which Hall could fruitfully bring not only his psychological expertise, but also his organizational talents and rhetorical skills. He made initial overtures to educationalists in a speech to superintendents of the National Education Association (NEA) in 1882. However, it was not until the 1890s that any organizational progress was achieved. Hall's appointment in psychology at Johns Hopkins temporarily diverted his interests and energy, but in 1891 he was brought back to the movement by the rapidly increasing number of reform-minded educators. Discussions at the meeting of the NEA in 1891 and at a summer school course at Clark University in the following year, and interest shown at the World's Columbia Exposition in 1893 paved the way for the formation of a Child Study Department in the NEA in 1894. As a result of internal dissension, no national organization for child study was founded, but individual states established their own groups, drawing the bulk of their support from upper-middle-class women. Clark University, under Hall's guidance, became the major center for research, while Harvard, Princeton, Yale, and some midwestern universities initiated their own courses in child development.[26]

The most important contributions made by the child study movement to a greater awareness of the uniqueness of childhood lay in three main areas. First, its studies helped to illuminate the basic emotions and interests that are characteristic of childhood and to distinguish the psychic makeup of different age groups. Utilizing the questionnaire method, Hall conducted systematic studies of, among other things, children's lies, fear, and anger. In doing so he revealed the complexity of a child's motivation and the need for a greater understanding of apparently antisocial behavior. It was Hall's hope that the sum total of the work done by the movement would be a comprehensive account of the periods in which certain powers and emotions dominated and the times at which rapid change was experienced. Although only partly successful, the movement did clarify the stages of development. In particular, Hall made what was probably the first systematic study of adolescence, which he considered the "golden stage when life glitters,"[27] "the apical stage of human development... before the decline of the higher power of the soul in maturity and age."[28] A full statement of his beliefs was published in 1904 under the awesome title, *Adolescence: Its Psychology, and Its Relation to Physiology, Anthropology, Sociology, Sex, Crime, Religion and Education*. Basically, Hall viewed this period as one of rapid physical and mental growth and of an increase in energy beginning at puberty. The relative harmony of childhood was replaced by a time of storm and stress, characterized by various antithetical impulses such as hyperactivity and inertness, selfishness and altruism, shyness and gregariousness.[29]

The other two areas of Hall's child study program centered on the school and its capacity to foster the child's physical and mental welfare. One channel of investigation involved the behavioral aspects of child development and education, concentrating on such facets as children's language and play activities. These pioneering studies provided the impulse for the growth of children's linguistics and for the playground movement, which blossomed in the 1890s. The second focus concerned health as a foundation for proper mental development. Child study experts, by expanding educators' concern about defects and disease to encompass wider problems of school hygiene, brought to fruition earlier independent attempts by physicians to rectify the poor conditions in American schools.[30]

As the twentieth century opened, support for the child study movement began to wane. Hall received criticism for his inadequate methods, for the conservative elements in his thought, and for his neglect of the social aspects of education in favor of narrow, scientific investigations. Nevertheless, the work carried out under his direction had provided the formative impulses for a whole range of more specialized educational, psychological, and medical fields of study. Hall had also helped to turn the eyes of many Americans to the future by making humanity brought to a new stage of evolutionary progress, instead of the traditional moral character, the goal of his work. To his way of thinking, the child study movement was not only an educational renaissance but a scientific reconstruction, which would be "the salvation and ultimate development and end and aim and creation of history."[31]

Hall's futuristic outlook was one that many Americans shared. In the last two decades of the nineteenth century they began to query the quality and successful interaction of America's citizens. What had gone wrong? Why, in a nation of apparent abundance and enterprise, was there increasing poverty, disease, crime, corruption, and conflict? What could be done to ensure a better human product and greater social harmony?

SOCIAL CLIMATE OF THE POST-CIVIL WAR PERIOD

Rapid, sweeping movements of epic proportions characterized the post-Civil War period. Free from war, external interference, and hemispheric rivalries, America concentrated its energies on creating a consumption-oriented economy within its vast and rich domain. By 1890 the frontier was declared a thing of the past. Where horses, wagons, and canoes had made the first inroads into the back country, steamboats and locomotives hewed a wider trail. A craze of canal building hit the country beginning in the 1820s, to be overtaken in later decades by feverish railroad construction. By 1915 the country was patterned with two hundred and fifty thousand miles of track.[32] The inventive skills of Samuel B. Morse and Alexander Graham Bell and the development of the modern press completed the communications revolution.

Improved communications made possible the coordination of the country's complex economic activity. By the end of the century the United States was the most powerful manufacturing nation in the world. In the 1860s the majority of the leading industrial concerns were small, operating locally and servicing a predominantly agrarian economy. At the beginning of that decade the total annual value of manufactured goods was approximately $2 billion, but by 1900 the industrial output was about $11 billion and was double that from the land. The goods produced were being used in industry or by the individual consumer rather than on the farm. Not only had the number of manufacturing companies multiplied, but several now operated on an unprecedented scale. Through processes of vertical and horizontal integration, business giants such as U.S. Steel, Standard Oil, and American Tobacco now catered to a national market. In turn, their continuous need for credit and the economy's concentrated surplus capital bred other titans, the great banking houses of America.[33]

Inextricably involved in this industrial explosion was the movement of large numbers of native and foreign people from traditional rural environments to the urban scene. Both offspring and parents of the manufacturing and transportation developments, cities and towns spread across the map in an epidemic manner. Whereas in 1860, 80.2 percent of the population could have been considered rural, in 1900 this had dropped to 60.3 percent, and by 1920 the farm or village was no longer the home of the average American. The beginning of the nineteenth century had seen the growth of cities barely keeping pace with the diffusion of thousands of settlers into new territory; the end saw a complex urban network of national and regional metropolises, special manufacturing centers, and smaller, subordinate cities differing in size and function.[34]

These grand movements and sweeping developments seemingly substantiated America's claim to superiority over Europe as a land of limitless possibilities. Yet, as the century drew to a close, voices began to denounce the dislocation, confusion, stratification, and antagonisms these processes had brought about.

The rich appeared to be getting richer. When Cornelius Vanderbilt's grandson moved into his new home on New York's Fifth Avenue in 1883, he occupied a mock fifteenth-century French chateau that had cost him a modest $3 million. A housewarming followed that consumed a further $.25 million.[35] For those shrewd enough to understand the economic currents of the present and the trends of the future, there were vast fortunes available. Andrew Carnegie made a profitable journey by way of the telegraph office and the railroad to a personal $250 million share in the merger of his organization with U.S. Steel in 1901. John D. Rockefeller amassed even greater wealth in his ruthless, single-minded domination of the oil industry. These men were aware of the "contrast between the palace of the millionaire and the cottage of the laborer," but claimed that the concentration of wealth was necessary for the advancement of the finer aspects of civilization.[36] Not all were convinced. Critics like Walt Whitman condemned "the depravity of the business classes" and their organizations, which seemed designed to lower wages, raise prices, and ruin competition.[37] Sharp practices were not confined to business but permeated all levels of government. Men of Wiliam Tweed's ilk were seen as the businessmen of politics, who made their own vast fortunes by setting prices for favors, selling franchises, and guaranteeing a controlled electorate.

At the bottom of the ladder were the increasingly conspicuous poor. Urban growth, with its human concentration, made their plight more obvious. Charity workers of the post-Civil War period, scouring the cities in order to distinguish the deserving from the degenerate, incidentally gathered a store of information on working and living conditions. A more sensational portrait was fed to a wider public through newspapers and magazines, through the prose of Edward Bellamy and William Dean Howells and the illustrations of Jerome Myers.[38] Journalist Jacob Riis guided his readers through the back alleys of New York and through tenements that were "hot-beds of the epidemics that carry death to rich and poor alike, the nurseries of pauperism and crime that fill our jails and police courts; that throw off forty thousand human wrecks to the island asylums and workhouses year by year, that turned out in the last eight years a round half million beggars to prey upon our charities."[39] As the nineteenth-century view of poverty as moral failure was gradually undermined and people began to query the efficiency and justice of the economic system, a more objective analysis was demanded. Statistics were lacking. Robert Hunter, in his study of poverty published in 1904, had no doubt "that there are in the United States ten million persons in...conditions of poverty," but he realized that there might be as many as 15 or 20 million.[40] Federal and state labor bureaus tried to provide the social statistics required, and while there remained unbridged chasms in this information, they did bring a greater degree of objectivity to the discussion of poverty.

Fear of growing stratification in American society was compounded by an increasing sensitivity to the foreign element among the lower classes. Although the foreign-born population was hardly proportionately greater in 1900 than in 1870, the comparatively more tolerant attitude of the 1870s was giving way to a serious questioning of America's ability to assimilate Europe's emigrants. Troubled by larger economic and social problems, groups of Americans reexamined U.S. immigration policies, which were attracting record numbers of refugees; for example, 8,202,388 persons entered the country in the first decade of the new century.[41] Native-born Americans were particularly disturbed by the new streams of Catholic and Jewish immigrants from southern and eastern Europe, whose cultural absorption appeared more difficult. The outlook seemed bleak to some. Believing that the European newcomers bred faster than the established Anglo-Saxons, they anxiously queried whether Americans were committing racial suicide by allowing the ethnic balance to swing in favor of the "Latin and the Hun."[42]

Action to bring about social order was thought to be imperative. To men in power the possibility of social conflict appeared to be a stark reality. From the 1880s they began to interpret the rise of organized labor as a prelude to mass sedition and political revolution. Disturbances such as the Haymarket bombing of 1886 evoked fatal reprisals and a swift consolidation of law-and-order groups. "Men who were so certain of an eruption saw volcanoes under every puff of smoke."[43] Economic depression in the mid-1890s, by creating up to 20 percent unemployment in the major manufacturing centers, threw up a specter of some 2.5 million revolutionaries.[44] Armed force met Jacob Coxey when he, with his wife and their child with the unforgettable name of Legal Tender, led a peaceful group of 500 men to Washington to protest the government's monetary policies. A similar show of strength was made at the Pullman strike of 1894 and at later labor clashes. These incidents had their share of casualties. During the short period from January 1902 to July 1904, 180 union men were estimated to have been killed; 1,651 injured; and about 5,000 arrested.[45] At the end of the century many thus agreed with Vida Scudder's assessment of the situation. "Cleavage of classes, cleavage of race, cleavage of faiths, an inextricable confusion! And the voice of democracy crying aloud in the streets: 'Out of all this achieve brotherhood, achieve the race to be!' "[46]

CHANGES IN FAMILY LIFE

And what of the race to be? When the attention of anxious Americans turned from the current adult population to the nation's children, the picture was hardly more encouraging. The children were the saddest victims of America's industrial and urban experience and correspondingly a potential threat to the country's development. Moreover, in the late nineteenth century there were proportionately less children, on whom to base the nation's future progress.

It was a rude shock to many Americans to discover that the national birthrate was declining. In the late eighteenth century the average family had 8 children; by 1900 this had dropped to 3.[47] In terms of age distribution, whereas in 1830 approximately 45 percent of the population had been below fifteen years of age, in 1880 the figure was only 38 percent, and in 1900, 34 percent.[48] In the early census figures, details of age had not been particularly good, but by 1890 quinquennial age distributions were available not only for the whole population, but also for the major racial and ethnic groups. As the facts became known, the causes and implications came under discussion. It was thought that economic changes had made children a burden to the wage earner, a social handicap to the middle class, and an encumbrance to those seeking to rise in the social scale. The desire of the rich for the endowment of their offspring also seemed to encourage a limitation in numbers. Not many saw this as being to America's advantage. The sound conditions of race progress, it was believed, involved "a condition in which the population is at least self-perpetuating and preferably one in which it is increasing, while the individual and social status is continuously improving." Of course, the fact that the birth rate of immigrants was greater than that of native-born Americans was even more distressing to those who jealously guarded their Anglo-Saxon lineage and ideals.[49]

The question of the relative benefits and disadvantages of birth control was only part of an acute anxiety that centered on the family at this time. The changes wrought by the country's industrialization and urbanization had not left the family untouched. Indeed, some thought they saw a wholesale breakdown in family life that had grave implications for the fate of the nation as a whole. For the first time there were figures at hand to show the increasing proportion of marriages ending in divorce. While before the Civil War divorces had been rare, in the succeeding decades they occurred at a steadily increasing rate. By 1890 not only was the Census Bureau taking note of marital status, but the Department of Commerce and Labor had conducted a special survey of marriage and divorce. Subsequently regular assessments were made, and debates began about the significance of the trend that had brought about 945,625 divorces in the period 1887-1906, as opposed to 328,716 in 1867-1886.[50] These agencies also became aware of another phenomenon—desertion. Although no reliable nationwide statistics were available, various charitable organizations published their own findings and attested to an increase in the number of abandonment and nonsupport cases in their files.

More than today, the breakdown of marriage was a topic of tremendous moral sensitivity. It was seen as an ethical failure with disastrous consequences for the larger community. Most Americans considered the family to be the unit of the state, the foundation stone of American civilization, the instrument by which America's inheritance of spirit and character was passed on to future generations. They questioned what would happen to the nation's children with its collapse. While, as I shall argue in a later chapter, their fears of total failure were unfounded, many Americans reacted to the possibility in an exaggerated manner.

Divorce and desertion, it was realized, were not the only hazards to children's growth and development. Death and destitution might remove their parents, throwing them into the hands of public or private welfare organizations. In addition, their own physical survival was by no means sure. Measles and diphtheria, scarlet fever and tuberculosis meant an early death, particularly for those millions of children crowded into the nation's tenements. The infant death rate, according to the U.S. Children's Bureau, was the truest index of the welfare of any community.[51] If this were so, the situation was serious. Although by the 1880s the mortality rate was on the decline, it was still a critical problem.[52] The newly established American Pediatrics Association and other health and welfare organizations had, by the turn of the century, initiated a publicity campaign to alert the general public and procure remedial action. (For a brief history of the establishment of the Children's Bureau, see Chapter 9.)

EFFORTS ON BEHALF OF CHILDREN

Simultaneously, other interested groups were taking the nation to task for its indifference toward the education and employment of its children. In 1892 a series of articles in *Forum* by Joseph Mayer Rice on the public school system illuminated the apathy, corruption and incompetence rife in America's schools.[53] For Americans who had become accustomed to the idea that the nation's progress was inextricably involved with education, this was a dramatic revelation. Other critics pointed to the decay of the rural schools that had been built during the educational renaissance of the 1840s and 1850s and to the inability of city institutions to care for the skyrocketing urban population.[54] Many children were evading the system altogether. In 1890 it was estimated that, of 18.5 million children between the ages of five and seventeen, only 12.7 million were enrolled and the average daily attendance was in the region of 8 million.[55] Of the missing children, a good proportion were a regular part of the labor force. One in six was, by 1900, employed on the farm, in the mill, in the cannery, in the mine, in the factory, or on the street.[56] While in earlier decades child labor had been justified on ethical as well as economic grounds, by the 1890s many people were questioning these claims. Could the old, clichéd argument that work produced industrious, self-reliant men and women stand up against factual information on the physical and mental effects of uncontrolled employment? Magazines and journals presented a dark picture of long hours, monotonous work, and dangerous conditions. Children were killed and maimed by machinery, poisoned by noxious fumes, crippled by endless hours of sitting hunched over their work. Their future contribution to society was questionable.

Despite the defects they saw in society and its treatment of children, most Americans expressed a faith in the regenerative powers of the nation. They were confident that intelligent men could achieve social control, could remake their own world. Herbert Spencer's application of evolutionary theory to the social sphere had tended, in earlier years, to support conservativism and laissez faire. Progress seemed a certainty; hence interference was thought unnecessary and even dangerous. By the 1890s, however, this view had been fatally undermined by the rise of critical reformism in economics and sociology and pragmatism in philosophy.[57] Men such as Lester Ward, William James, and John Dewey repudiated the idea that evolution was inherently beneficial. They put forward the idea that the task of a human being is to observe, understand, and direct the laws of nature rather than to submit passively to their action. Changes would be brought about, not by external circumstances, but by human control. Dewey claimed that "the biological point of view commits us to the conviction that mind, whatever else it may be, is at least an organ of service for the control of environment in relation to the ends of the life process."[58]

The outlook for a deliberate improvement in the quality of America's citizens seemed good. Although at the turn of the century there was a whole range of opinion on the relative effects of nature and nurture on the development of a personality, most expressed some faith in the power of the environment to determine character. A fair example of the middle ground taken was given at the National Conference of Charities and Correction in 1896. A delegate argued as follows:

> A man's nature is like a seed and his circumstances like the soil and climate in which the seed germinates and grows, the co-working of the two is indispensable to every vital process whatever, and they are so different in their function that they cannot without inaccuracy be said to be in opposition.... The union of nature and nurture is not one of addition or mixture, but of growth, whereby the elements are altogether transformed into a new organic whole.[59]

Other commentators, like Jacob Riis and Lester Ward, were more effusive and bitterly opposed the claims of biological determinism. It should be remembered, however, that hereditary thought was not necessarily pessimistic at this time. Contemporary European ideas on criminal anthropology, August Weismann's theories on genetics, and Mendelian laws of heredity formed the basis for a reform movement. The American Breeders Association, claiming to have as its aim the defense of civilization from the biologically inadequate, put forward a number of reforms relating to birth control and sterilization that were supposed to benefit the makeup of American society. Both environmental and hereditarian groups recognized the child as a central point. The formation, rather than the reformation, of adults was thought to be the logical starting place.[60]

Once again Americans came back to the child. They had already been brought to an awareness of children and their importance for adult life by the economic changes and scientific investigations of the nineteenth century. The idea of children as the purest form of human life had been absorbed into their consciousness. Current social problems and the poor condition of many of America's children had induced a common belief that "the state builds wisely which cultivates the habit of public concern over the quality of its citizenship."[61] At the same time, intellectual developments had occurred that generated an optimistic assessment of the possibility of producing a better human being. The child thus became a focal point in programs for the salvation of American society.

Each commentator had his or her own vision. In several of his speeches, Theodore Roosevelt emphasized the connection between national greatness and children. If the country could guarantee an adequate birth rate and produce industrious workers and good fighters, it could not fail. He had no time for families who were limiting their offspring. "The man or woman who deliberately foregoes the blessings (of having children) whether from vicious-ness, coldness, shallow-heartedness, self-indulgence or mere failure to appreciate aright the difference between the all important and the unimportant—why such a creature merits contempt as hearty as any visited upon the soldier who runs away in battle."[62] Roosevelt did not recommend indiscriminate breeding. He was more in-terested in boosting the birthrate of the "respectable" classes than that of the less fortunate. Four children seemed to him a minimum for any intelligent family; if only two were produced, society would be on the point of extinction in two or three generations. The children were to be strong, straightforward, industrious, courageous, "clean-minded and clean-lived." The American boy he advised to live life as he would play a football game: "Hit the line hard: don't foul and don't shirk." This, he thought, would produce the type of man who would make America the leading nation in the world.[63]

Others looked to the child to bring about the limitation of the nonproductive and potentially dangerous elements in society. The child problem was to them "the whole problem of charities and correction," the key to the cities' poverty, vice, and crime. Taking their cue from the flourishing conservation movement, many reform-minded Americans discussed children as the most valuable of the nation's natural resources and considered the implications of a poorly developing child as a wasted source of human energy. Every failure of society to guarantee the child a sound develop-ment was seen as a double failure. The community not only lost the productive force of the child, but it was compelled to support the criminal, insane, feeble-minded, and destitute adults which many of these children would become. If the child's requirements were taken care of, there would be no need for the adult institutions that consumed so much of the society's time and money.[44]

Educate the child properly, and democracy will be assured. This at least was the claim that John Dewey made in his educational treatises. He denied that individual growth and the interests of a democratic social order were necessarily antagonistic and put forward ideas for their synthesis. Society needed "a type of education which gives individuals a personal interest in social relationships and control, and the habits of mind which secure social changes without introducing disorder."[65] To achieve this, the school would have to undergo a drastic revision. By centering on the child, the school would allow children to cultivate their natural capacities, to improve on the qualities of the larger community instead of merely reproducing them. Dewey believed these educational reforms would encourage, among other characteristics, the cooperative spirit, which seemed increasingly undermined by class conflict.[66]

Whatever the area of child life that particular reformers considered, a common faith united them. This common faith was a belief that the child was "the promise of something that is to be... the possibility of something finer, something better, something greater on this earth than has yet been."[67] With this optimism they turned their attention to devising and procuring specific reforms to bring about the social order they desired. One group devoted its energies to the problems posed by dependent and neglected children.

NOTES

1. Ellen K. S. Key, *The Century of the Child* (New York: Putnam, 1909), translated from the 1902 German version by Frances Maro.

2. For a survey of Hine's work see Beaumont Newhall, "Lewis W. Hine," *Magazine of Art* 31 (1938): 636-37. Riis's most famous works are *How the Other Half Lives* (New York: Charles Scribner's Sons, 1890); *The Making of an American* (New York: Macmillan, 1903).

3. Robert H. Wiebe, *The Search for Order* (London: Macmillan, 1967), p. 169.

4. See for example, Philippe Aries, *Centuries of Childhood* (London: Jonathan Cape, 1962) on the changing family in France from the medieval

to the modern period. On the changing status of children in England see Frank J. Musgrove, *Youth and the Social Order* (London: Routledge & Kegan Paul, 1964) and Ivy Pinchbeck, *Children in English Society*, 2 vols. (London: Routledge & Kegan Paul, 1969-1973).

5. Joseph F. Kett, "Adolescence and Youth in Nineteenth Century America," *Journal of Interdisciplinary History* 1 (1971): 283-86. John Demos and Virginia Demos, "Adolescence in Historical Perspective," *Journal of Marriage and the Family* 31 (1969): 632-38.

6. John Sirjamaki, *The American Family in the Twentieth Century* (Cambridge, Mass.: Harvard University Press, 1953), p. 106.

7. Quoted in Edmund Morgan, *The Puritan Family: Essays on Religion and Domestic Relations in Seventeenth Century New England* (Boston: Trustees of the Public Library, 1944), p. 106.

8. Plymouth Colony Records vol. 4, p. 20, quoted in John Demos, *A Little Commonwealth: Family Life in Plymouth Colony* (New York: Oxford University Press, 1970), p. 102.

9. Bernard Bailyn, *Education in the Forming of American Society* (Chapel Hill: University of Carolina Press, 1960), p. 17.

10. Quoted in Demos, *A Little Commonwealth*, p. 134.

11. Susannah Wesley, quoted in Daniel P. Miller and Guy E. Swanson, *The Changing American Parent* (New York: John Wiley & Sons, 1958), p. 10.

12. Monica Kiefer, *American Children through Their Books* (Philadelphia: University of Pennsylvania Press, 1948), pp. 7, 29. Bert Roller, *Children in American Poetry 1610-1900* (Nashville, Tenn.: George Peabody College for Teachers, 1930), p. 178.

13. Bailyn, *Education in the Forming of American Society*, p. 178.

14. Demos and Demos, "Adolescence in Historical Perspective," p. 637.

15. Robert H. Bremner, *Children and Youth in America: A Documentary History*, vol. 1 (Cambridge, Mass.: Harvard University Press, 1971), pp. 370-73.

16. Alexis de Tocqueville, *Democracy in America* (New York: Mentor, 1956, first printed 1835-1840), p. 230. See also William E. Bridges, "Family Patterns and Social Values in America 1825-1875," *American Quarterly* 17 (1965): 3-11.

17. Francis Wyse, quoted in Richard L. Rapson, "The American Child as Seen by British Travellers, 1845-1935," *American Quarterly* 17 (1965): 527.

18. Robert Sunley, "Early Nineteenth Century American Literature on Child Rearing," in Margaret Mead, ed., *Childhood in Contemporary Cultures* (Chicago: University of Chicago Press, 1963), pp. 151-63.

19. Peter Coveney, *Poor Monkey: The Child in Literature* (London: Rockliff Press, 1957), pp. ix-xii, 52-84. George Boas, *The Cult of Childhood* (London: Warburg Institute, 1966), pp. 29-60.

20. Anne Trenskey, "The Cult of the Child in Minor American Fiction in the Nineteenth Century" (Ph.D. diss., City University of New York, 1969), p. 78.

21. Horatio Alger, "Ragged Dick," in *Struggling Upward and Other Works* (New York: Cronon, 1945), pp. 154-55. See also Richard R. Wohl, "The Rags to Riches Story—An Episode of Secular Idealism," in Richard Bendix and Seymour M. Lipset, *Class, Status and Power: A Reader in Social Stratification* (London: Routledge & Kegan Paul, 1954), pp. 501-6.

22. Albert G. Stone, *The Innocent Eye: Childhood in Mark Twain's Imagination* (New Haven: Yale University Press, 1961), pp. 270-71.

23. G. Stanley Hall, "The Ideal School Based on Child Study," *Forum* 32 (Sept. 1901): 24-25.

24. Dorothy Ross, *G. Stanley Hall* (Chicago: University of Chicago Press, 1972), pp. 118, 263-65.

25. Wilhelm Preyer, *Mind of the Child*, first English translation from German (New York: Appleton, 1888).

26. Ross, *G. Stanley Hall*, pp. 124-30, 281-83.

27. G. Stanley Hall, *Adolescence: Its Psychology, and Its Relation to Physiology, Anthropology, Sociology, Sex, Crime, Religion and Education*, vol. 2 (New York: Appleton, 1904), p. 132.

28. Ibid., p. 361.

29. Ibid., p. xiii.

30. Ross, *G. Stanley Hall*, pp. 298-300.

31. G. Stanley Hall, "Child Study in Summer Schools," quoted ibid., p. 261.

32. U.S. Bureau of the Census, *Historical Statistics of the United States, 1789-1945* (Washington, D.C.: Government Printing Office, 1949), p. 202.

33. Ibid., pp. 99, 183.

34. Conrad Taeubner and Irene Taeubner, *The Changing Population of the United States* (New York: John Wiley & Sons, 1958), p. 114. Charles N. Glaab and Theodore Braun, *A History of Urban America* (New York: Macmillan, 1967), pp. 107-32.

35. Lloyd Morris, *Incredible New York* (New York: Random House, 1951), pp. 152-54.

36. Andrew Carnegie, *The Gospel of Wealth* (New York: Century, 1900), pp. 14-15. Carnegie saw the concentration of wealth as necessary. It was "essential for the progress of the race that the houses of some should

be homes for all that is highest and best in literature and the arts and for all the refinements of civilization than that none should be so.... Much better this great irregularity than universal squalor."

37. Walt Whitman, "Democratic Vistas," in *Leaves of Grass and Democratic Vistas* (London: Everyman, 1927), p. 309.

38. See Robert H. Bremner, *From the Depths: The Discovery of Poverty in the United States* (New York: New York University Press, 1967), pp. 67-120.

39. Jacob A. Riis, *How the Other Half Lives* (New York: Hill & Wang, 1957, first printed New York: Scribner's, 1890), p. 3.

40. Robert Hunter, *Poverty* (New York: Macmillan, 1904), p. 11.

41. Taeubner and Taeubner, *The Changing Population*, p. 52.

42. To trace the growth of nativist feeling from the 1880s to World War I, see John Higham, *Strangers in the Land* (New York: Atheneum, 1965).

43. Wiebe, *The Search for Order*, p. 91.

44. Charles Hoffman, *The Depression of the Nineties* (Westport, Conn.: Greenwood Press, 1970), p. 97.

45. Slason Thompson, "Violence and Labor Conflict," *Outlook* 78 (1904): 969.

46. Quoted in Samuel P. Hays, *The Response to Industrialism* (Chicago: University of Chicago Press, 1957), p. 38.

47. Wilson H. Grabill, Clyde V. Kiser, and Pascal K. Whelpton, "Demographic Trends: Marriage, Birth and Death," in Michael Gordon, ed., *The American Family in Social-Historical Perspective* (New York: St. Martin's Press, 1973), p. 375.

48. Taeubner and Taeubner, *The Changing Population*, pp. 26-29.

49. See, for example, J. P. Lichtenberger, "The Instability of the Family," in *Annals of the American Academy of Political and Social Sciences* (henceforward *AAAPSS* 34 (1909): 93-103, quoted 103; W. S Rossiter, "The Significance of the Decreasing Proportion of Children," *AAAPSS* 34 (1909): 71-80; Lydia Commander, *The American Idea: Does the National Tendency toward a Small Family Point to Race Suicide or Race Progress?* (New York: Barnes, 1907).

59. U.S. Bureau of the Census, *Marriage and Divorce 1867-1906* (Washington, D.C.: Government Printing Office, 1908), p. 46.

51. U.S. Children's Bureau, *Baby Saving Campaign*, Publication No. 3 (Washington, D.C.: Government Printing Office, 1913), p. 46.

52. George B. Mangold, "Infant Mortality in the American Cities," *AAAPSS* 31 (1908): 485. The figures for New York City, for example, showed a decline from 288 deaths per 1,000 live births in the 1880s to 168 in 1902.

53. Joseph M. Rice's articles in *Forum* were subsequently republished as *The Public School System of the United States* (New York: Century, 1893).

54. Lawrence Cremin, *The Transformation of the School: Progressivism in American Education* (New York: Alfred A. Knopf, 1974), p. 48.

55. U.S. Office of Education, "Biennial Survey of Education 1930-1932," *Bulletin* No. 2, 1933, pp. 46-47.

56. H. L. Bliss, "Census Statistics of Child Labor," *Journal of Political Economy* 13 (1904): 246.

57. Richard Hofstadter, *Social Darwinism in American Thought* (Boston: Beacon Press, 1968), pp. 46, 124.

58. John Dewey, "The Interpretation of the Savage Mind," *Psychological Review* 9 (1902): 219.

59. Charles Cooley, "Nature vs Nurture in the Making of Social Careers," *Proceedings of the 17th National Conference of Charities and Correction* (henceforward NCCC), 1890, pp. 399-400.

60. Mark Haller, "Heredity in Progressive Thought," *Social Service Review* 38 (1964): 166-76. Donald Pickens, *Eugenics and the Progressives* (Nashville, Tenn.: Vanderbilt University Press, 1968).

61. Charles E. Faulkner, "Twentieth Century Alignments for the Promotion of the Social Order," *Proceedings of the 27th NCCC*, 1900, p. 7.

62. Theodore Roosevelt, "The Woman and the Home," in *The Works of Theodore Roosevelt* (New York: Scribner's, 1926), vol. 18, p. 230.

63. Theodore Roosevelt, "The American Boy," in *The Strenuous Life* (New York: Century, 1900), p. 181.

64. John H. Finley, "The Child Problem in the Cities," *Proceedings of the 18th NCCC*, 1891, p. 124. Hastings Hornell Hart, "The Economic Aspect of the Child Problem," *Proceedings of the 19th NCCC*, 1892, p. 191.

65. John Dewey, *Democracy and Education* (New York: Macmillan, 1910), p. 115.

66. Richard Hofstadter, *Anti-Intellectualism in American Life* (New York: Alfred A. Knopf, 1963), pp. 359-90.

67. Felix Adler, "The Attitude of Society toward the Child as an Index of Civilization," *AAAPSS* 29 (1907): 138.

2

CHILDREN AND CHILD-SAVERS

By the end of the nineteenth century, childhood and youth were subjects of widespread concern. In the field of social welfare, however, certain groups of children were singled out for particular attention. Philanthropists and social workers only gradually accepted the belief that the personal fulfillment of every American child was their proper sphere. Three categories of children were distinguished by welfare reformers as being in need of special care. They were the delinquent, the defective, and the dependent and neglected. The third group of children, the dependent and neglected, are the subject of this study.

THE LEGAL FRAMEWORK

Statutory definitions of dependency and neglect differed between states. The Illinois act of 1899 "to regulate the treatment and control of dependent, neglected and delinquent children" is perhaps characteristic of the various legal stipulations. In that year Illinois determined that

> the words dependent child and neglected child shall mean any child who for any reason is destitute or homeless or abandoned; or has not proper care or guardianship; or who habitually begs or receives alms; or who is found living in any

house of ill-fame or with any vicious or disreputable person; or whose home, by reason of neglect, cruelty or depravity on the part of its parents, guardians or other person in whose care it may be, is an unfit place for such a child; and any child under the age of eight who is found peddling or selling any article or singing or playing any musical instrument upon the street or giving any public entertainment.[1]

Often the distinction between dependency and neglect was not made explicit, and a large amount of discretion in the interpretation of these terms was left to the judge in question. In general, however, dependency referred to a condition such as orphanage or extreme destitution that was not to be blamed on any individual. Neglect, on the other hand, introduced the notion of culpability on the part of the parents. Their failure to protect children from physical harm or social and psychological damage was thought to be in conflict with the child-rearing standards of American society.

The necessity for the state to assume control of the dependent was set down in the earliest colonial records. Parents who were unable to maintain their children had to forfeit them. These children, together with the abandoned, the illegitimate, and the orphaned, were occasionally placed in workhouses but more usually bound out for their minority to other families in the community.[2] Recognition of neglect was a much later phenomenon. Where mentioned in colonial statutes, it normally referred to failure to provide a child with a suitable education or trade. Physical harm to the child was generally ignored. In common law the parent or guardian was justified in exercising a substantial amount of violence in order to discipline children or wards. The right to punish corresponded to the duty to support them. Rarely did the authorities consider a punishment sufficiently excessive to warrant prosecution. In the nineteenth century the responsibility of parents to guarantee their children's physical, mental, and moral welfare began to receive more attention. Various facets of neglect were incorporated into state laws relating to children, and the definition became more precise and at the same time more inclusive.[3]

Activity by societies for the protection of children provided the impetus for many of these legal changes. Humane societies had crusaded on behalf of animals for a number of years, and by the 1870s a substantial number of people had finally come to the conclusion that children were as important as dogs or horses. Similar services were then offered to children. Some states incorporated protection work for children into the already existent humane societies. This was not without murmurs of protest from those who feared that the animals might suffer in the merger. In other regions specific societies for the prevention of cruelty to children were established. By 1900 there were over two hundred organizations concerned with child neglect. Their impact on the recognition and definition of neglect may be seen in the work of the first, and probably most famous, association, the New York Society for the Prevention of Cruelty to Children (SPCC).[4]

This society was founded in 1874 by lawyer and philanthropist Elbridge Gerry and the president of the New York Society for the Prevention of Cruelty to Animals, Henry Bergh, in response to a particularly brutal case of ill-treatment. Neighbors, concerned for the safety of a young girl, Mary Ellen Wilson, who was regularly whipped and beaten by her guardians, had sought help from Bergh. He was dismayed by the fact that no organization existed that could cater to such cases, and he decided to set up his own. The New York Society for the Prevention of Cruelty to Children initiated various campaigns against parents and other individuals who were considered to be endangering the morals or physical well-being of New York's children. It also encouraged new legislation. The society directly brought about the 1876 law prohibiting the use of children in "singing, dancing, begging... or as a gymnast, rider or acrobat... for any immoral purpose." In 1881 the society helped clarify the word neglect in the act relating to "Abandonment and Other Acts of Cruelty to Children." This legislation provided penalties for a wide range of parental failings, including refusal to furnish food, clothing, shelter, or medical attendance, allowing a minor to engage in dangerous occupations or to be used for immoral purposes, and wilfully causing a child's life to be endangered, health injured, or morals impaired.[5]

This, then, was the type of legal framework in which social workers and philanthropists pursued their various activities on behalf of children. Certain situations were clearly defined, but in others there were only vague guidelines, within which there was considerable leeway for particular views on the norms of the community, for changing knowledge concerning the needs of children, and for idiosyncratic interpretations of dependency and neglect.

THE CHILDREN'S CLASS PROFILE

It remains to be seen who in fact were the children who fell into the hands of individual workers, welfare organizations and the courts. Clearly these children had one attribute in common: they belonged almost exclusively to the working class. Evidence for this may be found in the court records for the Chicago area, which occasionally took note of the occupations of the parents of dependent and neglected children. They showed a predominance of unskilled and semiskilled workers; many were employed as laborers and teamsters.[6]

Immigrants were heavily represented, as might be expected. Welfare reformers and philanthropists saw a close connection between immigration and the extent of destitution and crime. In part they feared the entry of defectives and delinquents from other nations. Feeling, like sociologist Charles R. Henderson, that "every atom of vicious and degenerate blood is poison in our veins," they supported restrictions on these groups.[7] However, the major problem, as social workers saw it, was the impact of urban living on an alien population. Toward the end of the century immigrants increasingly chose, or were compelled, to stay in the already congested cities rather than to move into unoccupied land. In the urban areas they were forced to live under the most squalid, unsanitary conditions and to take the most unskilled jobs available. Disease and financial difficulty were thus near at hand. Ignorant of language, customs, and legal rights, immigrants were, settlement worker Lillian Wald claimed, "more in danger of moral contamination than the rest of the community and...more liable to exploitation."[8] Immigration was thought to have a particularly detrimental effect on children. In one set of circumstances they might be forced out to work at an early age to help increase the family income; in another, they might break away from the traditional mores and discipline of their parents, take to the streets and, possibly, to crime.[9]

Despite the fears of reformers and social workers, immigrants do not seem to have provided a proportionately greater number of dependent and neglected children than lower-class native-born families. Of the dependency cases brought before the Cook County Juvenile Court for the first time in 1910, approximately 76 percent were listed as being of "foreign" stock. In the same year the national census estimated that 77.5 percent of the white inhabitants of Chicago were either foreign born or came from foreign or mixed parentage. In this instance, at least, ethnic factors apparently did not increase a child's probability of being considered dependent or neglected.[10]

All types of cases demonstrated a working-class profile. Orphans from more affluent families were not only rarer as a result of better living and working conditions, but those unfortunate enough to lose both parents were normally taken in by relatives rather than delivered to charity organizations. Upper- and middle-class parents did not provide the cities with the hundreds of pitiful infants left in hallways and on doorsteps, often wrapped in nothing but rags or newspaper. Jacob Riis, who was fully aware of the foundling problem in New York, was confident that "only the poor abandon their children. The stories of richly dressed foundlings that are dished up in the newspapers at intervals are pure fiction."[11]

These two types of dependency accounted for a small proportion of the children under care. Figures compiled by the New York State Board of Charities in 1910, for example, show that approximately 17 percent of the inmates of local institutions were full orphans or foundlings. In comparison, almost 50 percent of the children admitted were half-orphans.[12]

Working-class families were not cushioned by insurance, savings, or adequate earning capacity against the loss of one parent. Employing a housekeeper to perform the tasks of a mother was virtually impossible for a man on a laborer's wage. Children's-agency reports record many examples of children taken from, or surrendered by, fathers who were considered incapable of managing alone. Of course, the great majority of single-parent families were headed by women. Their position was extremely precarious. Not only did they occupy the most unskilled jobs, but they were forced to accept lower wages than their male equivalents. For example, a survey of the Pittsburgh steel district, carried out under the aegis of the Russell Sage Foundation in 1907-1908, revealed that the average earnings of women were from one-half to one-third the wages of men in that industry. In addition, women found it difficult to organize to defend their own interests. Powerless in the event of their husbands' deaths, mothers were frequently forced to give up their children, either temporarily or permanently.[13]

Death was not the only cause of single-parent families. Illegitimacy provided another deviation from the idealized family situation. Before 1910 the exact number of children born out wedlock was unknown due to an inadequate birth registration program. Surveys in the second decade of the twentieth century indicated that somewhere between 18 and 23 per 1,000 live births were illegitimate. A good proportion of these children found themselves in the hands of welfare organizations. In Boston, according to a Children's Bureau study, three-fifths of the illegitimate children born in 1914 reached some local agency in the first year of life. The difficulties facing unmarried mothers were almost insurmountable. Their relative youth, the social stigma attached to their pregnancies, and the lack of financial support from the children's fathers prevented most from raising their children alone. Their occupational status added to the burden. By far the greatest number of mothers studied were domestic servants or factory workers. Presumably illegitimacy was not confined to the cities' working class, but little mention was made of how wealthier families coped with the problem. Certainly they were not a significant group in the eyes of social workers.[14]

Many dependent youngsters in the care of children's agencies still had both parents living. Susceptible to the vagaries of the American economic system, poorer families often found themselves unable to maintain their children. If figures provided by contemporary economic surveys for 1906 may be relied upon, somewhere between one-half and two-thirds of the adult males working in leading industries received less than the $600 considered to be a living wage.[15] Depressions such as the crisis in the mid-1890s, in which thousands of men were thrown out of work, created a particularly heavy demand for aid. The Boston Church Home Society recorded a sharp increase in applications to take children in 1893. Staff found it "a hard duty to refuse the parents or relatives, as the closing of mills and factories for a time made it easy to understand their great anxiety."[16] In times of relative stability, sickness, injury, and temporary unemployment had the same effect. Often the children of poor families were forced to fend for themselves in the streets and became the quarry of children's agents, truant officers, and policemen. They were among the vagabonds that Jacob Riis noted, each "acknowledging no authority and owing no allegiance to anybody or anything, with his grimy fist raised against society wherever it tries to coerce him." They could be seen during the day begging, scavenging, peddling; at night they found warmth wherever they could. In winter these youths might be found "fighting for warm spots around the grated vent holes that let out heat and steam from the underground pressrooms." In summer a convenient outhouse, a packing case, or a truck in the street made an acceptable bed for the night.[17]

Finally there was the neglected child. The most dramatic examples of neglect involved physical abuse. The battered child was not an exclusively working-class phenonemon; the psychological and sociological strains that manifested themselves in violence toward the young were evident in all walks of life. Poverty and its associated problems did, however, afford a particularly fertile ground for brutality and, obviously, for other forms of physical neglect. Middle-class parents tended more toward verbal abuse and psychological manipulation.[18] Protective associations in the late nineteenth century found virtually all their clients among the lower-income groups. It was in a tenement "of most unsavory reputation" that the New York SPCC found Martha Nelson, "bearing upon her face and body marks of the most inhuman treatment. An artfully arranged rope device had been used for tying the child by her thumbs in such a position that her toes touched the floor, and a strap with a heavy buckle and a cat o'nine tails had been used in beating her bare back."[19] It was also working-class parents whose morals and behavior were found inadequate by the better situated social workers and philanthropists, who judged family life by community norms that did not include drinking, gambling, promiscuity, or consorting with "low characters." These activities, less openly displayed among the bourgeoisie and middle-class families, were the usual grounds for intervention by societies for the prevention of cruelty to children.[20]

THE CHILD-SAVERS' CLASS PROFILE

If dependent and neglected children may be pinpointed as belonging to one particular stratum of American society, what of those people who committed themselves between 1890 and 1920 to caring for and protecting these children? What may be said about their social rank and underlying motivations? What implications, if any, do class and attitudinal differences have for a consideration of child welfare reform, especially as it concerned dependent and neglected children?

The debate concerning the membership of so-called Progressive campaigns has been wide-ranging and at times confusing. So diverse a phenomenon has Progressivism proved to be that at least one historian has denied the existence of a movement as such. The data that American historians have gathered on various aspects of reform have constantly refused to be molded into any neat, comprehensive framework. Instead, the era appears to have been characterized by "shifting coalitions around different issues, with the specific nature of these coalitions varying on federal, state and local levels from region to region and from the first to the second decades of the century."[21]

The analysis that George Mowry and Richard Hofstadter advanced in the 1950s has been undermined by subsequent research. Mowry discovered his Progressives among the young, predominantly urban, middle class. They were generally Protestants, college educated and self-employed, either in professions or in business. He accepted as a motivating force a sense of lessened power in the face of the economic moguls who rose up after the Civil War.[22] Richard Hofstadter elaborated on that status anxiety in his Pulitzer Prize-winning study, *The Age of Reform*. To him "progressivism was to a very considerable extent led by men who suffered from the events of the time, not through a shrinking in their means but through the changed pattern in the distribution of deference and power." Until 1870, Hofstadter argued, "the United

States was a nation with a rather broad diffusion of wealth, status and power in which a man of moderate means, especially in the many small communities, could command much deference and exert much influence. The small merchant or manufacturer or the distinguished lawyer, editor or preacher was a person of local eminence in an age in which local eminence mattered a great deal."[23] With the massive economic and social changes of the post-Civil War period, these were bypassed by new men of wealth who appeared to be without the restraints "of culture, pride or even the inherited caution of class or rank."[24]

This account of the underpinning of middle-class reform has received challenges from various areas. It is no longer possible to define this movement by its class and geographic boundaries; the uniform composition of Progressivism has been alleviated by the inclusion of upper-class groups, the working masses, and rural elements. Also, the social distinctions uncovered by the status anxiety theory have been found to apply to ostensibly nonprogressive groups as well.[25] Furthermore, the idea that reform is derived from social tension has been queried. David Thelen has pointed out the difficulties in isolating and understanding a past psychological state. He feels that the interdisciplinary borrowings have been somewhat carelessly made, that the psychological assumptions on which the status anxiety thesis has been based have been "either disproved, disputed or ignored by modern psychologists." He emphasizes the complexity of motivation that is likely to cut across class interests in any period of great social change.[26]

Admitting the complexity of the reform phenomenon, the question remains as to whether the leaders in the campaign for child welfare constituted any distinctive social group. A survey of the more vocal and active workers tends to support the conclusion that urban-based professionals formed the mainstay of the movement. This also appears to have been the case among other welfare organizations, according to a 1973 study of the voluntary associations of Illinois between 1890 and 1920.[27]

The family, ethnic, religious, and educational background of the "child-savers" (as they frequently termed themselves) constitutes a somewhat familiar pattern. Most came from middle-class families.

Their fathers were lawyers and politicians or they were ministers, farmers, and doctors. Unlike social worker Carl Christian Carstens, who had spent his youth in Germany, the child-savers were generally native born and had been raised not in large American cities but in smaller towns and rural areas, although the larger urban areas became their working bases later in life. Protestants predominated, although a number of Jews and Catholics also recognized the need to act on behalf of children in their own groups, as well as all the nation's young. The educational level of the reformers was extremely high. Not only had most completed college, but a fair number had postgraduate qualifications.

Rather than suffering a lessening of power as a result of the economic and social changes of the period, the major figures in the child welfare campaigns seem to have achieved their career objectives. In this they resembled not Hofstadter's Progressive profile but rather that described by Robert H. Wiebe. Wiebe advanced the belief that in post-Civil War America, a society "without a core," it was not the older, conservative elements nor prophets with simple formulas for regeneration who ultimately gave direction to the nation's economic, political, and social forces. Instead it was a broad spectrum of middle-class specialists, who were to develop the new values of "continuity and regularity, functionality, administration and management." They included aspiring professionals in such spheres as law, social work, medicine, education, and administration, together with experts in business, labor, and agriculture. The emerging urban and industrial system did not provide a threat to their status; rather it offered the means by which they might achieve the respect they desired. Gradually coming to a consciousness of their common interests and talents, members of the emerging professions looked confidently to the future, in which their own fortunes would harmonize with the welfare of the nation as a whole.[28]

SOCIAL WORK AS A PROFESSION

According to occupational statistics compiled from 1870 on, during the late nineteenth century the rate of increase of professional groups was approximately double that of the total labor

force. Journalism and architecture were occupations that underwent a meteoric rise, while law, education, the ministry, and social
work demonstrated substantial growth. The medical profession
was inactive by comparison.[29]

The majority of the leading figures in child welfare activities
were part of the growing profession of social work. By the end of
the nineteenth century social workers were gradually widening the
gap between themselves and the older philanthropic organizations.
A common bond slowly demonstrated itself in the local leagues of
New York and Boston and in the National Federation of Settlements, which was founded in 1911. Journals such as *Survey* provided a catalyst for the increase of professional self-awareness,
while universities began to offer the means for vocational training.
The churches were another fruitful source of activity on behalf of
children. Often individuals had experienced both the occupation of
social worker and that of the ministry, as is the case of Hastings
Hornell Hart.

Although better known as a penologist, for over 25 years Hart
pioneered in the care and protection of dependent, neglected, and
delinquent children. He was born in Brookfield, Ohio, in 1851, the
son of a physician. After graduating from Oberlin College and
spending two years in the Indian Service as a clerk at Sisseton
Agency, South Dakota, Hart decided to train for the ministry at
Andover Theological Seminary and, in 1881, was ordained a
minister of the Congregational Church. The duties of a pastor,
however, did not bring the vocational satisfaction he required. Two
years later he relinquished a career in the church for one in social
work. His career in social work was an extremely distinguished
one. For 15 years Hart held the office of secretary of the Minnesota
State Board of Charities and Correction, gathering experience with
all areas of disease, destitution, and delinquency. More specialized
knowledge came with his appointment in 1898 as superintendent of
the Illinois Children's Home and Aid Society, an association he
helped transform into one of the nation's most advanced children's
agencies. This was only the beginning of his wide-ranging and
influential activity in child welfare.[30] His energies were channeled
into directing the newly-created child-helping department of the
Russell Sage Foundation from 1909 to 1924. Hart helped frame the

nation's first juvenile court law and was among the organizers of the 1909 White House Conference on Dependent Children, the first national convention on this subject.[31] He and his colleagues annually thrashed out professional problems at the National Conference of Charities and Correction (after 1917 the National Conference of Social Work). The twenty addresses he made at this important forum for debate, before his death in 1932, covered topics varying from standards in child placing, to the unity of the movement as a whole.

Hart was typical of a large number of people who found their success and satisfaction in social work for children. Others, like Wilfred S. Reynolds and Henry Thurston, came to the profession via teaching or, like Ernest Bicknell, through journalism. Their efforts to bring about changes in children's environments were complemented and supplemented by those of successful practitioners in other fields. Many were judges and lawyers who brought specific knowledge and skills to the problems of the legal status of children. They analyzed their experiences in the judicial process and drafted new legislation. Academics, such as Henderson, who was a professor of sociology at the University of Chicago, were similarly active in reform. Henderson's activities and interests, which spanned a variety of welfare problems, were primarily directed toward large movements for industrial and social betterment. Child labor, accident and unemployment insurance, and tenement and prison reform absorbed his attention, and he fought for improvements as a member of state, national, and international commissions.[32] Finally, doctors and journalists made their own significant contributions to a recognition and rectification of children's problems.

THE CONTRIBUTION OF WOMEN

The names mentioned so far as being representative of child welfare reformers have largely been those of men, but a distinctive feature of this area of activity was the high proportion of women who participated. Although women were making gradual inroads into a variety of occupations, child welfare drew a larger proportion of women than most.

It is clear that by the end of the nineteenth century industrialization and urbanization had brought about significant changes in the

life styles of women, particularly middle-class women. By producing the wealth that allowed greater leisure, by relieving them of
much domestic labor, by providing entry to higher education, and
by encouraging smaller families and a shorter period of child-
bearing, these processes had somewhat changed middle-class
domestic life. However, the feminist ideology of the late nineteenth
century had not broken down the cultural rationale for maintaining
women's traditional domestic role to an extent that would allow
women to pursue activities in a wide variety of male-dominated
spheres on the basis of anything like equality. Leading feminists
in earlier decades had not only tackled legal discriminations, but
had also questioned the family structure and the domestic obligations that prevented women from engaging in activities outside the
home. At the convention of women's rights at Seneca Falls, New
York, in 1848, for example, the Declaration of Sentiments considered topics ranging from suffrage to the double standard in
morals and demanded substantial changes in the social order.
Radical questionings of marriage and family life by such feminists
as Victoria Woodhull continued the probe. These women denied
the concept of separate spheres according to different capabilities
and responsibilities of women and men. Unfortunately, the
potential of these arguments for bringing about profound changes
was lost in the conservative reaction of the late nineteenth century.
This involved a defense of traditional morals and manners and an
almost paranoid sensitivity to the apparently declining family
unit.[33]

   In the face of this widespread conservatism, middle-class women
who were exeriencing a status revolution sought outlets that could
be justified in traditional sexist terms. Rather than asserting ideas
of equality, they stressed the particular utility of the feminine
personality to a society experiencing a certain dislocation. Clichés
concerning women's superior integrity, delicacy of perception,
gentleness, and selfless devotion were used by them to claim a
wider role in society. "Harmony and justice and purity and honesty
cannot be brought into human society...by the methods of force.
...The infusion of the gentler, more persuasive influences and
methods of feminine nature, and the higher quality and freedom

of motherhood are the only possible means of advancing the race."[34] Since many of the current social changes were impinging upon the home, women argued that they had the right to serve in the larger community. The idea was circulated that reform was merely housekeeping on a larger scale. "What is the city but the larger house in which we all develop, in which, under wise control, each member must live so as to contribute to the general welfare. Good city government is good housekeeping, and that is the sum of the matter. The experiences of the woman's narrow sphere are the same on a wider plane. If she follows her broom into the street, she is confronted with a problem upon which she has been at work for centuries."[35]

Social work, and more particularly child welfare, was an obvious area in which the defense of family life and of the traditional feminine image could be harnessed to new career openings. It was seen as an extension of the virtues of motherhood to a field requiring an expanding personnel. Throughout the nineteenth century the mother had been assigned the chief role in child rearing, being supposedly better at instilling discipline, while women were accepted as superior teachers for school children. Mother love and female understanding were seen as obviously vital to child welfare. This applied in institutions where, some believed, "few men can enter into the lives of children and young people and win their confidence as can a woman"[36] and was reflected in policy making and in legislative reform. Presented as a projection of the housekeeping function, child welfare was not seen as an intrusion into occupations usually taken by men. The activities of women would be complementary, not competitive.

Within the child welfare profession, however, women were in competition with men. Several of them reached the top of this profession, among them Julia Lathrop. Like other leading welfare reformers, such as Florence Kelley, Grace Abbott, and Jane Addams, Lathrop was born into an affluent family with a tradition of reform activity. Her grandparents had pioneered in the Illinois abolition movement, while her father, William Lathrop, a lawyer and Republican politician, was an ardent advocate of civil service reform. With the support of an educated mother and of a father who fortunately believed in women's capabilities, Julia graduated from Vassar in 1880 and later read law. In 1890 she turned her attention to social work, joining the Hull House settlement in Chicago and becoming a volunteer visitor for the Cook County agent's office.

It took very little time before her talents were recognized. In 1892 Governor John P. Altgelt appointed her the first woman member of the Illinois Board of Public Charities, a position she continued to hold, with one four-year break, from 1893 to 1909. Lathrop appears to have been a warm, vital woman with great insight into human motivation and with high principles. Her own success in Illinois did not prevent her from resigning in 1901 in protest against the political patrongage that permeated the public welfare system. Fortunately, with a change in governor, she resumed her place. During these years she made many thorough studies of state institutions for the blind, deaf, delinquent, and insane, while tours abroad allowed her to compare systems and suggest improvements.

One area of lasting interest to Lathrop was the welfare of children. Her early contact with children kept in poorhouses and state institutions stimulated a lifelong concern. In 1899 she was one of the major influences in the creation of the Chicago Juvenile Court. Subsequently she became president of the Juvenile Court Committee and was influential in the acquisition of the first mental hygiene clinic for the children who were passing through the state's judicial process. The peak of her career came in 1912 when President William Howard Taft offered her the position of chief of the new U.S. Children's Bureau. For nine years she guided the new department in its research into infant mortality and other welfare problems, constantly fighting for funds to make the bureau a viable entity. When Lathrop relinquished the post to her colleague Grace Abbott in 1921, many of the political battles had been won and the organization was in a position to expand its operations substantially in the following years.

Retirement from the Children's Bureau did not mean the end of Lathrop's activities. Until her death in 1932 she continued to lecture and advise on subjects ranging from immigration and women's suffrage to child labor and the better administration of laws concerning children. In addition, from 1925 to 1931 she was an assessor for the Child Welfare Committee of the League of Nations. Throughout her career, Lathrop expressed a constant optimism. It was her belief that "sooner or later, as we choose by our interest or its lack, the child will win."[37]

If professionals in certain fields formed the vanguard of the child welfare movement, its support was by no means confined to them. According to the particular institution or campaign concerned, a variety of individuals and groups contributed their aid. Women's clubs, for example, participated in many legislative battles. In Illinois alone there were over two hundred clubs at the turn of the century, representing some twenty thousand members. The most powerful, the Chicago Women's Club, which included some of the most socially prominent women in the area, provided a significant lobby for a wide range of welfare reforms, in such areas as child labor, compulsory education, and hours of female employment.[38]

An institution such as the George Junior Republic in Freeville, N.Y., attracted, "for various reasons and on various terms, a mixed bag of radicals and socialists, businessmen and conservatives, social gospellers and evangelists, students, feminists, professors, publicists and politicians."[39] Overall, Peter Filene's description of Progressivism as shifting coalitions of reformers (quoted earlier in this chapter) perhaps best reflects the total child welfare picture.

THE REFORMERS' ALTRUISM

Whatever the membership, there was undoubtedly a class difference between the children who were defined as dependent and neglected and the reformers who set about changing their environment. The implications of this social gap have recently received significant attention. Certain critical analyses have provided a useful counterbalance to previous interpretations that saw welfare reform as stemming solely from the good will of the people concerned and as being directed against the established order on behalf of the less privileged. These recent analyses have refused to accept the reformers' self-evaluation or to assume that institutional and legislative changes put forward in the name of justice were, in actual fact, either inevitable or an obvious improvement on the previous system.

We are now more conscious of the motivational ambivalence that was present during this period. In all areas there were those who "were torn between their wish to liberate the unused energies of the submerged portions of society and their enthusiasm for social planning."[40] American society was unstable; there was an apparent threat of social conflict; the less fortunate seemed also to be the most dangerous. Welfare reformers were not free from the anxieties and prejudices of their social group. They tended to be conservative, as might be expected of those who were profiting from the American system as it stood. Few, for example, took their criticism of the industrial situation to the logical extreme of condemning the capitalist system. Most, while recognizing that labor needed to organize for better wages and conditions, were still wary of trade unionists. Kelley was among the few exceptions. She had worked, studied, and corresponded with Friedrich Engels and throughout her social work career in the United States remained a committed, if undoctrinaire, socialist. Although not an active revolutionary, Kelley in no way saw her role as one of conciliation between capital and labor. In her early work at Hull House, as State Factory Inspector for Illinois, and later as general secretary of the National Consumers' League, she wholeheartedly supported the organization of workers to resist economic exploitation.[41]

The amelioration the majority of reformers hoped to see in American society was less dramatic than the demise of capitalism. Rather, they designed changes within the system that would integrate into capitalist society elements that were currently imperfectly assimilated. The direction of this social engineering was to be placed in the hands of those who, by virtue of their expertise, were best fitted to take on that responsibility. Undeniably there were manipulative overtones in the plans to extend the benefits of American society to the less fortunate. As Christopher Lasch has pointed out, at the same time that many spoke of the need to liberate the creative energies of humanity, they were also talking of "adjusting" people in healthful relations to one another. For example, this could be seen in progressive education, which was aimed not merely at the normal socialization of the individual but also at eliminating the self-centered attitude that generated social conflict. While Dewey saw education as an instrument for social change and a method of bringing equal opportunities to all Americans, he did not realize that his system still allowed for indoctrination, even though the values instilled would be Progressive rather than conservative.[42]

It is evident that this ambivalence behind reform extended to all areas of welfare work. The discrimination among groups that needed aid reflected the fact that more than welfare concerns were involved. Those who generally received least attention, the aged, blacks, and those of the sick who did not require institutional care, were those who posed least threat to the social order. Immigrants and unskilled workers were obviously in need of more consideration. Women and children were a subtler threat, their welfare determining the efficiency of families in the future. Among the children, the delinquent, the dependent, and the neglected were viewed with greatest concern because of the potential danger their uncontrolled development posed for America's general stability.

However, it would be wrong if as a reaction against earlier, uncritical interpretations of humanitarian reform, writers on child welfare were now to swing to the other extreme and allow the maintenance of social order to be the only motivating force. The interaction between self-interest and idealism is too complex to permit dismissal of the humanitarianism of the late nineteenth century as a hypocritical front for the self-interest of privileged classes. When considering the welfare reforms put forward during the Progressive era, it is clear that a genuine altruism was involved.

Much of this altruism had a religious orientation. As was mentioned earlier, a fair number of welfare reformers entered social work via the ministry. To many others, welfare work was a practical substitute for a life in the church, a way to carry out a sense of mission to society that had been nurtured in their youth. Prominent child welfare worker Homer Folks was one who showed an early concern with religion but decided against the ministry in favor of social work. During his undergraduate years at Harvard, Folks took courses in the ethics of social reform under Francis G. Peabody, a famous theologian of Christian morals. He was impressed with the idea that, in the final analysis, social problems were questions of ethics, the answers to which were to be found in charity and Christian cooperation. Welfare was his vocation after graduation. Appointment as general superintendent of the Children's Aid Society of Pennsylvania was followed by a 54-year relationship with the New York State Charities Aid Association. Through his work with this organization, his contributions to the National Conference of Charities and Correction, his support of child labor regulation, and his efforts on behalf of the juvenile court and the Children's Bureau, he received the deserved respect of the members of the new profession of social work.[43]

Jane Addams was yet another notable figure who found in social work a surrogate for religion. To her, Christianity was not "a set of ideas which belong to the religious consciousness (or)...a thing to be proclaimed and instituted apart from the social life of the community." Instead it was a faith that should "seek a simple and natural expression in the social organism itself." The religious impulse was one of the motives Addams singled out as being of prime importance in the foundation of the Hull House settlement and in the activity of other Chicago organizations.[44]

Another impulse was the desire to "make the entire social organism democratic, to extend democracy beyond its political expression." The infusion of the social ethic into American life was the essence of the reform movement Addams and others supported. She claimed that "it is not difficult to see that, although America is pledged to the democratic ideal, the view of democracy has been partial and that its best achievement thus far has been pushed along the line of the franchise. Democracy has made little attempt to assert itself in social affairs."[45] In her opinion, current society needed new rules of conduct, which should both be set down in law and absorbed into the consciousness of its citizens. Instead of the individualistic, competitive ethic of the nineteenth century, there was urgently needed a new morality based on humanitarianism and cooperation.

It was with this belief in the necessity of a new social ethic that reformers like Addams attempted to change the life style of America's less-fortunate citizens. Not all had her keen understanding of the poor and socially handicapped, her recognition that the poor were not to be regarded as misfits and failures because they refused to act like middle-class citizens. Most, however, did grasp something of the unjust and unfavorable conditions under which numerous American citizens lived, and they were moved by a genuine sympathy and concern. Unfortunately, they saw no potential conflict between the desire for a stable capitalist society and the urge to better the situation of the less privileged. Justification of their own favored position in the American system led middle-class reformers to equate what was good for "society" with what was good for the disadvantaged sections of society.

In their search for ways to produce the harmonious capitalist society they desired, reformers looked to, among other things, the successful socialization of children. With respect to dependent and neglected children, one question to be decided was the best means of caring for these youngsters outside their own families. This decision will be examined in the following two chapters.

NOTES

1. "An Act to Regulate the Treatment and Control of Dependent, Neglected and Delinquent Children," Laws of Illinois, 1899, in Robert Bremner, ed. *Children and Youth in America: A Documentary History* (Cambridge, Mass.: Harvard University Press, 1971), vol. 2, p. 507.

2. Ibid., vol. 1, pp. 64-71.

3. Homer Folks, *Care of Destitute, Neglected and Delinquent Children*, (New York: J. B. Lyon, 1900), p. 97.

4. For a history of societies for the prevention of cruelty to children, see Roswell C. McCrea, *The Humane Movement: A Descriptive Survey* (New York: Columbia University Press, 1910), and William J. Schultz, "The Humane Movement in the United States 1910-1922," *Columbia University Studies in History, Economics and Public Law*, Study no. 1 (New York: Columbia University Press, 1924), pp. 1-320.

5. Bremner, *Children and Youth in America*, vol. 2, pp. 189-94.

6. *Annual Report of the Cook County Juvenile Court*, in Cook County, Ill., Board of Commissioners, *Charity Service Report*, 1908, p. 182.

7. Charles R. Henderson, "The Relation of Philanthropy to Social Order and Progress," *Proceedings of the 26th NCCC*, 1899, p. 13.

8. Lillian Wald, "The Immigrant Young Girl," *Proceedings of the 36th NCCC*, 1909, p. 261.

9. Louise de Koven Bowen, *Safeguards for City Youth at Work and at Play* (New York: Macmillan, 1914), pp. 160-70.

10. *Annual Report of the Cook County Juvenile Court*, Cook County, Ill., Board of Commissioners, in *Charity Service Report*, 1910, pp. 203-4. U.S. Bureau of the Census, *Thirteenth Census of the United States, 1910*

(Washington, D.C.: Government Printing Office, 1913), pp. 854-55, 942.

11. Jacob A. Riis, *How The Other Half Lives* (New York: Hill & Wang, 1957, first printed New York: Scribner's, 1890), p. 141.

12. George B. Mangold, "Conditions Underlying Juvenile Delinquency," *Proceedings of the 16th Illinois Conference of Charities and Correction*, 1912, p. 90.

13. Edward T. Devine, "The Pittsburgh Survey," *Charities and the Commons* 21 (1908-1909): 1035-36. See also Robert H. Bremner, *From the Depths: The Discovery of Poverty in the United States* (New York: New York University Press, 1967), pp. 230-43.

14. Emma O. Lundberg, *Children of Illegitimate Birth and Measures for Their Protection*, U.S. Children's Bureau Publication No. 166 (Washington, D.C.: Government Printing Office, 1926), pp. 2-7. Emma O. Lundberg and Katharine F. Lenroot, *Illegitimacy as a Child Welfare Problem*, Part II, U.S. Children's Bureau Publication No. 75 (Washington, D.C.: Government Printing Office, 1920), p. 50. Percy Kammerer, *The Unmarried Mother* (Montclair, N.J.: Patterson Smith, 1969, first printed Boston: Little, Brown, 1918), p. 329.

15. Figures from John A. Ryan, *A Living Wage: Its Ethical and Economic Aspects* (New York: Macmillan, 1906) in Bremner, *From the Depths*, pp. 153-54.

16. *Annual Report of the Boston Church Home Society*, 1893, p. 5.

17. Riis, *How the Other Half Lives*, pp. 148-49.

18. See, for example, William J. Goode, "Force and Violence in the Family," *Journal of Marriage and the Family* 33 (1971): 624-37. Jeanne M. Giovannani, "Parental Mistreatment: Perpetrators and Victims," ibid., pp. 649-57.

19. *Annual Report of the New York Society for the Prevention of Cruelty to Children*, 1900, p. 44.

20. See case histories given by the Massachusetts Society for the Prevention of Cruelty to Children, *Annual Report*, 1904, pp. 19-25.

21. Peter Filene, "An Obituary for the Progessive Movement," *American Quarterly* 22 (1970): 33.

22. George Mowry, *The California Progressives* (Berkeley: University of California Press, 1951); George Mowry, *The Era of Theodore Roosevelt* (New York: Harper, 1958), pp. 85-105.

23. Richard Hofstadter, *The Age of Reform* (London: Jonathan Cape, 1962), p. 135.

24. Henry Demarest Lloyd, *Wealth versus Commonwealth* (New York: Harper, 1894), p. 511.

25. Samuel P. Hays, "The Politics of Reform in Municipal Government in the Progressive Era," *Pacific Northwest Quarterly* 55 (1964): 159-61.

Joseph Huthmacher, "Urban Liberalism and the Age of Reform," *Mississippi Valley Historical Review* 49 (1962): 231-41. William T. Kerr, "The Progressives of Washington, 1910-1912," *Pacific Northwest Quarterly* 55 (1964): 16-27.

26. David P. Thelen, "Social Tensions and the Origins of Progressivism," *Journal of American History* 56 (1969): 323-41.

27. Robert L. Buroker, "From Voluntary Association to Welfare State: The Development of Public Social Services in Illinois, 1890-1920," (Ph.D. diss., University of Chicago, 1973).

28. Robert H. Wiebe, *The Search for Order* (London: Macmillan, 1967), pp. 111-32.

29. U.S. Bureau of the Census, *Comparative Occupational Statistics for the United States, 1870 to 1940* (Washington, D.C.: Government Printing Office, 1943), p. 111.

30. *Dictionary of American Biography* (New York: Scribner's, 1960), Supplement 1, pp. 377-78. Emma O. Lundberg, *Unto the Least of These* (New York: Appleton Century Co., 1947), pp. 217-20.

31. For an account of the calling of the 1909 conference, see U.S. Children's Bureau, *The Story of the White House Conferences on Children and Youth* (Washington, D.C.: Government Printing Office, 1967), pp. 2-5.

32. *Dictionary of American Biography*, vol. 4, pp. 524-25.

33. William O'Neill, *Everyone was Brave* (Chicago: Quadrangle Books, 1971).

34. Lucinda B. Chandler, "The Woman Movement," *Arena*, 4 (1891): 706.

35. Mary Mumford, "The Place of Woman in Municipal Reform," *Outlook* 49 (1894): 587.

36. Lucy Sickels, "Woman's Influence in Juvenile Reformatories," *Proceedings of the 21st NCCC*, 1894, p. 164.

37. Jane Addams, *My Friend Julia Lathrop* (New York: Macmillan, 1935). Julia Lathrop is quoted from p. 213. *Dictionary of American Biography*, Supplement 1, pp. 484-86.

38. Dorothy E. Powers, "The Chicago Women's Club" (master's thesis, University of Chicago, 1939).

39. Jack M. Holl, *Juvenile Reform in the Progressive Era: William R. George and the Junior Republic Movement* (Ithaca, N.Y.: Cornell University Press, 1971), p. 33.

40. Christoper Lasch, *The New Radicalism in America 1889-1963* (New York: Alfred A. Knopf, 1966), p. 168.

41. Dorothy R. Blumberg, *Florence Kelley: The Making of a Social Pioneer* (New York: August M. Kelley, 1960).

42. Lasch, *The New Radicalism*, pp. 141-80.

43. Walter I. Trattner, *Homer Folks: Pioneer in Social Welfare* (New York: Columbia University Press, 1968).

44. Jane Addams, "The Subjective Necessity for Social Settlements," in Christopher Lasch, ed., *The Social Thought of Jane Addams* (New York: Bobbs-Merrill, 1965), p. 41.

45. Ibid., p. 29.

3

INSTITUTIONAL CARE

In the Progressives' search for order, much of their hope was rooted in a belief in the malleability of the human character. The years of childhood were considered the most important; children were less resistant to change than adults. The pliable nature of children's personalities made it crucial to select the right environment for their development. Social workers and philanthropists who were involved with dependent and neglected children debated the best surroundings for their care, education, and training. Where were they to be taught the basics of good citizenship? The choice, as they saw it, lay between the institution and the foster home. This was by no means a new debate. From the 1850s the relative merits of institutional and foster care had been the subject of much reasoned argument and personal invective. The skirmishes continued into the twentieth century, although by the first decade a consensus had been reached among leading welfare figures. Their decision was made in favor of the foster home.

The swing toward placing-out has been viewed as an inevitable and obviously beneficial step in the progress of child welfare.[1] It has been argued that colonial poor-law arrangements gave way to a more humane institutional system, which in turn was improved by the substitute family. Contrary to this assumption, however, the superiority of the foster home is not self-evident and institutions are not inherently destructive. Many of the criticisms leveled at institutions are well founded. Institutions have tended to be plagued by a variety of difficulties; for example, they have inclined towards authoritarianism, a binary structure, and "batch" living. Also, isolated from external scrutiny, they have often fallen below adequate standards. As one modern observer has noted, "many are in fact snake pits, special hells, social systems of captives."[2] However, these conditions can be alleviated. Group care is not doomed by virtue of its structure. Similarly, foster-family care fails or succeeds according to its particular application, not because of its family basis.

The general decision in favor of foster homes, then, was not logically necessary, nor was it based on any systematic empirical demonstration of the benefits of this type of care for the child's growth and development. The research efforts of these years were superficial and narrow in scope; their conclusions were tenuous. Foster care had been accepted in principle and applied all over the country before individual welfare workers began insisting on the necessity of evaluating results and comparing them with those of institutions. The choice was not made on the basis of a comprehensive investigation; rather, it resulted from the failure of institutions in general to achieve the ambitious goals for which they had been established from the abuses to be found within the system and the mystique surrounding the American family, which permeated late-nineteenth-century thought.

EVOLUTION OF THE ASYLUM

Widespread use of the asylum for dependents, defectives, and delinquents was a development of the Jacksonian period. Colonial society had not felt the need to isolate the destitute or the deviate. According to the belief of the time, poverty was a providential and integral part of society with certain beneficial side effects. The misfortunes of one section of the community stimulated the charitable instincts of others. Accordingly, society provided relief to individuals without attempting to relieve the conditions that made it necessary. Similarly, while there was apprehension about the existence of crime, it was not expected that society could eradicate it. Noninstitutional mechanisms of control were preferred; corporal punishment took precedence over incarceration.[3]

As David M. Rothman demonstrates in his book *The Discovery of the Asylum*, by the early decades of the nineteenth century this general attitude had been significantly undermined by the rapid economic and social changes taking place. Americans had lost confidence in the ability of a sense of hierarchy or location to maintain the social balance. An initial criticism of the then-current legal codes was succeeded by a more anxious analysis of the social structure. Although individual personality failings were taken into account, deviant behavior was thought to be rooted in society itself. The failure of the family to act as an efficient means of control, an imperfectly organized economy, widespread vice and corruption—all these apparently provided a fertile ground for the growth of the dependent and the delinquent. However, if this were so, there was now the possibility that society could rid itself of these potentially dangerous groups. The answer seemed to depend on separating deviates from family and community and placing them in artificially created and corruption-free environments. Model institutions would provide the setting for successful rehabilitation while also teaching society valuable lessons in the training of its citizens.[4]

An epidemic of asylum building swept across the country after 1830. Penitentiaries, juvenile reformatories, mental institutions, almshouses, and orphanages were established with grand expectations. The greatest optimism, of course, surrounded the removal of children from those "baneful influences which would inevitably tend to make them pests to society and ultimately tenants of our prisons."[5] County and municipal poorhouses took many thousands of these youngsters. Here they were to be well fed and clothed, attend school, and be given recreation and religious instruction until such time as they were old enough to be bound out. They were theoretically to be separated from the various dependent adults who were being cared for at public expense.[6] By 1880 approximately nine thousand Americans under the age of fifteen were being cared for in this way.[7]

The majority of these children found their way to the wide variety of private and public institutions that catered specifically to children. Before 1800 there had only been half a dozen; in the following half-century, 104 were founded, 81 of these after 1830.[8] By 1910 over 110,000 dependent, neglected, and delinquent children were being cared for in 1,151 institutions of some kind.[9]

Social need, sympathy, and sectarianism were the major forces in the creation of these institutions. Some, like the Protestant Orphan Asylum of Chicago, were opened in response to outbreaks of cholera or other fatal diseases. Others originated in the bequests of individual philanthropists or in the charitable inclinations of the increasingly active women's organizations. The Civil War stimulated the foundation of a number of state orphans' homes for children of men killed in action, while sectarian rivalry provided an even stronger impulse to institutional development. By the postwar period the Catholic church had established itself firmly enough, with sufficient funds at its disposal, to compete for control of the country's dependent and neglected children. Likewise, the large number of Jewish immigrants who arrived later in the century created a demand for separate welfare provisions.[10]

THE ASYLUM FALLS INTO DISREPUTE

Signs of disillusionment with the institutional network became visible as early as the 1850s and increased as the century progressed. It had not fulfilled the heady aspirations of its supporters. A regenerated society, free from large-scale poverty, crime, and mental disease, seemed as far away as ever. Facilities were strained. Programs for character training could not cope with the increasing number of chronic cases that were admitted. Rehabilitation was, in many instances, reduced to a mere custodial operation. In the face of rapid urbanization, immigration, and the accelerating stratification of society, convenience took over from the more constructive dynamic that had brought about the creation of the asylum. Many institutions became a means of keeping society's casualties out of sight and mind. Evidence of abuse was easy to find. Obedience, regularity, and discipline, once seen as the basis for character formation, frequently degenerated into a mechanical and often harsh application of authority.[11]

Part of this general disappointment encompassed the institutional care of dependent children. The situation of children in almshouses received the first blast of criticism. In 1856 a select committee appointed by the New York State Senate investigated and reported on the condition of the state's poorhouses. The report was a bitter condemnation of the "filth, nakedness, licentiousness, general bad morals and disregard of religion and the most common religious observances, as well as a gross neglect of the most ordinary comforts and decencies of life" to be found there. For the young these poorhouses were "the worse possible nurseries," encouraging pauperism rather than producing self-supporting adults.[12] About twenty years passed, however, before this recognition of the system's inadequacy was translated into legislative action. The solution put forward by William Pryor Letchworth, a leading member of the New York State Board of Charities, was to prohibit the commitment of normal children over two years of age to county almshouses. He described the plight of children in one such institution as follows:

> A group of boys were found in the wash-house, intermingled with the inmates and around the cauldrons where the dirty clothes were boiling. Here was an insane woman raving and uttering wild gibberings; a half crazy man was sardonically grinning; and an overgrown boy was torturing one of the little boys, while securely holding him, by thrusting splinters under his fingernails. The cries of the little one seemed to delight his tormentor as well as some of the older inmates who were looking on. The upper apartment of this dilapidated building was used for a sleeping room. An inmate was scrubbing the floor which was so worn that water came through the cracks in continuous droppings upon the heads of the little ones below, who did not seem to regard it as a serious annoyance.[13]

Removal rather than reform seemed the better solution. With the backing of the state Charities Aid Association, the press, and the state Convention of County Superintendents of the Poor, Letchworth's proposal finally became law in 1875. Other states witnessed similar agitation, and several managed to pass prohibitive legislation before the turn of the century.[14] The number of children cared for in this way gradually decreased. Even so, according to census figures for 1910, still to be found among the motley inhabitants of the almshouse were 2,486 children under the age of sixteen.[15]

Confidence in the beneficial effects of orphan asylums and other institutions for dependent children declined more slowly. Indeed, when thousands of children were released from almshouses throughout the country, most were transferred to other institutions rather than cared for in other ways. Ammunition was slowly being gathered, however, so that by the end of the nineteenth century, noninstitutional methods were once again being accepted as viable and valuable alternatives.

It is difficult to give an adequate impression of institutional life during this period. The type and quality of care varied tremendously from one asylum to the next. On the one hand there was the small rural home catering to the needs of a dozen or so homeless children. On the other were massive congregations like the New York Catholic Protectory. The Protectory was founded in 1862 by Levi Silliman Ives for "the regeneration both moral and physical of the juvenile waifs of our streets." It was also designed to prevent Catholic children being exported to Protestant families in the West, where their souls would supposedly be in danger. From its inception, the Protectory harbored large numbers of children behind its walls. During 1891, for example, it cared for a total of 3,123 cases, and it housed well over 2,000 at any one time.[16] Contrary to the usual impression given, however, the majority of institutions were relatively small. For example, in 1880, over half catered to the needs of less than 50 children. The median size of institutions was 42.[17]

Each organization determined the age and condition of the children it received and the time limit for their care. At one end of the scale were the foundling asylums, which accumulated vast numbers of abandoned babies and transferred them in later infancy. At the other were groups, such as William R. George's Junior Republics, that were designed mainly for youths in their teens. Institutions might be little more than common residences, the children being educated in the local communities. Alternatively, they might be agricultural or industrial training schools, self-sufficient and geared toward production of skilled and semiskilled workers. Whatever the structure, the amount of joy, satisfaction, and freedom the children experienced necessarily varied according to the personality, intelligence, and experience of the superintendent and directors.

For the purpose of this study, I shall not attempt to give an aerial view of institutional life but rather to point out some of the more harsh elements, which were encouraging criticism of the system. Needless to say, there were many orphanages and children's homes throughout the country that managed to avoid the rather stereotyped and repressive life style described here.

Home, for the large majority of dependent and neglected children in this period, was an institution built according to the congregate plan. Whether a simple two-story frame house or a massive brick edifice, it contained virtually everthing necessary for the daily existence of all of its children. If unfortunate, they might eat, sleep, play, work, and learn in the same building. If luckier, they might go to school or church in the local community. Rarely, however, was the institution an active and integral part of that community. Old ideas of the benefits of isolation lingered on. Outsiders, even relatives, were discouraged from visiting certain institutions by restrictions on the time and frequency of visits.

Within the institution, variety was hardly a great part of daily life. Many asylums believed that although children hate routine, "routine is the beginning and necessary condition of all effective life."[18] The Catholic Protectory was one organization that congratulated itself on being "a wonderful little world of system and regularity [where] . . . each day and month and season had its own appointed duties, its industries, studies and recreation."[19] The annual reports of asylums listed, for the benefit of the institutions' supporters, the everyday habits of the inmates. From approximately six o'clock in the morning to eight or nine o'clock at night, the children complied with an unvarying schedule. Each activity, from getting dressed to recreational reading, was allotted a rigid time limit. Children could virtually predict exactly what they would be doing and what they would be eating on any given day of the next week, month, or even year.

For example, this is the schedule given for the inmates of the Glenwood Industrial Training School for Boys in Illinois in 1892:[20]

Rising bell	5:45 a.m.
Dressing	5:45– 6:30
Breakfast	6:30– 7:00
Recreation and military drill	7:30– 8:00
Work in all departments	8:30– 9:00
Chapel exercises	9:00– 9:20
School	9:20–11:30
Recreation	11:30–12:00
Dinner	12:00–12:40
Work in all departments	12:40– 1:30
Recreation	1:30– 2:00
School	2:00– 4:30
Military drill and recreation	4:30– 5:55
Supper	5:55– 6:30
Military drill	6:30– 7:00
Chapel exercise	7:00– 7:30
Reading and social exercise	7:30– 8:00
Retire	8:00 p.m.

The object of much of this regularity was to instill into receptive minds and bodies obedience, industry, and morality, qualities considered essential to successful functioning in the outside world.

Discipline was generally believed to be of paramount importance to any program of character training. It was imposed on every aspect of daily living. In institutions such as the Illinois Soldiers' Orphans' Home, for example, eating was carried out in silence and at the appropriate command. Dining was hardly a pleasant period of social interaction. The children were marched to the dining hall in formation. There "while waiting for meals the little boys sat in rows with crossed legs, like little images of Buddha, and if any boy disturbed the holy calm, he was stood up behind the gas pipe as a token of disapprobation. The larger boys stood in line while waiting for their meals and were inspected and subjected to semi-military orders by one of their number."[21] After eating they disbanded in a similarly orderly fashion. In the New England Home for Little Wanderers, in Boston, the same rigidity and obsession with obedience applied to sleep. On Sunday mornings children were allowed to stay in bed for an extra half hour—or rather, they were forced to stay in bed during that time. "No doubt many of them would prefer to get up," reported the superintendent, "but not everything a child wants is it best a child should have."[22] A sense of autonomy was hardly encouraged. To leave children to themselves on the grounds that it developed personal initiative seemed to be an invitation to moral disaster. To give them a voice in the actual running of the institution was thought even more preposterous.

For boys, military drill frequently reinforced a closely supervised routine in an attempt to produce compliant inmates. In uniform, carrying guns, and sometimes accompanied by their own band, they paraded as often as three times a day. Ex-army men were occasionally employed to supervise their training. The results were enthusiastically praised. According to the directors of the Catholic Protectory, the drill was beneficial in that it gave the boys, "a manly and easy carriage, . . . taught them self-respect . . . [and] made them athletic and healthy." But they felt that "The highest results of the military training are to be found in the great precept and practice of obedience—prompt, cheerful and unquestioning obedience. It is not so difficult for boys, or even men, to obey their superiors but to obey instantly the word of command from one's companions, one's equals, and even perhaps one's inferiors, is the attainment of the best manhood; for the school of obedience is the surest road to an honorable command."[23]

If these methods proved inadequate, the institutions resorted to punishment or expulsion. Deprivation of food or privileges and extra work were common means of coercion. Corporal punishment does not seem to have been generally condoned in institutions for dependent children, but it was inevitably used. Cases of abuse were reported to state authorities and vigorously defended by the institutions involved as being justified or accidental.[24] Obviously, many of these cases were neither. In the event of behavior problems that the authorities were unwilling or felt themselves unable to handle, children were often summarily transferred to juvenile reformatories. The stigma of delinquency may have been unjustly conferred on any number of children who failed to conform to the institutions' rather rigid regimes.

Apart from encouraging habits of unthinking obedience, most institutions claimed to be dedicated to teaching their children the importance of industry. Constant hard work was considered an agency of reform, "leaving little time for reminiscences of a past which has been bad, and little room for thoughts which turn inward or downward rather than outward and upward."[25] Institutions saw themselves as preparing dependent and neglected children for success in the outside world. In the better asylums this "preparation" meant a varied program of manual training complementing an adequate formal education. In the poorer institutions, not only was education made to suffer but the work demanded of the children was often hard, consisted of menial tasks, and did little more than keep them continually occupied. In general there was little inducement to bright children to carry their education through to secondary school. The lack of facilities and the attitude that dependent children should be grateful for anything they received, meant that children accepted a meager amount of learning. A man who had been an inmate of an institution at the turn of the century recollected his own educational experiences: the "three R's" were considered adequate for children of his type; and when by sheer persistence this child managed to break through this tradition and secure a high school education for himself and others, "it so greatly upset the routine of the institution as to make the practice very unpopular and very difficult for the boys and girls who were involved."[26] Other institutions, while not actively prohibiting further education, regarded it as a privilege. At the Glenwood Industrial Training School for Boys, in Illinois, for example, permission to attend high school dependend on a minimum one year's residence in the institution and was given in return for carrying out extra duties at the weekend such as operating the switchboard.[27]

Much of the work given to children to prevent idleness and to "prepare" them, involved support of the institutions themselves. Children worked in the kitchen, maintained the grounds, cleaned the buildings, carried out repairs, made clothes, and laundered. Articles that they had made and vegetables or fruit grown at the asylum were often sold and the proceeds received by the institution. While, in themselves, these duties were not harmful, the load of tasks many children were expected to perform virtually amounted to exploitation. The superintendent of one farm school in Illinois expressed a common attitude when he explained with pride that he would be able to conduct an orphanage with little expense to the public if his institution had "a few more children and a bunch of cattle."[28] Public investigations reported very young children working three or four hours a day, not always in healthy conditions and often taxed beyond their strength.[29] In one asylum, at least, labor-saving devices were positively forbidden. It was considered better for the girls to carry out their chores in the traditional manner, that is, by sheer muscle power. It was not the intention of the directors "to furnish the institution with such appliances as shall discontent them with those they will find in...farmhouses or in the homes they have left."[30]

The actual value of this type of training to the children involved is questionable, but no doubt many of the institution staffs viewed it as invaluable. The superintendent of the Chicago Home for Jewish Orphans proudly reported the benefits of housework for one of his ex-inmates. "One of our boys who works in a wholesale grocery tells me that he could never hold his present position had he not learned in our home how to use the broom and duster."[31] More often than not this smattering of domestic skills was of far less use to the child than to the institution that child helped to maintain.

Morality was the third mainstay of the institution's training program. In those asylums founded on a sectarian basis, the development of moral values meant, primarily, religious instruction. Physical, intellectual, and industrial training might produce conditions favorable to the development of a worthy Christian or Jewish life, but it was thought dangerous to substitute them for religious teaching.[32] Hence there was a heavy emphasis on daily services and vast amounts of rote learning. A Lutheran minister, recalling his boyhood in a sectarian institution, remembered its stiffness and cold formality. All instruction "was in the German language (of which most of us were completely ignorant) and consisted of constant memorization."[33] To this religious training were added any number of more secular practices designed to promote righteous living. The New England Home for Little

Wanderers wanted its children well prepared to fight the evils of the outside world. Twice-a-month meetings of the institution's temperance society were convened to renew the pledge to abstain from the use of liquor, tobacco, and profane words and to publicly court-martial those who had strayed in the interim.[34]

In all of the activities so far described, conformity and uniformity generally prevailed. Exacerbated by an inadequate staff and meager facilities, the collective mentality of institutions remained unchallenged for many years. The days of children being known by numbers rather than by names had disappeared,[35] but nevertheless, in the early twentieth century, orphanages could still be found in which children dressed exactly alike, slept two or three to a bed in large dormitories, and were herded around like cattle. By that time, however, a large body of welfare workers and philanthropists had questioned the social utility of such practices and their values to the individual child. This recognition of abuses not only evoked demands for reform, but also helped swing the pendulum of welfare opinion away from the entire concept of group care.

In the period under study, leading welfare reformers such as Homer Folks, Hastings Hornell Hart, Carl Christian Carstens, and Julia Lathrop threw their support behind foster care. They were far more vocal than the Roman Catholic and other denominational groups that basically comprised the institution's defense. Through papers given at state and national conferences, and articles published in such journals as *Charities Review* and *Charities* (later *Charities and the Commons* and *Survey*), reformers carried out a powerful publicity campaign. Criticism was leveled at the rising figures for children being held in institutions, the expense, and the questionable adequacy of their care and training.

Self-interest on the part of institution directors and staff members was held to blame for various abuses, among them the increasing numbers. John H. Finley, secretary of the New York State Charities Aid Association, in an address to the National Conference of Charities and Correction in 1891, discussed the development of the nation's large congregate asylums. He asked his colleagues, "Why do these enormous institutions exist and continue to grow?

Why is it that we are practically not in advance of people one hundred years ago in this matter?'' The answer, as he saw it, lay in ''the pride, the unconsciously selfish interests of institutions that fill to overflowing their great structures.'' Where once they might have been intended as steppingstones in the treatment of dependent children, they had since forgotten their original charters and had gone into the more profitable victualing business.[36] Others condemned public subsidies, particularly the per capita grants, for increasing the temptation to accumulate children. The need for institutions to sustain their size led to children being kept far longer than necessary in overcrowded, often unhealthy conditions. It also encouraged their economic exploitation.[37]

Institutions, according to some, were too expensive. Generally disregarding the question of whether the quality of the service justified the cost, they pointed to the running costs of the large plants and the salaries of the sizable staffs as evidence of economic wastefulness. It was estimated that $40 million was being spent in 1892 to house the country's dependent children. In comparison, placing a child in a family seemed a sound financial step. One money-minded official thought that ''if for $20 or $50 we can get an institution to find a home for a child, it is a pretty good investment. If we can save some 8 or 10 years of board of a child by spending $50, I look on that as a good business plan.'' Many agreed.[38]

Most welfare leaders were less concerned with the expense than with the apparent failure of institutions to produce independent and hard-working children. Whereas earlier in the century an artificially created environment had seemed ideal for the training of dependent children, it was now condemned. Asylums and orphanages were criticized as being ''organized on a plan which is not that of the world which sooner or later their proteges have to re-enter.''[39] Segregation prevented the child from making contact with different types and groups of people and from dealing with a variety of common social situations. Physical isolation was reinforced by psychological alienation. Institutions, it was argued, cultivated in children a sense of being different that often remained for the rest of their lives. Their subsequent readjustment to normal life was emotionally difficult.[40]

Not only were the asylum children seen as ignorant of the outside world, but their independence and energy were supposedly
sapped by institutional living to such an extent that they failed to
function adequately in society. In the institution, shelter, food,
and clothing were provided by an unseen hand. This, it was felt,
could only lead children to expect that the state or certain of its
citizens would always provide for them. It encouraged an inclination toward permanent dependency.[41]

Similarly, it was claimed that initiative was sapped by constant
vigilance, routine, and collective activity. Children whose every
movement was merely a response to an order from the institutional
authorities would be confused and incapable of action once outside
the asylum walls. The regularity of their existence deadened
vitality, originality, and inquiry. It destroyed hope, the anticipation
of a different and better tomorrow that every human being needed.
"If there is magic for a boy in any one word, it is in the word
tomorrow. He by nature thinks about it; talks about it—in short he
lives for it. Take it out of his life and what have we left him? Evi-
dently the past which we wish him to forget and today, which
without the incentive of tomorrow loses more than half its interest."[42]
Training "in the lump" was thought equally disastrous. While it
might be convenient for the institution and might be adequate
physically for the child, it could not provide the individual choices
and responsibilities necessary for a successful life. "Whenever
Master Henry Jones has entirely sunk his individuality to become
number forty five in a line, he becomes an automatic part of a
great machine which at once lays the foundation for an utter lack
of self-reliance and essential individuality, so important in after
years for American citizenship."[43] Institutional life was condemned for producing uniformity of the soul. Critics thought that
the institutionalized child would never amount to much but would
always be one of a crowd, leading a colorless, shriveled existence.[44]

One part of "batch" living that many welfare workers found
obnoxious was the lack of contact and affection between staff and
inmates. Like Rudolph R. Reeder, superintendent of the New York
Orphan Asylum, these workers believed that children suffered
severely from a lack of adult influence and social intercourse. In
Reeder's opinion, "daily association and companionship with a

strong, sympathetic and lovable character is a brief but comprehensive description of a happy condition of child life."[45] How, it
was asked, could congregate living provide children with the
intimate relationships they would normally establish with a father
and mother? Critics pointed to the frequently high ratio of children
to adult personnel. One woman might be charged with the care of
fifty or more noisy, demanding children. How could she be expected to know and love each one as a mother knew and loved her
own family? It was impossible. In the case of very young babies,
lack of mother love could be fatal. Reformers had before them
mortality figures for organizations such as Saint Vincent's Infant
Asylum in Chicago, which in 1900 lost 345 of the 869 babies it
cared for. The high death rate was attributed not only to the poor
physical condition of the children received but also to the lack of
personal nursing by a mother figure. If the infants survived, social
workers argued, their lot was still a tragic one. They were compelled to grow up alone, without the love of parents and siblings.[46]

Institutions were also condemned for overemphasizing religious
instruction. The "religious" challenge was not the vehement
sectarian attack of earlier decades; at that time the asylum had
largely been denounced as part of a system that was strengthening
the power of the Catholic Church in the United States. The influence of the institution was attributed to a "lingering superstition"
about the power of the moral machinery in monastic establishments. Protestant-based organizations like the New York State
Charities Aid Association had opposed legislation that safeguarded
the faith of children being dealt with by the state. In response, the
Catholic Church had railed against the blatant proselytism of
Protestant associations that were attempting to deal with the
increasing numbers of immigrant children in U.S. cities.[47] Criticisms
in the 1890s and in the early twentieth century, while often made on
a sectarian basis, were more broadly stated. Both the quantity and
the quality of religious education were seen as objectionable. Byron
C. Mathews complained that institutionalized children were "often
taught too much about heaven and too little about earth."[48] An
undue amount of instruction produced weaklings. Religion, it was
claimed, was taught more by the atmosphere of a child's surroundings than by formal instruction. It was not imparted by "a set

form of blessings drawled out or mechanically entuned before each meal, and thanks in the same manner after, with chapel exercises twice a day in which psalms or other portions of the scriptures are repeated until they have worn hard-beaten grooves in the brain without penetrating the understanding, a rising prayer in the morning and a retiring prayer at night, all in concert and aloud."[49] As late as the 1930s, social workers were still pointing an accusing finger at sectarian institutions, claiming that their policy was based more on church affiliation and education than on the actual needs of the child.[50]

Not all arguments involved the effect of institutional life on the child. An objection commonly heard in the early days of the National Conference of Charities and Correction and still in circulation at the turn of the century was that institutions promoted the dissolution of family life. It was claimed that the asylum's willingness to accept children who still had one or both parents living encouraged irresponsible parents to shift their duties onto public and private welfare organizations. The practice of accepting a small weekly sum from parents, and caring for the child as long as this sum was forthcoming, was condemned. One child welfare worker with a vivid imagination painted the consequences of these cheap boarding schools. "Assured that the child is being cared for, the income is expended upon fine dresses, picture hats and a hired carriage and coachman to carry the parent to the orphanage for [the] visit." This worker was even doubtful as the advisability of accepting children temporarily when the parents were ill, because of "the tendency on the part of irresponsible parents to shirk, if possible, the burden of support of their offspring."[51] As social workers gained a greater insight into the conditions that forced parents to relinquish their children, the argument based on irresponsibility gradually disappeared. However, it has never been totally discarded.[52]

Despite the fact that the majority of their arguments concerned weaknesses in the practical workings of the institution, most critics tended to believe that the disadvantages were inherent in its group structure. They acknowledged that individual asylums varied in the quality of care provided but still denied the viability of long-term institutional training for the majority of dependent and neglected children.

THE CASE FOR THE INSTITUTION

Few went so far as to suggest that the institution be abandoned altogether. In view of the immense numbers of children in need of temporary and permanent shelter, this was simply unrealistic. However, it was advocated that the institution's function be reduced in terms of the types of children accepted and the length of the care given. Various types of problems seemed more suited to a period of institutionalization. While the foster family was seen as the best choice for most children, many, because of poor physical or mental condition, could not be placed immediately. Insofar as preparation was necessary, the institution appeared to be the most efficient and convenient method available. Here

> the head, heart and hands of children are trained to right ways of thinking, feeling and doing: the officials and teachers who are masters of their craft become expert in the diagnosis of disposition, inclination and capability, as well as in the discovery and relief of physical needs. Neglected children suffer from exposures to which they are subjected and their ailments, whether moral or physical, are the fruitful cause of disappointment, and the failure of effort to improve their condition, or to successfully domicile them in approved homes.[53]

The institution, in this case, was to be subsumed in the process of foster care.

Short-term institutionalization was also thought adequate for children who were only temporarily separated from their parents. Illness or sudden economic misfortune threw many children into the hands of welfare organizations. Until home circumstances improved, the asylum would provide a suitable environment for these youngsters. Other children whose needs might be possibly satisfied by the institution were those in specific age groups or those deprived of education by the negligence and vices of their parents. Conviction, more than evidence, underlay this classification of children to be placed in institutions; only later in the period did the question of admission come under close scrutiny. Nevertheless, welfare workers conceded that the institution did have a part to play in the care of dependent children.[54]

In response to the criticisms leveled at them, institution personnel defended what seemed to be the better aspects of their training schemes and sought to reform the abuses which they acknowledged in the system. Little attention was given, however, to the justification of group care as such. Mary E. Cobb was among the few voices in favor of communal child rearing. In an article entitled "The Legitimate Use of an Institution for Children," she wrote: "Someone said to me, 'I am always so sorry for children who have to do things in rows.' But children love to do things 'in rows.' The boys wish to train in companies, and play firemen or soldiers; the larger the companies, the better. The little girls hold their sewing societies, and give tea parties, and there are never enough of them until every doll is made to do duty. It is an unnatural child, I think, that shuns the crowd of its fellows.[55]

Few of her contemporaries paused to consider the positive potential of large numbers of children living and learning together. Instead they stressed the superiority of the formal and religious education provided by the better asylums.

According to certain supporters, children's institutions were simply schools with homes attached. They were for the destitute, dependent, and neglected "what Harvard, Yale, Vassar, Columbia, Oberlin and other colleges and seminaries are to the children of the more fortunate in life's struggle."[56] It was argued that in New York, Chicago, and other cities throughout the country, thousands of children owed their livelihood and happiness to the educational and training facilities of these organizations. Farmers sent their sons to agricultural college for scientific training, since they could no longer trust tradition and example to give an adequate grounding. The best housewives sent their daughters to school to learn cooking or dressmaking. The institution could provide this type of training, together with any number of other industrial skills. The well-equipped manual training school was thought, by some, to be the best that institutions had to offer.[57]

In view of the large number of sectarian organizations catering for dependent and neglected children, it was only to be expected that much of the institution's defense should center on the benefits of a religious education. Those in favor of the asylum claimed that without religious instruction, children could not be educated in the true sense of the word; that was to say, no complete and harmonious development of the intellect and the heart could be achieved. They declared that, given proper religious training, children were prepared for this world and for the life beyond. Religious institutions were powerful agencies for morality and righteousness, instilling into their charges faith, obedience, justice, and purity—the pillars of real character. Home training often neglected this.[58] According to one supporter of sectarian asylums, "all the efficient, lasting work for children today is accomplished under the direction of the various churches. The best results attained in institutions are to be found where religion is the groundwork of the system."[59] While not all made such extreme claims for their welfare activities, most were adamant on the value of a religious education for society's waifs and strays.

THE COTTAGE INSTITUTION

Although extolling the virtues of their own organizations, institution superintendents and directors did recognize the need for improvements. At the second meeting of the National Conference of Catholic Charities in 1912, it was admitted that institutional life was too regimented. One delegate denounced the fact that children "would remain from five to ten years in an institution and perhaps during that time would never have performed an individual act." Others acknowledged that asylums had a heavy death rate among infants and a high incidence of infectious diseases.[60] These criticisms of structure and particular practices did provoke a response. Programs for change were set in action. Not surprisingly, in the face of the then current, somewhat uncritical, defense of the family unit, the trend of institutional reform was toward a simulation of family life. Supporters of the asylum accepted the premise of the foster care argument and attempted to harmonize it with the facilities already in existence. The "cottage" institution gained steady ground.

One of the most enthusiastic and vocal advocates of this institutional design was Reeder. After a lengthy career in education, Reeder had, in 1898, accepted the appointment as superintendent of the New York Orphan Asylum, a congregate institution founded in the early nineteenth century. Two years later the asylum was moved to Hastings-on-Hudson and restructured on a cottage plan. In various articles and speeches and by way of a monograph entitled *How Two Hundred Children Live and Learn*, Reeder painted a rose-colored picture of the benefits of this reorganization.

To Reeder, the congregate institution was the poorest type of substitute home. It needed to be born again or go out of business. The amount of individual attention that might be given to any child seemed to be in inverse ratio to the number cared for. Quality and quantity were incompatible. When children were treated en masse, the result was a combination of "rote, routine and dead levelism, based on law and coercion, without liberty or individual initiative." This situation could be avoided by making the institution as complete an imitation of the natural home as possible. The home he referred to was not the "modern deteriorated type of home," empty, uninteresting and much like a boarding house. Rather it was the home of a century earlier, in which obedience, industrial training, and daily mutual services were significant features of daily living.[61]

The physical plant was to consist of a group of self-contained cottages providing for most of the daily needs of its children. These cottages were not merely to be separate dormitories attached to a central building; each would contain all the features of a model home—library, dining room, kitchen and pantry, bedrooms and toilets, cellar and attic. The running of each would be entrusted to a matron, a mother figure, who was to have a strong natural love of children. Her personality and abilities were critical if the home was to function as a family. The number of children to be grouped in one cottage depended on her skills and the amount of general domestic work required of her. Reeder considered that somewhere between 15 and 25 children would provide the necessary family spirit without overtaxing the energies of the institution staff.[62]

Where possible, the cottages were to be situated in the country. Like many of his contemporaries, Reeder suffered from a sense of urban disenchantment and held a rather romantic vision of rural life. Only gradually was it recognized that the problems of the country, particularly with respect to children, were as pervasive and pressing as those of the city. By moving the institution to the country, Reeder and others hoped to increase the chances for the child's regeneration. The best place for a child to perform the natural functions of change and growth seemed to be in an environment that changed and grew. Nature alone could furnish this. He declared: "The miracle of the changing seasons, the myriad forms of life that burst into being with the first days of spring, the opening buds, the first notes of the songsters among the trees, the plowing and planting, the gorgeous glow of the sunrise, and the varied tints of sunset—all these teach lessons that are not found in books nor imparted by words. Let the child run and skip in Nature's own laboratory."[63] Away from city life, children would become more active, more dynamic, more content.

Reeder was extremely satisfied with the results of his own institutional experiment. It offered, in his own opinion, such a wealth of interests, industries, opportunities, and privileges that there was nothing left to say in favor of the congregate type except that it was cheaper. Even here, no system that failed to develop the child to full capacity could validly be regarded as economical. Under the cottage system the children's health improved significantly. Their play life was more spontaneous and varied. They used every type of building material and equipment to be found around the homes in imaginative and creative games. There was no restriction on how they used their spare hours. For the first time there were real choices to be made in daily life. For example, the children could help to choose what they ate. They also had a voice in the types of punishment to be meted out to offenders. Family life and the making of decisions in concert encouraged good fellowship among the individual children. Reeder therefore heartily recommended the cottage system to all organizations that dealt with their inmates in large groups.[64]

An increasing number of agencies attempted similar reforms. In 1910, according to a survey of children's institutions, 15 percent claimed to be structured on the cottage plan.[65] Despite objections with regard to the expense and the larger staffs required, the concept was generally accepted. In January 1909, approximately 220 social workers met in Washington, D.C., to take part in the first national conference on the care of dependent children. President Theodore Roosevelt had been requested to support such a conference by a group of concerned men, including Folks, Hart, and Theodore Dreiser, editor of the magazine, the *Delineator*. Roosevelt had willingly done so. The conference debated a number of issues, among them the best type of institutional care. It was formally concluded that "so far as it may be found necessary temporarily or permanently to care for certain classes of children in institutions, these institutions should be conducted on the cottage plan, in order that routine and impersonal care may not unduly suppress individuality and initiative.[66]

In practice, the family ideal was imperfectly applied. Cottages were often much larger than the 25-child home allowed to be reasonable. There was frequently segregation by sex and age, which would not be found in a normal home. Nevertheless, changes were made in the belief that "the institution that comes nearest to the home...is the one that is successful." These changes undoubtedly brought about a significant improvement in the conditions of children under care.[67]

THE JUNIOR REPUBLIC

The need to reconcile the institution with the family did, however, discourage experimentation with other types of group care. Individuality, responsibility, autonomy, industry, and initiative were not the exclusive property of a family-type structure. Child welfare leaders in the Progressive era had an example before them of how a community could function without the pseudofamilial skeleton. William R. George's Junior Republic attempted to give youths real choices and responsibilities within an institutional setting that simulated the outside world as closely as possible.

George was a businessman from the Finger Lakes area of New York State, whose reform activities included participation in the Five Points Mission in New York City, the New York State Child Labor Committee, and the board of trustees of the International Juvenile Court Society as well as the Junior Republic. Like Reeder, George believed in the redemptive power of rural life. He felt that the problem children of the city would stand a far greater chance of success if they were removed to the country. A Fresh Air Camp organized in 1890 soon developed into a permanent rural settlement at Freeville, N.Y. Housed in a few old farmhouses and cottages, George's collection of city children lived according to general republican principles. The inmates profited or failed according to their own industry. Each boy or girl was free to work, play, or do nothing as he or she desired, but at the end of the day money was needed for food and shelter. Members of the Republic governed themselves. They wrote their own constitution and laws, elected their own executive and legislative officers, conducted their own courts, and punished offenders. Education was geared to the individual's needs. The school programs allowed the children to work at their own rate and on the subjects that interested them most. The emphasis was on spontaneity, exploration, and interest rather than routine and regimentation. The children formed a community. They learned, worked, and played without reference to a family structure.[68]

The trend of opinion opposed this type of institutional development. Institutions for dependent and neglected children had come to be regarded more as a necessary evil than as a positively constructive form. They could be accepted more easily if they emulated family life, even if this emulation was somewhat superficial, but the majority of child welfare leaders were more interested in avoiding institutional contact altogether. They were contributing their time, energy, and talent to the expansion of an alternative method of treatment—foster care. It is to this that we now turn.

NOTES

1. See, for example, Henry Thurston, *The Dependent Child: A Story of Changing Aims and Methods in the Care of Dependent Children* (New York: Columbia University Press, 1930).

2. Martin Wolins, "The Benevolent Asylum: Some Theoretical Observations on Institutional Care," in Donnel M. Pappenfort, Dee M. Kilpatrick, and Robert W. Roberts, eds., *Child Caring: Social Policy and the Institution* (Chicago: Aldine Publishing Co., 1973), p. 96.

3. David M. Rothman, *The Discovery of the Asylum: Social Order and Disorder in the New Republic* (Boston: Little, Brown, 1971), p. xix.

4. Ibid., pp. 57-78.

5. *Annual Report of the Boston Children's Friend Society*, 1845, p. 14.

6. Robert H. Bremner, ed., *Children and Youth in America: A Documentary History* (Cambridge, Mass.: Harvard University Press, 1971), vol. 1, pp. 639-47.

7. U.S. Bureau of the Census, *Paupers in Almshouses, 1923* (Washington, D.C.: Government Printing Office, 1924), p. 10.

8. U.S. Bureau of the Census, *Benevolent Institutions, 1904* (Washington, D.C.: Government Printing Office, 1905), pp. 56-127. These figures do not take into account organizations that may have ceased to exist before 1904.

9. U.S. Bureau of the Census, *Benevolent Institutions, 1910* (Washington, D.C.: Government Printing Office, 1913), p. 27.

10. Bremner, *Children and Youth in America*, vol. 1, pp. 271-81, 653-70. For information on the sectarian development see Francis E. Lane, *American Charities and the Child of the Immigrant* (Washington, D.C.: Catholic University of America, 1932); George Jacoby, *Catholic Charities in Nineteenth Century New York* (Washington, D.C.: Catholic University of America, 1941); Boris D. Bogen, *Jewish Philanthropy* (New York: Macmillan, 1917). According to figures for 1910, Roman Catholics ran 24.4 percent of children's institutions, caring for 45 percent of the nation's dependent children; Protestants ran 23.7 percent, caring for 15.1 percent; Jews ran 2.2 percent, caring for 4.5 percent. The remainder was divided among other private organizations (39.7 percent, caring for 24.2 percent) and public institutions (10 percent, caring for 11.3 percent). U.S. Bureau of the Census, *Benevolent Institutions, 1910*, p. 69.

11. Rothman, *Discovery of the Asylum*, pp. 237-64.

12. New York State Senate, "Report of the Select Committee Appointed to Visit Charitable Institutions Supported by the State," 1857, in Bremner, *Children and Youth in America*, vol. 1, p. 648.

13. William Pryor Letchworth, "The Removal of Children from Almshouses in the State of New York," *Proceedings of the 21st NCCC*, 1894, p. 134.

14. See Grace Abbott, *The Child and the State*, vol. 2, pp. 65-72, and David M. Schneider and Albert Deutsch, *The History of Public Welfare in New York State 1867-1940* (Chicago: University of Chicago Press, 1941), pp. 60-70.

15. U.S. Bureau of the Census, *Paupers in Almshouses, 1910* (Washington, D.C.: Government Printing Office, 1915), p. 35.

16. *Annual Reports of the Catholic Protectory*, 1880, p. 9; 1882, p. 9; 1891, p. 10.

17. See Rachel B. Marks, "Institutions for Dependent and Delinquent Children: Histories, Nineteenth Century Statistics and Recurrent Goals," in Pappenfort, Kilpatrick, and Roberts, *Child Caring: Social Policy and the Institution*, p. 37.

18. *Annual Report of St. Mary's Home for Children, Chicago*, 1911, p. 11.

19. *Annual Report of the Catholic Protectory*, 1893, p. 13.

20. *Annual Report of the Glenwood Industrial Training School for Boys*, 1892, p. 5.

21. Division of Child Welfare, Illinois Department of Public Welfare, *Report of the Sub-Committee on Dependent Children* (Chicago, 1921), p. 60.

22. *Annual Report of the New England Home for Little Wanderers*, 1896, p. 8.

23. *Annual Report of the Catholic Protectory*, 1890, p. 11.

24. For example, see *Biennial Report of the Illinois Board of Public Charities*, 1906-1908, on a special investigation in 1906 of institutions for children, p. 252.

25. Anne Richardson, "The Massachusetts System of Caring for State Minor Wards," in *A History of Child Saving in the United States*, the Report of the Committee on the History of Child Saving Work to the 20th NCCC, 1893 (reprinted Montclair, N.J.: Patterson Smith, 1971), p. 63.

26. Quoted in Thurston, *The Dependent Child*, p. 71.

27. Benjamin Hayenga, "The Glenwood Industrial Training School: Its Development and Present Programs" (master's thesis, University of Chicago, 1935), p. 67.

28. Quoted in Bertha Hosford, "Protestant Institutions for Dependent Children in Illinois" (master's thesis, University of Chicago, 1927), p. 80.

29. See for example, Illinois Department of Public Welfare, *Report of the Sub-Committee on Dependent Children in Institutions*, p. 59.

30. Richardson, "The Massachusetts System," p. 63.

31. Quoted in Nathan Berman, "A Study of the Development of the Care of Dependent and Neglected Jewish Children in the Chicago Area" (master's thesis, University of Chicago, 1933), p. 41.

32. William Fairbank, "Religious and Moral Training in Institutions," *Proceedings of the 31st NCCC*, 1904, pp. 327-30.

33. Thurston, *The Dependent Child*, pp. 75-76.

34. *Annual Report of the New England Home for Little Wanderers*, 1893, p. 8.

35. This had been the case in Boston's House of the Angel Guardian in the 1840s. See Edward C. Dullea, *Catholic Child Welfare in Masschusetts in the Early Days* (Boston: Knights of Columbus, 1938), p. 10.

36. John H. Finley, "The Child Problem in the Cities," *Proceedings of the 18th NCCC*, 1891, pp. 131-32.

37. "Children of the State," *Biennial Report of the Illinois Board of Public Charities*, 1896-1898, p. 67. C. W. Wendte, statement in "Discussion on Reports from the States," *Proceedings of the 16th NCCC*, 1889, p. 213. William Pryor Letchworth, "Children of the State," *Proceedings of the 13th NCCC* 1886, p. 143.

38. Hastings Hornell Hart, "The Economic Aspect of the Child Problem," *Proceedings of the 19th NCCC*, 1892, pp. 192-93. Bird S. Coler, "The Subsidy Problem in New York City," *Proceedings of the 28th NCCC*, 1901, quoted, p. 138.

39. Emil Hirsch, statement, *Proceedings of the Conference on the Care of Dependent Children*, Washington, D.C., January 25-26, 1909 (reprinted New York: Arno Press, 1971), p. 89.

40. Ibid., p. 88. Homer Folks, "Why Should Dependent Children Be Reared in Families Rather Than in Institutions?" *Charities Review* 5 (1896): 141. J. J. Kelso, statement in "Discussion on Child Saving," *Proceedings of the 26th NCCC*, 1899, p. 381.

41. Byron C. Mathews, "The Duty of the State to Dependent Children," *Proceedings of the 25th NCCC*, 1895, p. 371.

42. Walter A. Wheeler, "Problems of an Institution: Scraps of Experience," *Proceedings of the 22nd NCCC*, 1895, p. 206.

43. E. A. Murdoch, statement, *Proceedings of the 5th Illinois Conference of Charities and Correction*, 1900, p. 360.

44. Rudolph R. Reeder, "Good Citizens from Institution Children," *Charities* 11 (1903): 154.

45. Rudolph R. Reeder, *How Two Hundred Children Live and Learn* (New York: Lloyd Adams Noble, 1917), p. 200.

46. Richard C. Cabot, "Body and Soul in Work for Children," in Sophonisba P. Breckinridge, ed., *The Child in the City* (London: P. S. King & Sons, 1911), p. 17. *Annual Report of the St. Vincent's Infant Asylum of Chicago*, 1898-1900, p. 105.

47. Lane, *American Charities and the Child of the Immigrant*, pp. 45-134.

48. Mathews, "The Duty of the State," p. 371.

49. Reeder, "Good Citizens from Institution Children," p. 153.

50. Martin Wolins and Irving Piliavin, *Institutions or Foster Family: A Century of Debate* (New York: Child Welfare League of America, 1964), p. 13.

51. William B. Streeter, "Admission of Children to Orphanages," *Proceedings of the 31st NCCC*, 1904, p. 333.

52. Wolins and Piliavin, *Institution or Foster Family*, p. 25.

53. Charles E. Faulkner, "Institution Care for Dependent Children," *Proceedings of the 31st NCCC*, 1904, p. 336.

54. See, for example, Adolph Lewisohn, statement, *Proceedings of the (1909) Conference on the Care of Dependent Children*, p. 146; Edward T. Devine, statement, ibid., p. 47; Finley, "The Child Problem in the Cities," p. 135.

55. Mary E. Cobb, "The Legitimate Use of an Institution for Children," *Charities Review* 2 (1893): 272.

56. Edward A. Hall, "Destitute and Neglected Children," *Proceedings of the 26th NCCC*, 1899, pp. 187-88.

57. Lyman P. Alden, "Institutions for Children," *Proceedings of the 23rd NCCC*, 1896, p. 321.

58. Thomas Kinkead, "The Institutional Care of Children," *Charities* 10 (1903): 396. D. J. McMahon, statement in "Discussions on Children," *Proceedings of the 28th NCCC*, 1901, p. 370. James Sullivan, "Institutional Care of Children," *Proceedings of the 1st National Conference of Catholic Charities*, 1910, p. 286.

59. Thomas M. Mulry, "The Home vs. the Institution," *Proceedings of the 25th NCCC*, 1898, p. 365.

60. Brother Barnabas, statement, *Proceedings of the 2nd National Conference of Catholic Charities*, 1912, pp. 248-50, quoted 248. Robert Biggs, "The Policy and Practice of Catholic Institutions in Receiving, Caring for and Discharging Children," *Proceedings of the 4th National Conference of Catholic Charities*, 1916, p. 177.

61. Reeder, *How Two Hundred Children Live and Learn*, quoted pp. 195-96; Rudolph R. Reeder, statement, *Proceedings of the [1909] Conference on the Care of Dependent Children*, pp. 141-42.

62. Ibid., p. 142.

63. Reeder, *How Two Hundred Children Live and Learn*, p. 49.

64. Ibid., pp. 27-28, 59-69, 79, 83-87, 151-54.

65. U.S. Bureau of the Census, *Benevolent Institutions*, 1910, p. 27.

66. *Proceedings of the (1909) Conference on the Care of Dependent Children*, p. 194.

67. Galen Merrill, statement, ibid., p. 144. For difficulties in the practical workings of cottage institutions see Alice Channing, "The Illinois Soldiers' Orphans' Home" (master's thesis, University of Chicago, 1926), p. 50.

68. Jack M. Holl, *Juvenile Reform in the Progressive Era: William R. George and the Junior Republic Movement* (Ithaca, N.Y.: Cornell University Press, 1971).

4

FOSTER CARE

THE CHILDREN'S AID SOCIETY

In 1852 Charles Loring Brace, a young graduate of the Union Theological Seminary in New York, began work for the homeless and destitute at the Five Points Mission, a converted brewery in one of the most squalid of New York's neighborhoods. It took him only a short time to realize the immensity of the work involved. One problem was the hundreds of youngsters drifting about the streets without any apparent care or protection. Their plight aroused not only his pity but also his fear, for he saw in that "great multitude of ignorant, untrained, passionate, irreligious" children, potential additions to the "dangerous classes" of the country.[1] If not helped they would enlarge the burden on law-abiding taxpayers and poison the society around them. Since there existed no organization devoted to this group of youngsters, Brace took it upon himself to create one. With several of the city's clergymen, he founded the New York Children's Aid Society in 1853. The society's program rested on a belief in the value of religion, self-help, and education for the underprivileged. It included religious meetings, workshops, industrial schools, lodging houses, and employment of children outside New York City. More importantly, the new association initiated a program for placing-out dependent and neglected children in rural homes throughout the nation.[2]

Brace was influenced in his choice of method by European experiments in family care. While on a "grand tour" of Europe in 1851, he had visited the Rauh Haus in Germany, Johan Wichern's famous attempt to rehabilitate juvenile delinquents by placing them in a family atmosphere. He was also aware of the activities of the New York House of Refuge and the New York Juvenile Asylum, both of which indentured many of their young inmates to families out west. Fully convinced that "a child, whether good or bad, is above all things an individual requiring individual treatment and care,"[3] Brace saw family life as necessary for the reformation of his vagrant children. In his opinion, "the best of all asylums for the outcast child [was] the farmer's home."[4] Operations for the large-scale emigration of New York's children began in 1854 when a group of 46 children between the ages of five and seventeen set out for Michigan. In the first twenty years of its activities, the New York Children's Aid Society claimed to have placed well over twenty thousand children. After a preliminary screening process to weed out the mentally defective, diseased, and incorrigible, the children were washed, clothed, and sent with an agent to communities along the east coast and in western and southern states. According to Brace, the sight of the little company of unfortunate children always touched the hearts of the naturally generous population, and his staff had no problem in disposing of all their charges.[5]

The story of Brace's efforts to transplant thousands of New York children into rural homes is too well known to require any great elaboration here. The activities of the Children's Aid Society deserve attention, however, for they constituted the first large-scale attempt to place children. Of course, individual family care for dependent and neglected children was by no means a novel phenomenon. In colonial days children were auctioned off through the vendue system, whereby members of the community were asked to tender a figure for the support of a child for the coming year. The child was knocked down to the lowest bidder. A more common method was formal indenture. Following the practice of the English

Poor Law, American settlers bound out their waifs and strays to serve as domestics, to learn husbandry, or to be apprenticed to craftsmen. The craftsman's family contracted to supply adequate food, clothing, shelter, and a useful trade, while the children in return, were to obey their masters in all things and to abstain from gambling, drinking, fornication, matrimony, and other supposedly disruptive practices. Infractions on either side were adjudicated by the local magistrates, who could render the contract null and void in the event of excessive abuse. If the apprenticeship followed a normal course, the child reached independence as a self-supporting adult with whatever money or goods had been earlier stipulated. Sums of up to $100, cattle, tobacco, clothing, or Bibles changed hands at this time.[6]

As slavery and immigration increased, there were fewer offers to take children. At the same time, public officials became less willing to entrust children to families who were only interested in their stamina. Evidence of physical and sexual abuse combined with nineteenth-century views on the value of the institution to undermine this method of caring for dependent and neglected children. While indenture remained on the books of a number of child welfare organizations into the twentieth century, it increasingly lost favor.[7] When family care was revived in the second half of the nineteenth century, it was not indenture but another variant— foster care—that was advocated. The New York Children's Aid Society played a crucial, if ambivalent, role in this transaction to foster care. On the surface, Brace's idea of placing-out had much in common with the older apprenticeship system, in that labor was to be given in return for room, board, and education. However, it departed from the traditional idea of binding out, in that no contract of apprenticeship was drawn up. The society retained complete control of the child and could end the association at will. In addition, Brace hoped the children would be assimilated into the various families as members, rather than remaining as boarders.[8]

Brace's efforts were catalytic in the development of foster care. They stimulated similar activities by other organizations and provoked discussion of the potentialities of placing-out. Before 1890 several societies, such as the Baltimore Children's Aid Society (1860) and the Boston Children's Aid Society (1864), were founded along the same lines. By 1882 Massachusetts had established the first government placing-out system for its minor wards. At the same time, however, the sectarian overtones of Brace's programs and the frequently lax and haphazard methods used provided grounds for much vehement criticism of family care. This helped to prolong the debate and postpone the general decision in favor of foster care until the turn of the century.

The founder of the New York Children's Aid Society was well aware of the religious problem involved in placing-out. "One-rock which the manager of such a movement must always steer clear of," he wrote, "is the sectarian difficulty. He must ignore sects and rest his enterprise on the broadest and simplest principles of morality and religion."[9] Brace claimed that both Catholic and Protestant homes were offered to the children and that their religious views were not interfered with. However, his antipathy to the Catholic Church was clearly evident. He saw asylums as the "bequest of monastic days," through which the Catholic Church was expanding its power.[10] Outside New York City, Catholic homes were comparatively rare. Thus, transferring children to rural areas necessarily placed many Catholic children in Protestant environments.

Catholics were swift to denounce Brace's society as an instrument of Protestantism. They saw his agents as deliberately scouring New York's streets for Catholic children to spirit away to the West, where their faith would be torn from them. Levi Silliman Ives, of the Catholic Protectory, accused the Children's Aid Society of taking steps "to sever the precious tie which binds [children] to the parental heart and parental influence." He declared that "transportation to that indefinite region, 'the Far West' with changed names and lost parentage, will effectively destroy every association which might revive in their hearts a love for the religion of which they have been robbed."[11] From the 1860s to the 1880s, the Catholic world kept up a regular attack on the proselytization of the Children's Aid Society and other Protestant placing-out agencies.

A second stream of criticism questioned the efficiency of the Children's Aid Society's placing methods. In 1874, at the meeting of the National Prison Reform Congress, a Wisconsin delegate condemned the Children's Aid Society for transporting trainloads of juvenile delinquents to disturb the peaceful neighborhoods of that state. In response Brace adamantly denied the charge, claiming that his agents had found a lower rate of delinquency among his children than among other youngsters. His critics remained unconvinced, and for the next 15 years Brace's achievements were fiercely debated at every major child welfare conference. Supporters of institutions argued that Brace's selection criteria were inadequate, that his placements were hastily made, and that his standards of supervision were appalling. Concerned, Brace initiated a longer investigation in 1883 of placing-out in Wisconsin, Minnesota, and Kansas and claimed few failures. In the following year Hastings Hornell Hart, then Secretary of the Minnesota State Board of Correction and Charity, carried out his own survey. While this examination confirmed that few of the children were juvenile delinquents and that no delinquents had been deliberately sent West, it did reveal lax placement methods and poor supervision.[12]

As a reaction to the possibility of juvenile delinquents and other unsuitable children being shipped across their borders, several states passed laws regulating the interstate placement of children. The first of these, enacted by Michigan in 1895, stipulated that any individual or society placing children within its borders should file, with the relevant county authorities, a bond protecting the county from future support. Shortly after this, Indiana, Minnesota, and Illinois prohibited the placement of criminal, diseased, insane, or incorrigible children in their jurisdictions. Many states followed suit in subsequent years.[13]

FOSTER CARE GAINS SUPPORT

Despite the obvious flaws in the early attempts at placing-out, the concept of foster care gained steady ground until the 1890s, when the support of young reformers such as Homer Folks gave it an accelerating impetus. Concern for the survival of the family unit and a growing disillusionment with the institution as a means of socialization and reform guaranteed its acceptance. Reformers did not have before them any systematic empirical data testifying to the superiority of the foster home. Research and investigation would come later. Instead the value of the substitute family was apparently self-evident.

Advocates of placing-out saw the family as imbued with certain inalienable, positive characteristics. The relationships and associations of the home were felt to be exactly those that promoted the best development of each of its members. The family was "the common denominator of everything good in human life."[14] To some it was a Divine creation, "the God-given plan of taking care of children." When children were homeless, it was "God's orphanage."[15] To others the key word in their description of family life was "natural." According to Emil Hirsch, vice-president of the Jewish Home Finding Society of Chicago, "if there is one certainty, it is this, that the family is the direct outcome of nature's own plan to secure the safety and growth of the child. Man stands in need of maternal care much longer than any other animal. This dependence of the child on the mother forced, in the course of the ages, man to adopt the family and the family to adapt itself to it."[16] Since family life was "the only natural environment for the child," it was the duty of state and private organizations to provide a home for each of their dependent wards. No artificial substitute would do.[17]

Social workers and philanthropists who argued the case for the institution or the foster home were less concerned with their ability to make children happy than with their potential to produce well-trained citizens. Supporters of foster care spelled out its advantages for the production of sociable, independent, and responsible Americans. Folks, in a paper read before the Conference of Charities of New York City in 1896, praised the "ever-changing variety" of interest of family life. In a normal home a child could associate with persons of various ages and both sexes in the ordinary everyday activities of life. The child also came to see, little by little, "the ways and means of getting on in the world."[18] The institutionalized child did not have the good judgment that came from experience and was at a loss when thrown into the outside world, but the foster child's transition from dependent infant to self-sufficient adult was gradual and complete. One of the most important lessons learned in a family atmosphere, Folks believed, was the necessity of making ends meet. By continually observing the relation between labor and the power to purchase, children were encouraged to be industrious in later life. Further benefits of foster care lay in children's development of local relationships and

attachments in the community, which would assist them when
starting out in life. Perhaps the most important asset of the foster
family, in Folks's opinion, was access to affection. In good homes
the foster parents could provide the sympathy, love, and understanding that death or misfortune had taken from these children.
"No superintendent, no matron, however good or wise," Folks
claimed, "can be to fifty or a hundred, still less to five hundred or
a thousand children, what a father or mother, brother or sister can
be to two or three."[19]

If there were advantages of foster care for each individual child's
happiness and well-being, there were also certain benefits for
society in general. Foster care supposedly avoided the problem of
moral contagion inherent in the institutional system. Asylums, it
was thought, brought together children from a wide variety of
unfortunate backgrounds. Many had been exposed to vice and
crime, and it was difficult to prevent bad habits from being spread
among the more innocent inmates. What was needed was some sort
of current to disperse the collected "scum." Placing-out seemed,
to some, the best way of diluting antisocial behavior.[20] Foster care
was also advocated as a means of promoting family life. It was
claimed that parents who saw the institution as a cheap means of
educating their children might not be so keen on giving them up to
a family of no better means than their own. Alternatively, and
more constructively, knowing that their children were not lost in an
institution but were in a family with which they could retain contact, would encourage parents to rebuild their homes and regain
possession of their children.[21]

INSUFFICIENT DATA

These beliefs in the virtues of the family constituted a strong
and pervasive faith that was hardly affected by inadequate knowledge of the precise workings of that social structure. Even Folks,
who was more explicit than most on the effects of family life on
children, could still write:

The fact that it is not easy to give a full explanation as to why
the conditions of family life are best fitted for the normal
development of children does not diminish the force of the

argument. It might not be easy, even for the scientist to give a complete explanation of the fact that a mixture of certain gases in certain proportions, commonly known as air, is the best material for breathing purposes. Yet of the fact there is no question. It might be difficult to catalogue accurately the virtues of sunlight yet no-one, for that reason, questions its superiority over gaslight or the electric light for the general purposes of the vegetable and animal kingdoms.[22]

Foster care was accepted by many reformers as a self-evident improvement on group care within the institutional framework, despite the paucity of data available to substantiate such a belief.[23] Considerations of the results of placing-out were hardly more informative than Brace's attempts to justify his methods. In support of his claims that the majority of his emigrants turned out well, he pointed to various well-known figures, including a governor of Alaska, as products of his system. These, he thought, easily counteracted the odd cases of delinquency and dependency that his investigations uncovered. However, his superficial criteria of success (such as the absence of a criminal record) and loose sampling techniques made these studies of little value to welfare workers.[24]

Until the second decade of the twentieth century, this type of perfunctory assessment of results was all that children's agencies had to offer by way of a concrete demonstration of success. By that time social workers were beginning to realize that a lack of facts led to sentiment and sentimentality in child care. At the 1909 White House Conference on the Care of Dependent Children, Rudolph R. Reeder challenged societies who claimed to place children successfully. "Yesterday and today," he said, "we have heard a great many delegates say 'the Society I represent had five hundred children placed in families,' or another 1,400, another 1,200 and so forth. We have had a good many statements of that kind, all of which are interesting, but it would be still more interesting as well as of much more practical worth if we had more data as to the outcome of such work."[25] Delegates at the conference who represented placing associations acknowledged the need for studies of results to demonstrate their superiority over institutions.

A tentative start was made, before 1920, to study groups of foster children and to assess the effects of this type of training. A few private agencies, such as the Boston Children's Aid Society, examined the success or failure of representative samples of children.[26] The Massachusetts State Board of Charities conducted a survey of the "after careers" of minor wards discharged between 1898 and 1900. Although it was admitted that the study was not "made as a test of the placing-out system," the investigation into the progress of 240 foster children did provide useful evaluative information. The main emphasis of the survey was on the economic position and moral character of the wards and their continued relationship with foster parents. The results claimed that 84.7 percent of dependent and 75.3 percent of neglected children were of "good" character. They had been criticized favorably by friends, relatives, and acquaintances. The majority of dependent and neglected children were not in touch with their former foster parents at the time of the survey, and only one-fifth had remained in the communities where they had been placed. Similarly, only one in three children retained contact with the natural parents. Most wards seemed to have begun their adult life alone. The Massachusetts State Board made little comment on these figures except to express some surprise that more children had not kept in touch with their relatives. It did not query the success of foster relationships even though close ties were obviously not established in most cases. Another drawback in placing-out, which this survey incidentally revealed, was the unsuitability of farm work for many city-bred youths. While most wards were placed in rural areas, many returned to take up jobs in urban communities.[27]

With these exceptions, there was little factual information available before 1920 with which proponents of foster care could compare the relative merits of placing-out and institutional care. Sophie Van Senden Theis's study of 910 children placed by the State Charities Aid Association of New York, published in 1924, was a more extensive study of the effects of foster care.[28] Through interviews with parents, friends, relatives, and the foster children themselves, Theis came to the conclusion that 77.2 percent of the children investigated had become adults capable of managing their own affairs, who lived according to the standards of their communities. Six years later, Elias Trotzkey of the Marks Nathan Jewish Orphans' Home of Chicago produced a comparative account of the impact of institutions and family life on dependent children.[29] Although Trotzkey was trying to justify the methods of his own organization, he nevertheless threw considerable light on the physical, mental, and emotional development of 2,512 children in institutional care and 1,214 in foster homes, thus allowing comparisons to be drawn. Trotzkey concluded from the data he collected that good institutional care was superior in terms of physical and emotional development and educational progress to foster care. To welfare workers of the Progressive era, however, these data were not yet available. Immediate pressures demanded a decision, and the decision was increasingly made in favor of the substitute home.

TYPES OF FOSTER CARE

Having made this commitment, the next question to be answered concerned the type of foster care to be implemented. To many social workers, legal adoption was "the most desirable arrangement which can be secured."[30] However, this solution was not thought feasible for most dependent and neglected children. Physical and mental handicaps or age ruled out a large number. Moreover, the majority, as was noted in Chapter 2, still had one or both parents living. Only a small proportion of these mothers and fathers had lost their rights to their children through cruelty or gross neglect. Many parents continued to hope for the return of their children some time in the future. Orphans and abandoned children were thus the main source of adoptions. These children were placed in homes for trial periods of three to six months and, if results were favorable, legal proceedings were initiated.[31]

The most popular options open to placing agencies were free or boarding homes. The former method was praised in that it guaranteed that affection was involved. It was thought that parents who willingly opened their home to a child and demanded no payment in return were more likely to appreciate the child fully. Some child-savers were hesitant about introducing money into the bargain. Practical considerations led others to advocate boarding-out. This plan had the advantage that "it insures enough homes for all dependent children, since without the incentive of compensation it might be difficult to secure enough homes."[32] Better to pay where necessary than to deprive children of homes altogether, it was thought. Boarding-out was also supported because it left control with the state. If the government paid for the child's care, it would supposedly be more anxious to supervise the child's progress. One disadvantage of free homes was claimed to be their inability to provide temporary care. Foster parents were normally interested in taking children on a permanent basis. Where natural parents were forced to surrender their children for short periods because of illness or financial difficulties, boarding-out seemed to provide an obvious alternative to short-term institutional care. The Children's Aid Society of Pennsylvania advocated boarding-out for unattractive children. By paying from $1.75 to $2.50 per week, the society introduced children into homes where it hoped they might ingratiate themselves and be taken in as members at a later date.[33]

DISADVANTAGES

The trend of opinion in favor of foster care, whether free or boarding, was not without opposition. Supporters of institutions had no defense against arguments based on divine inspiration and natural law. Accepting the family as the foundation of American society, they could hardly attack the theoretical basis of foster care. Instead, defenders of institutions criticized the practical workings of the ordinary home. Although accepting that the family home came direct from God, they argued that "much of God's work in this world has been tampered with, and not all the final results of family training are ideal, even for the children born to the household."[34]

Homes presented dangers just as the asylum did. One particular weakness that was stressed was the possibility that the foster child was taken solely for labor. Institutions threw the charge of economic exploitation back at their critics. While Brace had seen the need for child labor as a guarantee that rural homes would accept his bands of city children, the balance of opinion was now heavily against children being used for mercenary purposes. One institution superintendent expressed this general wariness. He declared, "We may always be afraid . . . of young married people who come and want a strong, healthy girl to adopt. They want to take that child into their own family and treat her as their own. That sounds on the surface very beautiful. What does it usually mean? It usually means they want cheap labor. They want to adopt her so that no-one may come to visit. They want that child to do the work for them."[35] Critics claimed they knew of numerous instances of overworked foster children.[36] Certain defenders of institutional care also denied that removal to the country was necessarily a great benefit to children born and raised in the city. They refused to accept the widely held belief in the natural superiority of country life. Instead they argued that few children, particularly those out of infancy, would get any satisfaction from working on a farm. The solitude and monotony of country living was more likely to make them return to their old neighborhoods as soon as possible.[37] In view of the findings of the Massachusetts survey cited earlier, this argument seems to have had some foundation.

Much of the abuse that was described was blamed on the careless methods used by the placing agencies. Institutions charged their rivals with insufficient investigation, hasty placing, and inadequate supervision. Such accusations were quite often justified. Some organizations operated a fairly comprehensive selection process involving a questionnaire, personal references, and an inspection of the home. But this was not the case throughout. For example, the methods of the Glenwood Industrial Training school for Boys, in Illinois, in the late nineteenth century left much to be desired. To secure a child from this agency it was not even necessary to visit the school or be visited by one of its staff. A letter written to the general agent, describing the child desired, was thought to be adequate. The school would then try to match the description with one of its inmates. On receipt of written references and money for travel expenses, the school sent the child by rail to his new home.[38] "Tagging," that is, labeling children and placing them on a train to their destinations, was not unknown in late-nineteenth-century America, although it is impossible to say how widespread this practice was.[39]

Critics took placing agencies to task for the haste with which they disposed of their children. They pointed to the ease with which the round peg could be fitted into the square hole. Dependent and neglected children in need of care were often difficult cases, whose manners and habits were not easily acceptable to every family. It was argued that placing agents did not always have the time nor the ability to match parent to child.[40] Unfortunately, this was true. The staff members of many societies were burdened with the tasks of making speeches and fund raising in addition to finding the children suitable homes. They had large territories to cover and frequently passed through communities at great speed, dropping off their charges as they went.

The record of one agent of the New England Home for Little Wanderers gives a clear picture of the pressures involved. He recalled an instance when

> we had travelled 185 miles and we were waiting at the junction to connect with a local branch. The train was overdue and the nurse stood on the platform with the baby in her arms. Our time was out and our train was about to start when the local whistled around the hill and steamed in. Then there was hustling and rushing of baggage. I saw a woman and felt by instinct that it was she who we had expected to meet. I jumped off and said, "Is this Mrs. Kumbull?" "Yes Sir." "Here's your baby." "All aboard," shouted the conductor of the Northern express and we were gone.[41]

On a typical journey west, children placed by this agency were taken to the church of a particular community. Here they might sing plaintive songs to arouse compassion, and a brief description was given of each individual. Families judged eligible by a local committee of prominent citizens took their pick there and then. Usually the collection of youngsters was disposed of in one or two days, and the agent would leave to take charge of his next group of waifs.[42]

One of the sadder aspects of this early placing was the frequency with which brothers and sisters were split up and parents completely lost touch with them. Institution personnel told Horatio Alger-type stories of siblings who rediscovered each other after many years and of parents who were denied all knowledge of their children even though they had not been formally adopted. In contrast, institutions were claimed to keep children together.[43]

When hasty matches proved unsuitable, most placing agencies took the children back and replaced them. Often a large percentage of the children experienced more than one home. The Illinois Children's Home and Aid Society, one of the more advanced agencies, could still report in 1900 that of 494 cases dealt with in that year, 195 were cases of replacements.[44] To opponents of foster care, the experience was disastrous for the child. Failure to adapt to the family, it was argued, "reacts upon the child who goes reluctantly and with increasing distrust into its next trial place." Also, "an unfavorable feeling is...created in the minds of the disappointed family who perhaps decline to receive another child for fear of undergoing a similar experience."[45]

A final condemnation of foster care concerned the lack of supervision. Critics claimed that many dependent and neglected children were lost track of altogether when they or their foster families moved out of an area. Other children were physically or sexually abused or mentally ill-treated because an agency was not sufficiently vigilant. Again, these accusations could be substantiated. Often supervision was no more than occasional correspondence. Visits were made only after there had been a charge of abuse. At least, it was claimed, the institution had complete control over its wards and could ensure their right treatment.[46]

WIDESPREAD ACCEPTANCE

All these arguments were to no avail. Welfare opinion increasingly supported the foster home. Those in favor of foster care were aware of the problems involved. Few took the extreme stance of one of their colleagues that "the poorest home in the land...is better than the best institution."[47] They realized that placing-out was "difficult work and unless it is surrounded with every possible safeguard, it is extremely dangerous."[48] Nevertheless, by the turn of the century most agreed that, with a vigorous preliminary examination of homes, judicious fitting of children to places, and abundant supervision, the family system was by far the best. The 1899 National Conference of Charities and Correction witnessed the virtual end of the controversy that had raged for fifty years. At that meeting Thomas M. Mulry, founder of the Catholic Home Bureau, gave the report of the Conference Committee on the Care of Destitute and Neglected Children. While emphasizing the valuable work accomplished by institutions in the past, the report concluded that the preponderance of opinion among leading welfare figures was in favor of placing children in family homes.[49]

The gradually gained support of Catholic and Jewish groups was an important development in the growth of this consensus. Foster care was not unknown to a few Catholic agencies. Despite its vehement opposition to Protestant placing-out organizations, the Catholic Protectory had early considered the possibility of finding "such Catholic mechanics and farmers as might be disposed to receive one or more...children." From 1868 it had sporadically placed children in Maryland, New York State, and the Midwest, but the difficulty of finding Catholic homes outside New York had limited these operations.[50] The majority of Catholic organizations did not follow suit but chose to cling to the institutional format.

By the end of the nineteenth century, several changes had occurred that made the idea of foster care more palatable to the Catholic welfare system. Not only had large-scale immigration provided a greater number of potential foster homes, but the fear of proselytization had receded. Protestant and nondenominational children's agencies generally insisted that the religious beliefs of the children should be respected where possible. The same sentiment was embodied in various laws concerning dependent children and was accepted at state and national conferences.[51] As a result, Catholic associations made increasing use of this alternative method of child care. In 1899 the Catholic Protectory established a special department for placing-out along progressive lines. In the same year the Catholic Home Bureau for Dependent Children of New York was founded under the auspices of the Saint Vincent de Paul Society. It was realized that "our Catholic institutions were in danger of being overcrowded, and their highest usefulness, in measure at least, impaired by the necessity of retaining and properly caring for children long after the age when they might be safely placed in private families." Working as a clearing house for the majority of New York's Catholic institutions, the bureau, in its first ten years, placed 2,500 children, a small but nonetheless significant number.[52] By the time of the first National Conference of Catholic Charities in 1910 it was generally conceded that the foster family was the best substitute home for most Catholic children.[53] "Catholics," it was declared, "are not at all lax, but are doing their fair share of placing out."[54]

A similar movement toward acceptance of foster care was visible among Jewish agencies. At the second National Conference of Jewish Charities, held in Detroit in 1902, the possibilities of placing out were debated. Lee K. Frankel, manager of the United Hebrew Charities in New York, had solicited opinions from a variety of Hebrew institutions as to the viability of placing Jewish children. He found that a number had experimented with varying success. Some supported placement with families; some continued to prefer the asylum. The difficulty of finding Jewish homes outside New York City seemed to deter many associations. The Committee on Dependent Children at the conference determined to investigate the matter further. It felt that "the home is a natural product, the institution an artificial one, and that all things being equal, the former is to be preferred to the latter."[55] In the following two years, Frankel continued to examine the subject. His conclusion, presented at the 1904 conference, affirmed the benefits of foster care, at least for those without immediate family ties.[56]

The next step was to translate this commitment into action. In 1904 a joint committee, made up of representatives of various child care agencies, began to search out and investigate potential Jewish foster homes for New York children. Three years later a special organization, the Home Finding Society of Chicago, was set up. The society faced certain difficulties, since it entered a field where there were already three Hebrew children's organizations. Because of the expense of their establishment and operation, the orphanages had first claim to the available children, and the remainder were diverted to the Home Finding Society. Nevertheless, this society and other Jewish agencies gradually extended their fostering activities.[57]

A slow expansion likewise took place among other sectarian and nondenominational organizations. In addition to established child placing agencies, many institutions, such as the Boston Church Home Society, began to place children in foster families. Founded in 1855 by members of the Episcopal Church of Boston, the society had considered placing-out early in its history but had rejected the

idea in favor of a farm school. By the 1890s its board of managers
had returned to the idea of foster care. Not having the facilities to
select and investigate homes, the society began, in 1896, to cooperate with the Boston Children's Aid Society. The experiment
proved so successful that in 1915 the whole of the Boston Church
Home Society's operations were devoted to placing-out.[58] In 1923,
according to a census report, there were 339 such placing agencies
in the United States.[59]

While many agencies were locally based, others operated statewide. Furthermore, many of these became affiliated to form a
national organization. The National Children's Home Society, as it
was known, was inspired by Martin Van Buren Van Arsdale, a
Presbyterian minister from Green Valley, Illinois. For many years
he had been concerned with the plight of children in almshouses,
who could only be released if they were placed out on contract at
no expense to the county. His first solution was to personally place
these children in Christian homes. Eventually, finding this work
too great for one man, Van Arsdale established the American
Educational Aid Association. This organization was designed "to
co-operate with young women of special promise in fitting themselves for the requirements of life." Later renamed the Illinois
Children's Home and Aid Society, it expanded its work to include
a wide range of dependent and neglected children of both sexes.
Receiving homes were set up to admit youngsters and prepare them
for placement in various localities. In the early years children were
largely acquired through voluntary surrender by their parents.
After 1899 the newly established juvenile court committed children
to the society. (See Chapter 9 for more information about juvenile
courts.) Children were placed throughout Illinois. The state was
divided into districts under the control of a superintendent, and in
each community advisory committees of respectable citizens were
established to collect funds and select suitable families.[60]

From the time of its inception, Van Arsdale thought of his work
in national terms. Not only did his society place children in Illinois,
but also across state borders. By the early 1890s auxiliary associations had been organized in Iowa, California, Indiana, Missouri,
and Michigan. A national charter was taken out in 1893. By 1907
there were 28 societies operating under the aegis of the National

Children's Home Society, and their work extended to 32 states and territories. These offshoots were not under the direct control of the parent society. Instead they incorporated under their own state laws and were loosely federated for mutual help and encouragement. From national headquarters in Chicago they received advice on methods, news of meetings, and regular issues of the society's publication, *The Children's Home Finder*. This magazine carried stories about children, articles on child welfare, notes about staff members, and reports of funds collected. In 1918 the name of the organization was changed to the National Children's Home and Welfare Association. Soon afterwards, its influence began to decline. The Child Welfare League of America, a larger cooperative agency, was established in 1920, and most of the association's members joined it. The activities of the association slowly declined until its final dissolution in 1939.[61]

Although the decision of child welfare personnel was made in favor of foster care, institutions retained considerable influence. The theoretical contest may have been won, but the practical changes were slow in coming. According to a U.S. Bureau of the Census survey in 1923, the first accurate account of child-placing, 64.2 percent of dependent and neglected children under care were still housed in asylums. In comparison, 23.4 percent were cared for in free homes and 10.2 percent in boarding family homes. After that date the percentage drop of children in institutions accelerated until in 1962 only 31 percent of the children were not placed in families. In some states in the early part of the century there was even a visible countertrend. In Illinois, for example, the instituttional percentage rose 14 points from 1910 to 1923, before undergoing a sudden decline. In dictating the type of care dependent children received in certain states, the availability of facilities was perhaps as influential as the theoretical consensus.[62]

Not all supporters of foster care saw the total demise of institutions as desirable. In Chapter 2 it was noted that critics of the asylum did envisage a limited role for children's institutions. Some, like Charles W. Birtwell of the Boston Children's Aid Society, were sufficiently farsighted to realize that plans to solve the individual child's problems should be flexible. He looked forward to the day when others would "feel the thrill of unity and sympathy as we consider together how under both methods this identical claim may be considered—the passionate service of each individual child."[63] Such a plan of action would also offer another alternative —the care of children in their own homes. This option will be examined in the following chapter.

NOTES

1. Charles Loring Brace, *The Dangerous Classes of New York and Twenty Years Work among Them* (New York: Winkoop & Hallenbeck, 1872), p. 28.

2. Miriam Langsam, *Children West: A History of the Placing Out System of the New York Children's Aid Society* (Madison, Wis.: State Historical Society of Wisconsin, 1964), pp. 1-15.

3. Brace, quoted in Emma Brace, *The Life of Charles Loring Brace Chiefly Told in His Own Letters* (New York: Scribner's, 1894), pp. 170-71.

4. Brace, *The Dangerous Classes*, p. 225.

5. Langsam, *Children West*, pp. 21-31. Joseph M. Hawes, *Children in Urban Society: Juvenile Delinquency in Nineteenth Century America* (New York: Oxford University Press, 1971), pp. 98-102.

6. Robert H. Bremner, ed., *Children and Youth in America: A Documentary History* (Cambridge, Mass.: Harvard University Press, 1971), vol. 1, pp. 64-71, 262-70.

7. Ibid., p. 262.

8. Langsam, *Children West*, p. 18.

9. Brace, *The Dangerous Classes*, p. 440.

10. Ibid., pp. 76, 244.

11. *Annual Report of the Catholic Protectory*, 1864, p. 72. Also see Francis E. Lane, *American Charities and the Child of the Immigrant* (Washington, D.C.: Catholic University of America, 1932), pp. 117-34.

12. Langsam, *Children West*, pp. 56-64. Hastings Hornell Hart, "Placing Out Children in the West," *Proceedings of the 11th NCCC*, 1884, pp. 143-50.

13. Grace Abbott, *The Child and the State* (Chicago: University of Chicago Press, 1938), vol. 2, pp. 133-37.

14. R. M. Little, "The Family and the Community," *Proceedings of the 42nd NCCC*, 1915, p. 24.

15. F. M. Gregg, "Placing Out Children," *Proceedings of the 19th NCCC*, 1892, p. 415.

16. Emil Hirsch, statement, *Proceedings of the Conference on the Care of Dependent Children*, Washington, D.C., January 25-26, 1909) (reprinted New York: Arno Press, 1971), p. 89.

17. Byron C. Mathews, "The Duty of the State to Dependent Children," *Proceedings of the 25th NCCC*, 1895, p. 369.

18. Homer Folks, "Why Should Dependent Children Be Reared in Families Rather Than in Institutions?" *Charities Review* 5 (1896): 142.

19. Ibid., pp. 140-44, quoted p. 144.

20. Finley, "The Child Problem in the Cities," *Proceedings of the 18th NCCC*, 1891, p. 133.

21. Homer Folks, statement in "Discussion on Children," *Proceedings of the 25th NCCC*, 1898, p. 404.

22. Folks, "Why Should Dependent Children be Reared in Families?" p. 140.

23. Martin Wolins and Irving Piliavin, *Institution or Foster Family: A Century of Debate* (New York: Child Welfare League of America, 1964), pp. 5-9.

24. "Results of Placing Out Work," *Annual Report of the New York Children's Aid Society*, 1899, p. 99. Langsam, *Children West*, pp. 57-61.

25. Rudolph R. Reeder, statement, *Proceedings of the [1909] Conference on the Care of Dependent Children*, p. 122.

26. Ruth Lawton, "A Study of the Results of a Child Placing Society," *Proceedings of the 42nd NCCC*, 1915, pp. 164-73.

27. Massachusetts State Board of Charities, "After Careers of Minor Wards of the Massachusetts State Board of Charities," *Annual Report*, 1910, pp. 119-36, quoted p. 119.

28. Sophie Van Senden Theis, *How Foster Children Turn Out* (New York: State Charities Aid Association, 1924).

29. Elias Trotzkey, *Institutional Care and Placing Out: The Place of Each in the Care of Dependent Children* (Chicago: Marks Nathan Jewish Orphans' Home, 1930).

30. Herbert W. Lewis, "Terms on Which Children Should be Placed in Families," *Proceedings of the 21st NCCC*, 1894, p. 140.

31. For a typical example of this adoption process see *Annual Report of the Glenwood Industrial Training School, Illinois*, 1888, p. 22.

32. Mathews, "The Duty of the State to Dependent Children," p. 372.

33. Ibid. C. H. Pemberton, "The Boarding System for Neglected Children," *Proceedings of the 21st NCCC*, 1894, pp. 138-39. Resolutions, *Proceedings of the [1909] Conference on the Care of Dependent Children*, p. 10. Homer Folks, "Family Life for Dependent Children," in Anna Garlin Spencer and Charles W. Birtwell, eds., *The Care of Dependent, Neglected and Wayward Children* (Baltimore: Johns Hopkins Press, 1894), pp. 77-80.

34. James Sullivan, "Institutional Care of Children," *Proceedings of the 1st National Conference of Catholic Charities*, 1910, p. 286.

35. Martha P. Falconer, statement, *Proceedings of the [1909] Conference on the Care of Dependent Children*, p. 130.

36. Edward A. Hall, "Destitute and Neglected Children," *Proceedings of the 26th NCCC*, 1899, pp. 182-83.

37. Charles E. Faulkner, "Institution Care for Dependent Children," *Proceedings of the 21st NCCC*, 1904, p. 339.

38. *Annual Report of the Glenwood Industrial Training School for Boys*, 1888, pp. 20-22.

39. *Statement of Work of the Boston Home for Destitute Catholic Children, 1864-1889* (Boston: Cashman, Keating & Co., 1890), p. 28.

40. Francis H. White, "The Placing Out System in the Light of its Results," in Spencer and Birtwell, *Care of Dependent, Neglected and Wayward Children*, p. 88.

41. *Little Wanderers Advocate* 39 (January 1903): 6.

42. "Out West," *Little Wanderers Advocate* 26 (Aug. 1892): 190-93.

43. *Annual Report of the Angel Guardian's German Catholic Orphan Society of Chicago*, 1920, p. 2.

44. *Biennial Report of the Illinois Board of Public Charities*, 1898-1900, p. 99.

45. V. T. Smith, "The Economy of the State in the Care of Dependent and Neglected Children," *Proceedings of the 14th NCCC*, 1887, p. 239.

46. Thomas Kinkead, "The Institutional Care of Children," *Charities* 10 (1903): 395. Bertha Hosford, "Protestant Institutions for Dependent Children in Illinois" (Master's thesis, University of Chicago, 1927), p. 96.

47. F. Nutting, statement in discussion on children, *Proceedings of the 18th NCCC*, 1891, p. 329.

48. Hugh Fox, statement in discussion on children, *Proceedings of the 29th NCCC*, 1902, p. 411.

49. Thomas Mulry, "The Care of Destitute and Neglected Children," *Proceedings of the 26th NCCC*, 1889, pp. 166-70.

50. Letter of Archbishop John Joseph Hughes to Levi Silliman Ives, quoted in George Jacoby, *Catholic Charities in Nineteenth Century New York*, p. 150. See also pp. 151-57.

51. Wolins and Piliavin, *Institution or Foster Family*, pp. 7-8.

52. Catholic Home Bureau, quoted by Hastings Hornell Hart, "The Evolution of the Child-Placing Movement," *Proceedings of the [1909] Conference on the Care of Dependent Children*, p. 110. William Doherty, "Placing Out of Children," *Proceedings of the 1st National Conference of Catholic Charities*, 1910, p. 294.

53. Ibid., p. 295.

54. William Doherty, "Selection of Children for the Foster Home,"

Proceedings of the 2nd National Conference of Catholic Charities, 1912, p. 266.

55. "Report of the Committee on Dependent Children," *Proceedings of the 2nd National Conference of Jewish Charities*, 1902, pp. 107-21, quoted p. 118.

56. Lee K. Frankel, "Placing Out of Jewish Children," *Proceedings of the 3rd National Conference of Jewish Charities*, 1904, pp. 72-82.

57. Boris D. Bogen, *Jewish Philanthropy* (New York: Macmillan, 1917), pp. 161-64.

58. Lillian Barrow and Ralph Barrow, *The Challenge of a Heritage—100 Years of Service* (Boston: The Church Home Society, 1955), p. 7-22.

59. U.S. Bureau of the Census, *Children under Institutional Care, 1923* (Washington, D.C.: Government Printing Office, 1927), p. 25.

60. Wilfred S. Reynolds, "A History of the Society," *Home Life for Childhood* 7 (Nov.-Dec. 1918): 2-5, quoted p. 2. Elizabeth White, "The History and Development of the Illinois Children's Home and Aid Society" (master's thesis, University of Chicago, 1934), pp. 14-29.

61. Henry Thurston, *The Dependent Child: The Story of Changing Aims and Methods in the Care of Dependent Children* (New York: Columbia University Press, 1930), pp. 149-54.

62. U.S. Bureau of the Census, *Children under Institutional Care, 1923*, p. 21. Wolins and Piliavin, *Institution or Foster Family*, pp. 36-39.

63. Charles W. Birtwell, statement in discussion on children, *Proceedings of the 29th NCCC*, 1892, p. 399.

5

SAVING
THE
FAMILY

Whereas nineteenth-century child-savers were mainly concerned with removing children from dangerous influences, their successors in the Progressive era believed that dependency and neglect might be prevented. By the first decade of the twentieth century, many social workers and philanthropists agreed with Mary Richmond, general secretary of the Philadelphia Society for Organizing Charity, that "the old cry of 'Save the children' must be superseded by the new cry 'Save the Family,' for we cannot save the one without the other."[1] By preserving and reconstructing the family unit, the child-savers hoped to reduce the numbers of dependent and neglected children in institutions and foster homes.

This objective was pursued in various ways. On the one hand individual children's agencies began to strengthen and rehabilitate families that came to them for help. On the other, reformers demanded and promoted legislative action. They linked their cause to larger campaigns against the social problems that indirectly produced dependency and neglect. In addition, social workers and philanthropists launched a specific campaign to provide public funds for certain groups of mothers who were forced to support their families alone. As will be shown later in this chapter, the mothers' pension scheme typified the various, and often conflicting, attitudes of the Progressive movement for child welfare. It expressed hopes and fears, sympathy and suspicion. Reformers envisioned that the welfare of thousands of children and mothers would be guaranteed by the creation of state funds to provide regular relief. At the same time, their anxiety for the stability of American society undermined the adequate application of this relief and made it conditional upon the assumptions of middle-class behavioral norms.

CONCERN ABOUT THE FAMILY

The new emphasis on keeping children in their homes was partly the result of an acute anxiety about the future of the family system. In the late nineteenth century, most Americans strongly believed that the family was "the unit of the state and upon its safety and perpetuity not only government and order, but the race itself depend."[2] Consequently, many were disturbed by the appearance of concrete evidence of its dislocation. From being a rare occurrence in the eighteenth century, divorce had become a noticeable phenomenon. Almost 946,000 marriages were dissolved between 1887 and 1906. For several decades the divorce rate had risen five times as fast as the rate of the population.[3] These figures, naturally, represented only the tip of the problem. The amount of voluntary separation and desertion was virtually unknown. Charity organizations, public welfare departments, and children's agencies were only beginning, in the 1890s, to consider the effects of broken families on relief rolls and institutions. No state or national analysis had been attempted or even contemplated.

A flood of literature appeared discussing the problems of family life and their implications for the moral health of the nation. Critics isolated a number of causes of family breakdown. Some pointed to the growth of secularism as encouraging immorality. Others claimed that cities had released families from the close control of country neighborhoods and had replaced the absolutism of rural life with a relative moral code. Industrialization was accused of taking the father out of the home, diminishing his influence, and forcing the mother and children into the factories. The role of the woman in the downfall of the home was particularly debated through the media. In the nineteenth century it was believed that women were largely responsible for the dissolution of marriages, since two-thirds of all divorces were filed by them. The more conservative overlooked larger trends, such as the wholesale absorption of women into the work force, in favor of more personalized condemnations of women as selfish and irresponsible and as possessed by overinflated ideals. Not surprisingly, such commentators thought they saw a plot to subvert the family. Feminists, together with socialists and other radicals, were seen by some as the enemy in the "battle between those who would preserve the family and those who would destroy it."[4] Few social workers and welfare reformers took this extreme stance. However, they, too, shared the fear that family life was in peril. They shared the belief that family life was essential to the successful continuation of the capitalist economy and the existing sexual hierarchy and committed themselves to its preservation.

A NEW ASSESSMENT OF THE CAUSES
OF DEPENDENCY AND NEGLECT

Just as fears of family breakdown served to focus the attention of reformers and welfare workers on the family unit, so a new analysis of the causes of dependency and neglect produced a similar shift in emphasis.

Throughout most of the nineteenth century, misfortunes or individual character failings were generally accepted as the reason why there were dependent and neglected children in America. Parents died or were incapacitated; they were immoral or poor. Little inquiry was made into the exact nature of their demise or the possibilities for improvement in the home situation. Death by accident was an integral part of life, tragic but inevitable. The attitude toward sickness was almost as fatalistic. Public health was an unknown quantity during most of the nineteenth century, and prevention of disease was largely confined to control of epidemics by the use of quarantine. A tendency toward vice could be laid at the doorstep of inheritance or the individual's sinful nature. Poverty, which provided the mass of dependent children, was again a personal matter. While accepting the idea that people were blessed with unequal occupational abilities, most Americans saw poverty as unnecessary. In a land of visible plenty, to be without indicated a want of application and efficiency that could be remedied by personal effort. It was thought that any discontent on the part of the lower classes could be dissipated by America's limitless resources and opportunities. The needs of the poor demanded a charitable impulse from the more fortunate but no social analysis or structural change.[5]

As the twentieth century began, a distinct change was becoming visible. Edward T. Devine, secretary of the New York Charity Organization Society, illustrated this in an address to the National Conference of Charities and Correction in 1906. In his speech he condemned child-care agencies for their "ignorance of the causes which have led to the orphanage or the neglect of their wards." Devine doubted that they knew whether children were "on our hands because of the essential vices and weaknesses of their parents, or because they were the victims of needless accidents, preventable disease or industrial exploitation."[6]

Devine's emphasis upon environmental factors in cases of distress was typical of a new approach to the problems of America's dependent and lower classes. Shaken by economic depression and social unrest, Americans were being forced to reevaluate the nation's failures and misfits. Increasingly they recognized that many of the country's citizens were suffering from events over which they had no control. Organized charity and state and federal bureaus gradually gathered factual information on unemployment, wages, ill-health, accidents, and living conditions. Conferences heard an increasing number of questions concerning the implications of economic and social conditions for social work. As a result many came to believe, like Devine, that the previous view of poverty "is one which rests upon an unproved and unfounded assumption." No doubt there were individual causes of dependency and distress. Few would deny the personal element. But more frequently misery arose "because our social institutions and economic arrangements are at fault."[7] Believing this, welfare workers could no longer confine themselves to alleviating the problem. Dependency and distress were curable to a large degree; hence "the work of prevention is what we should seek to accomplish."[8]

A similar sentiment was expressed with respect to children. Judge Benjamin Barr Lindsey of the Denver Juvenile Court explained to his colleagues at the 1909 Conference on Dependent Children the necessity of looking beyond relief to prevention. "Child dependency," he stated, "is just as much due to the weakness and injustice in our social and political system as to the folly, ignorance, immorality and intemperance of parents."[9] Humane associations and societies for the prevention of cruelty to children also pointed to the broader conditions producing abuse and neglect. At the Illinois Humane Society Conference in 1909, it was argued that "cruelty grows out of poverty, ignorance and discouragement. And it may well be said that ignorance and discouragement are, after all, but incidents of poverty. In order then to overcome cruelty we must overcome poverty."[10] Likewise, the Massachusetts SPCC saw neglect as being frequently due to bad social conditions in the community. It was "a preventable social disease."[11]

If child-welfare workers had previously insisted that it was necessary to save the child in order to save society, they now argued that it was impossible to save children apart from their surroundings. The keynote for the future was to be conservation of the home. At the 26th National Conference of Charities and Correction in 1899, the Committee on Neglected and Dependent Children advised the delegates as follows:

> Do not be in a hurry to send the children to an institution until you are convinced of the hopelessness of preserving the home. Remember that, when the home is broken up, even temporarily, it is no easy task to bring it together again, and that a few dollars of private charity, a friendly visit, a kind word and a helping hand will lift up the courage of the deserving poor; and this is half the battle, because discouragement begets carelessness.[12]

While social workers readily agreed that poverty alone should never be justification for the removal of children, they were more cautious when moral aspects were involved. Their class background made them wary of clients of "questionable" character, that is, those who failed to abide by middle-class norms of behavior. They reminded themselves that the quality of America's future citizens and the stability of the nation was at stake. In cases where children were being corrupted by their families, separation seemed necessary.

Nevertheless, many child-savers felt that the parental instinct was seldom entirely dead and might be stimulated to make the home a viable unit once again.[13]

IMPROVEMENT OF WELFARE SERVICES

Children's agencies attempted to translate this concern for the welfare of the home into concrete terms. At the lowest level they tried to use whatever personal, institutional, and community forces might strengthen the family. They slowly began to revise their policies in order to find a way to keep children in their own homes. Some established specific departments, the major task of which was to isolate and treat those cases not in need of long-term care. In 1902, for example, the Illinois Children's Home and Aid Society created an Aid Department "to give information, advice and assistance in regard to children who should not be properly placed in foster homes." Keeping a family together might involve seeking help from friends and relatives or securing medical aid, psychiatric advice, or religious counseling. It might mean procuring positions for mothers where children could be with them or training "less efficient mothers" to support themselves. If necessary, cases were referred to other agencies, those offering a specific service or the wider charity organizations, such as the Chicago Bureau of Charities, which dispensed various types of material aid.[14]

When it proved impossible to prevent a "deserving" family from being separated, agencies accepted the child on a temporary basis while attempting to restore the home. The superintendent of the Boston Children's Friend Society praised his own agency, which "never gave up hope of re-establishing a family and [was] eagerly watching for the opportunity of returning a child to his kindred."[15] Previously, parents and guardians had frequently been required to sign an agreement relinquishing all rights to their children. They undertook not to interfere with their upbringing and were restricted in their amount of personal contact and correspondence with them. Often they were not notified of the children's whereabouts. Now asylums and placing agencies made some effort to keep the ties as close as possible. It was realized that many children would go back to their previous homes and that this return should be as easy and free from friction as possible. At the Chicago Home for Jewish

Orphans, the staff claimed they tried "to make the children feel that a close tie exists between them and their parents and that only through misfortune have the parents been forced to part with them." The orphanage congratulated itself for the "remarkable spirit of liberality displayed in the policy of allowing parents to visit as often as desired." Children of the same family were now often placed together in asylums or foster homes. If that was impossible, two or three families in close proximity might be used. There was a growing feeling that "when so many ties have already been broken with these children, it seems essential that the brother-sister contact be retained at whatever cost."[16]

A similar movement to prevent separation was visible to a lesser extent among protective societies. In the 1890s the general attitude of societies for the prevention of cruelty to children was, "if child-rescue is the object, stick to that and that alone."[17] The turn of century brought a gradual change in policy. In Massachusetts the SPCC, under the direction of Carl Christian Carstens, began to see its function as more than being an adjunct to the police force. Carstens gave a broader interpretation to protective work for children, seeing the society as a preventive agency. He argued that "if by means of its close relation to the courts, it can awaken neglecting parents to a better understanding of their responsibilities before it is too late, and insist on an improvement being made, the Society becomes in every sense an agency for preventing cruelty and conserving family life."[18]

The society subsequently dramatically reduced the number of cases taken to court and thus the number of families separated. In 1921, of 12,435 children involved in cases of abuse and neglect, only 2,143 were brought before the court. Of these, approximately 40 percent were allowed to remain with the parents under the court's supervision. The trend toward a widening of their program gradually encompassed most protective societies who made reconstruction and rehabilitation their aims. "When we find a home that has gone to pieces we pick up the pieces carefully, draw them together and build the structure anew. Not to take the child from an unfit home but to make the home fit for him and keep him in it is our aim."[19] By 1919 even the conservative New York SPCC had been sufficiently influenced by the swing in welfare opinion to claim that "every effort is made to save the children to their homes."[20]

In addition to a shift in emphasis among established children's agencies, there was a burst of enthusiasm for the foundation of day nurseries and creches. According to the Committee and Dependent and Neglected Children at the National Conference of 1899, "by providing a place for the children while the mother is at work, this institution has become a potent factor in the preservation of the home and has been productive of incalculable good." It not only gave shelter and moral training to children during the day but was also an employment agency, finding work for mothers in distress. Day care was thus a more humane and constructive form of relief for youngsters who would otherwise find themselves in the hands of local charities.[21]

The day nursery was not a product of the Progressive era. Several establishments based on the Paris creche had sprung up around the country from the 1850s. Nevertheless, during the 1880s and the 1890s the concept gained widespread popularity. Nurseries catered to children from two weeks to six years of age and occasionally looked after older children before and after school. If not a free service, the charge was a moderate five or ten cents a day. Some provided emergency night care in case of illness and employed their own visiting nurses; others held classes in sewing, laundering, cooking, and child care for mothers and found them work when necessary.[22]

The use of day nurseries was not without qualification. The parents were to be in need of their services as a result of death, desertion, or illness. The nursery was considered a temporary expedient that, ideally, would eventually become unnecessary when the mother took her rightful place in the home. It was not to be used to enable the mother to work when the father was lazy, shiftless or incompetent, or when she herself chose to do so. Even social workers like Florence Kelley, who supported women's wider involvement in society, did not see day care as a service available to all. Rather the nursery was a form of charity founded to deal with a specific welfare problem. Within its own sphere of influence it was a highly successful preventive force.[23]

LEGISLATIVE ACTION

Improvement of welfare services was one means of preventing dependency and neglect. A second method was legislative action.

Many child-savers agreed with Grafton Cushing of the Massachusetts SPCC that "we must develop in a new direction and take a
more active part in all movements which look towards the betterment of the conditions under which the children of the state
live."[24] Social reform at city, state, and national level attracted
their attention.

HEALTH

The promotion of health and decent housing were logical
extensions of a desire to improve child life. Homer Folks was one
social worker who believed that measures for improvement of public
health were intimately associated with reduction of child dependence. His own activities in child welfare had shown him that
parental illness was one of the major factors in the removal of
children. Ill health was the main cause of 40 percent of the institutional commitments made by the New York Bureau of Dependent Children in April 1903.[25] Tuberculosis was particularly rife
among poorer parents. One-fifth of the 185 children dealt with by
the Boston Children's Friend Society in 1902 had lost one or both
parents from this disease.[26] Though serious, the situation was
hopeful. By the turn of the century it was recognized that much
could be achieved by way of prevention. The discovery of the
tubercle bacillus by Robert Koch of Germany in 1882 led the way
for an assault on this widespread disease. In the United States,
the publication of the Briggs Report of 1889, the foundation of the
first voluntary antituberculosis association in Pennsylvania in 1897,
the creation of the National Anti-Tuberculosis Association in 1904,
and the holding of the Sixth International Congress on Tuberculosis in Washington in 1908 were milestones in an expanding
program of control. While federal action was unsuccessful until the
1940s, municipalities and states made important strides in the
dissemination of information, registration of cases, inspection of
cattle, isolation of diseased persons, and improvement of sanitation.[27]

Child welfare workers made their contribution. Folks himself
threw his weight behind the antituberculosis campaign. In 1907,
for example, with the cooperation of the Russell Sage Foundation,
he managed to organize, under the auspices of the State Charities
Aid Association of New York, the first comprehensive statewide
campaign against the disease. Other states later adopted his model.[28]

The fight against tuberculosis was only one aspect of a wider concern with health, which manifested itself in a variety of measures to improve medical services, sanitation, and food and milk supplies.

HOUSING

Closely associated with this interest in disease was the movement to regulate the nation's housing. Social workers involved with children were only too aware of the debilitating effects upon a family of inadequate shelter. They saw the overcrowding, the lack of fresh air, and the absence of decent sanitation and their implications for children. In 1918 Albion Fellows Bacon of Indiana asked her fellow delegates at the National Conference of Social Work to "remember that the normal family forced to live in a sub-normal environment, sinks to the subnormal if it remains long enough; first physically and through the illness and death of the breadwinner and then morally by lowered standards and loss of self-respect."[29] The Boston Children's Aid Society was similarly aware of the effects of poor housing. In a hundred of the families treated by the agency during 1913, living conditions were considered to have made "normal life impossible and helped to some extent to create the varied conditions we are called upon to relieve."[30] Child-savers thus acknowledged their obligation to support the legislation being drawn up to improve the design and construction of urban housing. The solution of "the housing problem [was] another fundamental step in the conservation of the parental relationship for children."[31] They therefore added their influence to that of other philantropists and the professional expertise of such men as Lawrence Veiller to attempt to bring about more effective legislation on space, ventilation, light, and safety; to promote model tenements; and to improve city planning.

WORKING CONDITIONS

If living conditions affected children by incapacitating their parents, working conditions did likewise. America was sadly lagging behind Europe in its protection of employees from the hazards of industry. Robert Hunter complained that "no other nation has so many needless deaths or so many cases of illness wholly due to preventable industrial causes as the United States of America."[32]

For the first time Americans were made aware of the extent and consequence of accidents in certain of the nation's industries. Crystal Eastman's survey of Pittsburgh casualties during 1907 and 1908 was one of the earliest and most important indictments of the country's indifference toward industrial deaths and injuries. Her analysis demonstrated the impossibility of attributing precise responsibility for most cases. Danger was inherent in modern methods of production, construction, and transportation. The study also illustrated the total inadequacy of the compensation provided. The burden of accidents fell not on employers but on the wives and children of the men concerned. Later studies further illuminated the problem.[33]

Reformers interested in children publicized the consequences of industrial hazards for dependency and neglect. Florence Lattimore, assistant director of the Child Helping Department of the Russell Sage Foundation, saw institutions "being used as a form of compensation for industrial accidents."[34] Figures from a study of institutionalized children in the Pittsburgh area during 1908 demonstrated that 14 percent of the children in care were there as a result of occupational accidents or diseases. Justice to the child demanded that children should be sheltered from orphan asylums "by stopping the needless slaughter of fathers in shop or factory or mine."[35] Greater use of safety devices and more humane working conditions were advocated. There was a call for research into the nature and prevention of diseases associated with particular trades. To ensure greater protection of children, reformers supported and helped to secure legislation for workmen's compensation. Though generally inadequate in the provisions, these measures were an improvement on the legal uncertainties of previous rulings on employers' liability.[36]

A further area of interest to child welfare workers involved wages and hours of employment. They recognized that children benefited from "a working day which will give the worker a chance to be a householder and a citizen, which will give a man one day off in seven for his family."[37] Also, as Julia Lathrop pointed out, "the power to maintain a decent family living standard is a primary essential of child welfare."[38] However, the plight of the average working man attracted less attention prior to 1914 than did that of the working woman. Motherhood was apparently endangered by the industrial exploitation of the nation's women. In the first decade of the twentieth century, reformers such as Kelley began to agitate for legislation restricting women's working hours. The verdict in favor of the constitutionality of the Ohio ten-hour law in 1908 was seen as "the greatest single step yet taken in this country in a saner adjustment of claims between industry and the family."[39] The subsequent five years saw a burst of enthusiasm with respect to legislation regulating women's hours. During the same period, women's wages also came to the fore as an area of concern. Studies pointed to the total inadequacy of the amounts paid and suggested a legal minimum wage. After 1910 Kelley and other members of the National Consumers' League placed this guarantee among their most urgent tasks. Following the example of Massachusetts in 1913, laws regulating women's wages were enacted in 14 states, although opposition succeeded in rescinding many of the decisions made.[40]

MOTHERS' PENSIONS

These wider movements for social justice promised a future reduction in the numbers of dependent and neglected children. Of more immediate consequence was the legislative campaign for mothers' pensions. This movement achieved extraordinarily swift success throughout the nation. It also generated fierce controversy within the social welfare field. Vested interests and nineteenth-century ideas on the value of public relief clashed with a belief in the benefits of guaranteed economic security. Supporters of the latter position were victorious, yet in their victory they demonstrated the anxiety and suspicion many of their opponents and predecessors felt toward the dependent.

Although a consensus of opinion had been reached that poverty should never justify the removal of children, it was painfully obvious that this was a frequent occurrence. The plight of widows provoked the greatest sympathy, for they could not possibly be held responsible for their condition. There was no moral slur on their dependency. The difficulties they experienced in trying to combine the roles of breadwinner and homemaker were enormous. Few received any compensation for their husbands' deaths. If not already wage-earners, they were pushed into the work force, usually taking low-paid domestic jobs or joining the tenement industries. More often than not they were unable to achieve self-support. Figures from public and private agencies indicated the extent of the problem. In Cook County, Illinois, the county agent reported that in 1903, of 5,460 families given material aid, the heads of 2,010 were widows. Similarly, in a study of 985 widows undertaken for the Russell Sage Foundation, Mary Richmond found that two-thirds of the women gave up the struggle to support themselves within one year of their husbands' deaths.[41]

Certain private charities recognized that a regular supplement to the mother's income was needed. The United Hebrew Charities of New York City, for example, granted $123,914 in pensions to approximately five hundred widows and deserted mothers during 1908-1909. From 1909 this was dispensed under the auspices of the newly created Mother's Fund Association. Likewise, in Chicago the Children's Day Association was founded in 1908 with the object of raising a fund "to be used at the juvenile court to prevent the separation of little children from their mothers."[42] Limited experiments were also made by city and country authorities. In California, the San Francisco earthquake stimulated assistance to a small number of widows with children. Oklahoma and Michigan, in 1908 and 1911 respectively, provided scholarships to dependent children to obviate the necessity of the children being forced into the work force by their mothers' poverty. Jackson County, Missouri, in which Kansas City is situated, provided pensions to be administered through the local juvenile court in 1911. In the same year the St. Louis Board of Children's Guardians was established, with authority to help destitute mothers.[43]

THE CALL FOR PUBLIC AID

Increasingly, welfare opinion favored greater government participation in this area. Various groups of supporters combined their energies to bring about the state laws concerning mothers' pensions. In the vanguard were judges with first-hand experience of the juvenile justice system. Judges Benjamin Barr Lindsey and Merritt W. Pinckney were at the forefront of the movements in Colorado and Illinois. In Ohio Judge Babst, in California Judge Curtis

Dwight Wilbur, and in Missouri Judge E. E. Porterfeld, helped formulate opinion and draw up legislation. Social workers were fiercely divided on the issue. Those supporting the movement included public officials such as Robert Hebberd, secretary of the New York State Board of Charities, whose positions were part of the expanding public welfare system. Settlement workers, who were acutely aware of the social and economic causes of destitution, also tended to favor public pensions. Julia Lathrop, Kelley, Jane Addams, Mary Simkhovitch, Grace and Edith Abbott were among those members or ex-inmates of settlement houses who sought preventive measures beyond the material relief offered by private philanthropy. Among private charity organizations and children's agencies, there were a number of individuals whose allegiance to their own societies did not blind them to the practical necessities of the problem of dependent children. Representatives of Jewish agencies, such as Hannah B. Epstein, vice-president of the United Hebrew Charities of New York, and Solomon Lowenstein, super-intendent of the Hebrew Orphan Asylum of Chicago, were forced to admit the inadequacy of their own efforts and the necessity of public aid.[44] Folks's opinions showed a similar movement from a belief in the superiority of private relief to an admission that "if we do not secure from private sources sufficient funds then, without hesitation, we ought to have a system of public relief for widows." Before his resignation from the New York Association for the Improvement of the Condition of the Poor, its secretary, John A. Kingsbury, had come to an identical conclusion.[45]

Naturally, women's organizations were active in the support of pensions. Within the various states, groups of young women formed mothers' pensions leagues and women's clubs publicized the cause. At the national level, the General Federation of Women's Clubs and, more importantly, the National Congress of Mothers and parent-teacher associations put their weight behind mothers' pensions while their local groups lobbied for the enactment of state laws. In Oregon and Massachusetts the latter organization was undoubtedly influential in the passage of state legislation.[46]

Favorable arguments received exposure through various news-papers and magazines. The Scripps and Hearst chains of news-papers publicized the campaign, as did reform-oriented publications such as *Outlook* and *Nation*. One of the most effective magazines was the *Delineator*, which, under the editorship of Theodore Dreiser, had already championed the foster-home concept and had contributed to the creation of the 1909 White House Conference. Through the magazine's columns, William Hard, formerly of the Northwestern University Settlement House, poured out a constant flow of persuasive argument.[47]

Advocates of mothers' pensions largely based their claims on the inadequacy of aid being given by private agencies and the right of the unfortunate mother to economic security.

Like Hard, most believed that "private charity is too puny for the task that confronts it."[48] Critics pointed to the fact that charitable societies were constantly crying out for subscriptions and that their incomes were often dependent on the philanthropic whims of individuals rather than on regular financial sources. In many societies, it was claimed, a greater proportion of money was being devoted to research than to relief. What material aid was given depended on the needs of the society, not the needs of the recipient. According to a Massachusetts commission to investigate the conditions of mothers with dependent children, "how much relief is granted and upon what terms, is certainly not determined wholly . . . by the facts of the family's condition. Inevitably the condition is interpreted by a standard in which a personal element of caution or generosity, of care and indifference or tradition is present."[49] Often the responsibility for aid was split among a number of associations, resulting in inefficiency, insufficiency, and subsequent hardship. The record spoke for itself. New York's Commission on Relief for Widowed Mothers presented evidence to show that, in 200 cases of widows dealt with by private societies, the average contribution was approximately two cents per day per person. In 1914 there were 2,716 children, of 1,483 widowed mothers, in institutions who had been committed for reasons of poverty alone.[50] Massachusetts authorities collected similar data and concluded that 59 percent of the widows studied by them had been unjustly forced to relinquish their children. Reformers argued that if private relief was incapable of preventing this type of family breakdown, then public aid was a logical alternative.[51]

This relief was not to be the material and financial relief dispensed under the poor law system. Widowed mothers were distinguished from typical dependents. There was no obvious moral stigma attached to their condition. The pension was to be granted in return for services rendered. It was not charity but a right, "justice due mothers whose work in rearing their children is a work for the state as much as that of the soldier who is paid by the state for his services in the battlefield."[52] The widow or destitute mother was to be paid as an employee. Hard insisted that "to call such a person a 'dependent' is . . . as monstrous as to call the Librarian of Congress a 'dependent.' He is paid for his work, she for hers."[53] Advocates of mothers' pensions saw no insuperable problems in the public administration of such a fund. They acknowledged that the government had not always performed creditably in the past but argued that public administration had made significant gains in efficiency and competence. Lathrop chastised critics for being frightened by the ghost of the English poor law system. She agreed that it was necessary to employ "the type of person who possesses the choicest intelligence and cultivation of the community and who will serve the public with genuine devotion," but did not see this as an impossible task. In her opinion, the sympathy and aptitude needed for the job were to be found in particular individuals and were not the property of certain organizations and societies. If there was anyone who thought that the public sector could not learn how to administer a pension fund, he had cast aside his heritage in democracy.[54]

A final benefit of mothers' pensions was their apparent economy. When compared with the amount expended by an institution, or more ridiculously, given to a foster home for board and lodging, the expense was favorable. In 1912 Pinckney claimed that the economy of the practice had already been demonstrated in Illinois. "Take a widowed mother and her group of six little ones," he told fellow delegates at the National Conference. "Even after you eliminate the mother and her future welfare from your consideration, you will find that the amount of money demanded by institutions for their care and custody is nearly double that required to rear these children in their own homes." Furthermore, most mothers only needed supplemental aid, so that the cost, in actual fact, was much less.[55]

Pensions, however economical, were not viewed as the ultimate means of financial protection for unfortunate mothers. Instead, many looked upon them as an intermediary measure that would disappear with the eventual instigation of a comprehensive program of social insurance. However, a system that would guarantee security to a mother whether her husband suffered from an accident, ill health, or unemployment might take decades to achieve. In Germany it had taken thirty years. Meanwhile, the plight of dependent children was an existent fact. Their relief could not await the future ideal of social insurance. Pensions were considered an urgent necessity.[56]

OPPOSITION TO GOVERNMENT PARTICIPATION

Many disagreed vehemently. Opposition sprang mainly from members of private charities. Social workers who had agreed with their colleagues on the necessity of many reforms for children, stood violently against pension legislation. Resistance was greatest in the east coast states, where charity organization societies exerted their strongest hold. At the forefront were such figures as Frederick Almy, secretary of the Buffalo Charity Organization Society, Josephine Shaw Lowell and Edward Devine of the New York Charity Organization Society, and Mary Richmond, general secretary of the Philadelphia Society for Organizing Charity. New York's private charities had been undermining attempts to provide public relief to widows for over a decade. As early as 1897 they had lobbied against a bill authorizing the New York City Commission of Charities to provide an allowance to mothers equal to that given to institutions for the care of their children. The bill was subsequently vetoed by the mayor. Similarly, in 1899, they thwarted another attempt to create a pension fund. The battle assumed larger proportions in 1911, when mothers' pension bills began to be introduced regularly, until success was achieved three years later. During this time the private agencies consistently tried to forestall and abort the movement for legislation.[57]

In New York and elsewhere, differences of opinion did not center on the need for regular material aid but on the relative merits of public and private control. Throughout the nineteenth century there had been a strong and continuous antagonism toward public outdoor relief. Relief was condemned both for its substandard administration and for its detrimental moral effects on recipients. Officials were poorly trained and badly paid. Their positions opened the door to chicanery and fraud and were susceptible to political manipulation. The aid dispensed was considered expensive and superfluous. It encouraged a tendency toward permanent dependence in those who received it, sapping their energy and self-respect. The poor came to think of the public coffers as bottomless and their claims to its wealth as their rights. Correspondingly, the obligation of the rich toward the poor was made redundant and the gap between the social classes widened, fostering social instability.[58]

These, essentially, were the objections put forward to public outdoor relief. America's charity organization societies, which had flourished since the 1870s, assumed a similarly hostile stance toward public aid. They themselves were forced to dispense relief in cities where no other agency provided adequate aid. Because this was only part of their larger program for family rehabilitation, it was thought to be more strictly controlled than public relief would be. Using "techniques of functional specialization and centralized coordination and administration that characterized the business world," placing emphasis on the benefits of personal relationships between client and social worker, they acknowledged the constructive possibilities of relief. Public relief, however, deserved no such qualified praise. Even a greater understanding of the social and industrial causes of poverty failed to reverse their opinion of the hazards of placing a relief fund in government hands.[59]

Edward T. Devine was one charity organization society executive who denied that mothers' pensions were anything more than public relief under an assumed name. He thought that advocates of those funds were deluding themselves that changing the names of things in some way altered their essential character. To his mind "no hysterical denunciation or passionate protest will change the bald fact that the transaction is a gift for which the persons at whose expense it is made have received no direct equivalent. Sympathy and not the payment of a financial obligation explains it."[60] Others agreed that no vital distinction might be drawn. The term "pension" merely confused the issue by implying payment for services rendered and by making no reference to the needs or characteristics of the individuals concerned.[61]

Since these payments were believed to be a disguised form of public charity, they were considered susceptible to the same dangers. They would sap the nation's moral fiber by discouraging self-support. According to Mary Wilcox Glenn of the Brooklyn Bureau of Charities, "to demand of the State that it shall give relief to the widow and her child tends to lessen the family's sense of responsibility for its own." The passage of these laws would help "create a new class of dependents in our communities," would encourage the "pathological parasitism" that was destroying the country. It was not American; it was not virile.[62]

Critics of mothers' pensions claimed that entrusting the funds to public administration was hazardous in that it offered further scope for political interference in welfare matters. While it was admitted that politics existed in both public and private charity, public charity seemed more vulnerable.[63] A further objection was made to the standard of public administration. Carstens, after making a study of the early administration of the Illinois act (1911), criticized the inadequacy of the investigation undertaken. He also found the staff of the juvenile court poorly trained and inexperienced and their supervision of families inadequate.[64]

A final factor that opponents of mothers' pensions thought vital was the detrimental impact they would have on private charity in general. It was thought that relief from private agencies would inevitably dry up, since it could not compete with public resources. Furthermore, in individual cases the interest various societies and community groups showed in particular families would decline once they saw them being supported by anonymous hands.[65]

Having spelled out the flaws in the mothers' pension scheme, members of private charities praised their own resources and services. Although admitting the necessity for aid, many thought that the problem had been somewhat exaggerated. Some, like Carstens, claimed that "the number of children who have been removed from their mothers because of poverty alone is found to be only a very small percentage of those in the various institutions."[66] As corroborating evidence he pointed to the fact that there had been no significant reduction in institutional admissions since the Funds to Parents Law had come into operation in Illinois. In most states it was felt that not enough information was available to enable those concerned to judge whether or not existing facilities were adequate. Private organizations argued that it was essential to know what the total welfare resources were for particular areas. Reformers should not be swept off their feet by the great and pressing needs of centers such as Chicago and New York to the extent that they unthinkingly advocated wide-reaching legislation.[67]

Private charity, it was claimed, had hardly been expanded to its full potential. In particular, the "valuable pension system of private charity [was] not half developed as a money raiser."[68] Rather than dismissing it as ineffective, those concerned with the nation's welfare should focus their attention on meeting present needs as far as possible. By bringing to bear all personal, family, and community resources on each individual case, private agencies felt they could reduce the payments needed to a minimum while ensuring the best program of family rehabilitation. They claimed that regular allowances provided by the government on the national scale would assume gigantic proportions. Richmond pointed to the fact that over $4 billion had already been granted in Civil War pensions alone. Pensions to mothers might prove another extravagant snowball. It was considered far better to leave control of cash endowments to the scientific methods and sympathetic understanding of private societies.[69]

STATE AID PROGRAMS

Despite their pleas and political lobbying, opponents of mothers' pensions failed to halt the movement to provide aid to dependent children in their own homes. Illinois passed the first statewide law in July 1911. Agitation for such a move emanated from the juvenile court, where Pinckney presided, and from the National Probation League. It also received support from the county agent's staff. The bill was taken to Springfield by Henry Neil, secretary of the National Probation League, where it was referred to a judiciary committee comprised largely of lawyers familiar with the state's juvenile justice system. After committee approval it was brought before the legislature and passed without a single dissenting vote. Other states rapidly followed suit. In 1913, of 42 legislatures in session, 27 were considering bills for mothers' pensions. By the end of that year, 20 states, mainly in the central and western regions, had passed laws. By 1919 funds for dependent children in their own homes had been provided by 39 states and the territories of Alaska and Hawaii. A decade later only Alabama, Georgia, New Mexico, and South Carolina were without such pensions.[70]

The campaign for mother's pensions had been based upon considerations of the necessity and justice of keeping families together in the face of adversity. Financial support was claimed to be a right of mothers who were unavoidably left to raise their children alone. However, a survey of the conditions of eligibility and the actual administration of pensions shows that a concern for social control undermined this "right" to justice.

The Illinois Funds to Parents Act of 1911 stipulated that "if the parent or parents of such dependent or neglected children are poor and unable to properly care for the said child but are otherwise proper guardians and it is for the welfare of such a child to remain at home, the court may enter an order finding such facts and fixing the amount of money necessary to enable the parent or parents to properly care for such child."[71] However, two years later a new statute was drawn up that placed far greater restrictions on the type of parent who might qualify for such a pension. Most state laws were similarly specific. The majority were designed basically for widows, the least suspect and problematic group. As late as 1931, widows comprised 82 percent of the mothers receiving aid under this scheme. There was less agreement on other circumstances warranting a pension. Less than half of the states made provisions for women whose husbands were feebleminded or otherwise totally incapacitated. In Hawaii, Michigan, and Nebraska, unmarried mothers were specifically included, but most states considered them ineligible. In Massachusetts, for example, it was thought that pensioning mothers of illegitimate children would "offend the moral feeling of respectable mothers and would do violence to a traditional sentiment that is inseparable from a respect for virtue." The child's welfare was subordinated to the recognition that there existed in America a strong stigma attached to the illegitimate. Similarly, the child's needs were considered less important than deterrence of desertion by husbands. The Massachusetts legislation was intended to ensure that fathers would not easily be relieved of their responsibility to provide for their families. It therefore stipulated that the authorities would not consider an application by a deserted mother until one year had passed and she had shown her willingness to cooperate by requesting the court to prosecute her husband for nonsupport. Illinois was not even prepared to grant money to a woman whose separation from her husband was permanent. One of the clauses of the amended act of 1913 ruled against divorced women as recipients of relief.[72]

Further hindrances to mothers with dependent children hinged on residence, nationality, and property qualifications. The residence requirements varied considerably between states, but they could insist on up to five years' residency. Some demanded that the applicant be a citizen of the United States or currently taking out papers for citizenship. When the Illinois Funds to Parents Act was tightened in 1913 by rendering alien women ineligible, 567 children were cut off from aid. Many of these were removed from their families as a result of this action. Finally, most pension legislation required proof of extreme poverty. Being a householder or possessing more than the fixed amount of personal property often prevented a mother's claim from being met. Although it was reasonable that the woman be proved financially in need of aid, these regulations often meant, for example, that a woman with no income yet possessing a small house was forced to sell the home and live off the profits until she was reduced to sufficient poverty to warrant recognition by the relief agency.[73]

The behavior conditions attached to these allowances pointed to the ambivalent attitude toward dependency. Although proponents of the scheme claimed that they would offer advice and friendship rather than authoritative interference, in fact the pressure brought to bear on mothers to cooperate and conform was quite considerable. In the application of pensions there were often the same behavioral demands that had characterized nineteenth-century scientific philanthropy. Setting middle-class norms as standards of acceptability weakened the idea that pensions were a right rather than a gift of charity. It emphasized the idea that the mere fact of requiring aid demonstrated an individual's "abnormality." The stigma attached to relief continued.

Most pension laws made the provision that the mother must be a "proper" person, physically, mentally, and morally. Since the government was providing adequate aid, it was thought reasonable to ask a high standard of character and home care. One commentator on the Massachusetts law declared that "with such a reward in view, it is a poor sort of woman who will not do well. The public authorities can make adequate relief a powerful lever to lift and keep mothers to a high standard of home care. If we grant aid to any other woman whose care of her children will just pass muster, we throw away a chance to make these women improve."[74] Other advocates of mothers' pensions agreed on the valuable possibilities of changing the life styles of an underprivileged group.

Particular habits or conditions were pinpointed as undesirable. In Massachusetts and Pennsylvania, for example, the presence of male lodgers in the home justified refusal of aid. Pennsylvania authorities spelled out the dangers. "Our widows are all young. They are often depressed and tired, physically below normal. The presence of a man in the same home with a full pay envelope may offer an overwhelming temptation."[75] They left the exact nature of the temptation to the imagination. Other signs of immorality similarly rendered the mother ineligible, as did habits of wastefulness, uncleanliness, intemperance, or the use of tobacco. The New Jersey regulations demanded that the children be given religious education, while in Minnesota the court dispensing pensions required foreign mothers "to make a reasonable effort to learn the English language and customarily use the same on her family."[76] On occasion, after agencies had given consideration to the housing situation and the desirability of the neighborhood, the family might be required to move. Alternatively, a mother might be forced to prosecute relatives who had refused to provide her with aid. Even more harsh was the Illinois condition, which could enforce removal of a husband who was permanently incapacitated and who was considered "a menace to the physical and moral welfare of the mother and the children."[77]

If the woman was willing to cooperate unquestioningly, all was well. If reluctant to obey, her security was in question. Any resistance to pressure might be seen as an unwillingness to accept advice and hence might justify her being removed from the relief rolls. Unfortunately, this same pressure to conform still haunts the present system.

The failure of pension advocates to consistently defend economic assistance as an end in itself, and the uneasy conjunction of economic and moral criteria, also affected the administration of mothers' pensions. In most states the laws empowered the counties to raise the required appropriations. Legislatures tended to carry over the poor law principle of local responsibility. Before 1919 only one-quarter of the laws involved state funds. The funds, distributed most frequently through the juvenile courts, were generally inadequate for the task in hand. Not only were appropriations insufficient, but the actual apportioning of money to parents was unrealistic.[78]

A study undertaken by Chicago social workers Edith Abbott and Sophonisba Breckinridge illustrates the way in which pensions were actually applied. The 1911 Illinois statute authorized expenditure of a fixed amount of $15 per month for a single dependent child and $10 for each additional child, with a maximum of $50 per family. (In 1915 this was raised to $60.) In comparison with other states, this was a fairly generous amount. Kansas, for example, placed a $25 per month maximum on its allowance to an individual family. However, Abbott and Breckinridge found that, of 778 families pensioned in Cook County during 1915, only three were receiving the maximum amount, despite the fact that 23 of the families had six children or more. When the requirements of each family were studied, it was found that approximately 56.6 percent of the mothers were still dependent on an income below the budget standard prepared by the authorized dietitian. "It must be recognized," they declared, "that judged not by our present wage standards but by any reasonable standards of what is necessary to maintain physical and mental efficiency, the court pensions must be inadequate." For many families there was no income except the precarious earnings of the mother. Often she was in poor health or handicapped by infants, so that her earning capacity was vitually nil. The juvenile court provided relief that was only sufficient as supplemental aid. There was frequently a delay in receiving allowances due to unnecessary investigation requirements. Not only was an inquiry made by the conference committee of the juvenile court, but the county agent conducted an entirely independent investigation to establish the same facts. When it was eventually established that the mother was eligible, she was forced to collect it weekly from the county agent's office. This was a demoralizing process.[79]

Other welfare personnel, in Illinois and elsewhere, echoed this disappointment in the amount of aid dispensed. They protested against the attitude that "half a loaf is better than no bread" and condemned the fact that the state gave mothers approximately one-third to two-thirds of the amount found requisite to board children away from their families. At times the public funds had to be supplemented by private charity or ordinary poor relief, thus continuing the same inefficiency and insufficiency that had characterized earlier methods of relieving mothers with dependent children.[80]

FEDERAL AID

In 1935, with the enactment of the Social Security Act, mothers' pensions entered a new phase in their history. As passed, the bill provided for federal allotments to states for the relief of families with dependent children to the amount of $6 for the first child and $4 for each subsequent child. Caution again affected the provisions. Not only was the amount conservative, but an earlier stipulation that the grants should "furnish assistance at least great enough to provide, when added to the income of the family, a reasonable subsistence compatible with decency and health" had been deleted from the final bill.[81] From that time, Aid to Families with Dependent Children (AFDC) grew, to become the largest cash public assistance program in the United States. In 1970 it was estimated that, by the time they reached the age of 18, almost one-fifth of all Americans would have received benefits under the scheme for at least a short period. The AFDC program has continued to provoke controversy to date. For many it is seen as a symbol of what was wrong with the American welfare system. Critics point to the increasing numbers of families on its rolls and the huge expenditures. They question the scheme's efficiency in terms of preventing dependency, the amount of discretion permitted its administrators, and the continuance of moral criteria in the granting of relief.[82]

IMPACT OF THE MOTHERS' PENSION MOVEMENT

Despite its inconsistencies in philosophy and the faults that emanated from them, the mothers' pension movement was a significant step forward from older practices of dealing with dependent children. It did offer the means by which a large number of children remained with their parents. In 1921, for example, 45,825 families, with approximately 120,000 children, were receiving aid.[83] This rivaled the figure for children then being cared for in institutions. Although weakened by moral concerns, the campaign had challenged the idea that economic assistance was a peripheral social work function. Agencies could no longer claim that financial support was a negligible feature of family rehabilitation. Finally, the movement had dealt a decisive blow to the previous idea that the major responsibility for social welfare belonged to the private sector. While the opportunity to modernize the public welfare system had not been successfully exploited, the need for wider government action was becoming more acceptable. This change in attitude had considerable implications for the care and protection of dependent and neglected children in areas other than provision of financial relief, as will be shown in later chapters. Meanwhile, this study will examine further legislative innovations designed to support the family unit, namely, changes in the legal relationship between parent and child.

NOTES

1. Mary Richmond, "Charitable Cooperation," *Proceedings of the 28th NCCC*, 1901, p. 301.

2. D. J. McMahon, statement, *Proceedings of the Conference on the Care of Dependent Children*, Washington, D.C., January 25-26, 1909 (reprinted New York: Arno Press, 1971).

3. U.S. Bureau of the Census, *Marriage and Divorce 1867-1906* (Washington, D.C.: Government Printing Office, 1909), pp. 3-4.

4. William O'Neill, *Divorce in the Progressive Era* (New Haven: Yale University Press, 1967), pp. vii, 1-88. Ernest Mowrer, *Family Disorganization* (Chicago: University of Chicago Press, 1927), pp. 1-24. Michael J. Scanlan, statement, *Proceedings of the [1909] Conference on the Care of Dependent Children*, quoted pp. 41-42.

5. For the nineteenth-century view of poverty see Robert H. Bremner, *From the Depths: The Discovery of Poverty in the United States* (New York: New York University Press, 1967), pp. 17-21.

6. Edward T. Devine, "The Dominant Note of Modern Philanthropy," *Proceedings of the 33rd NCCC*, 1906, p. 7.

7. Edward T. Devine, *Misery and its Causes* (New York: Macmillan, 1918), pp. 9, 11.

8. Hastings Hornell Hart, "On the Care of the Poor," *Proceedings of the 2nd Illinois Conference of Charities and Correction*, 1897, p. 45.

9. Benjamin Barr Lindsey, statement, *Proceedings of the [1909] Conference of the Care of Dependent Children*, p. 217.

10. "Winnebago Report," *Proceedings of the Illinois Humane Society Convention*, 1909, p. 2.

11. *Annual Report of the Massachusetts Society for the Prevention of Cruelty to Children*, 1907, p. 12.

12. "Report of the Committee on Neglected and Dependent Children," *Proceedings of the 26th NCCC*, 1899, p. 169.

13. See, for example, Carl Christian Carstens, "The Breaking Up of Families," *Proceedings of the 36th NCCC*, 1909, p. 51, and "The Separation of Children from Parents," *Charities* 11 (1903): 490-92.

14. Elizabeth White, "The History and Development of the Illinois Children's Home and Aid Society" (master's thesis, University of Chicago, 1934), p. 67.

15. *Annual Report of the Boston Children's Friend Society*, 1904, p. 12.

16. *Annual Report of the Chicago Home for Jewish Orphans*, 1918, pp. 4, 12. For the change in policy see also *Annual Reports of the Boston Children's Aid Society*, 1891, p. 10; 1913, p. 17.

17. Elbridge Gerry, quoted in Roswell C. McCrea, *The Humane Movement: A Descriptive Survey* (New York: Columbia University Press, 1910), p. 139.

18. Carl Christian Carstens, quoted ibid., p. 142. For an account of changes in policy see William J. Schultz, "The Humane Movement in the United States 1910-1922," *Columbia University Studies in History, Economics and Public Law*, Study No. 1 (New York: Columbia University Press, 1924), pp. 200-12. For changes in the Massachusetts Society for the Prevention of Cruelty to Children, see *Annual Reports*, 1906, pp. 4-5; 1910, p. 13; 1911, p. 24; 1921, p. 20.

19. Massachusetts Society for the Prevention of Cruelty to Children, *Annual Report*, 1910, p. 13.

20. *Annual Report of the New York Society for the Prevention of Cruelty to Children*, 1919, p. 24.

21. "Report of the Committee on Neglected and Dependent Children," *Proceedings of the 26th NCCC*, 1899, p. 170.

22. Margaret Steinfels, *Who's Minding the Children? A History and Politics of Day Care in America* (New York: Simon & Schuster, 1973),

pp. 34-47. United Charities of Chicago, *Year Book*, 1911, on the Mary Crane Nursery, pp. 26-28.

23. Steinfels, *Who's Minding the Children?*, pp. 50-51.

24. *Annual Report of the Massachusetts Society for the Prevention of Cruelty to Children*, 1905, p. 8.

25. Homer Folks, "Disease and Dependence," *Proceedings of the 30th NCCC*, 1903, pp. 334-35.

26. *Annual Report of the Boston Children's Friend Society*, 1902, p. 6.

27. Lillian Brandt, *The Facts About Tuberculosis* (New York: New York School of Philanthropy, 1915). Anthony M. Lowell, Lydia B. Edwards, and Carroll E. Palmer, *Tuberculosis* (Cambridge, Mass.: Harvard University Press, 1965), pp. 1-4.

28. Ibid., p. 12.

29. Albion Fellows Bacon, "Housing, Its Relation to Social Work," *Proceedings of the 45th National Conference of Social Work* (henceforward NCSW), 1918, p. 200.

30. *Annual Report of the Boston Children's Aid Society*, 1913, p. 8.

31. J. Prentice Murphy, "Conserving the Child's Parental Home," in U.S. Children's Bureau, *Foster Home Care for Dependent Children*, Publication no. 136 (Washington, D.C.: Government Printing Office, 1924), p. 24. Harriet Fulmer, "The Housing Problem and Its Relation to Other Reform Movements," *Proceedings of the 38th NCCC*, 1911, pp. 145-50. Roy Lubove, *The Progressives and the Slums: Tenement House Reform in New York City 1890-1917* (Pittsburgh: University of Pittsburgh Press, 1962), pp. 248-52.

32. Robert Hunter, *Poverty* (New York: Macmillan, 1904), p. 157.

33. Crystal Eastman, "Work Accidents and Employers' Liability," *Proceedings of the 37th NCCC*, 1910, pp. 414, 424.

34. Florence Lattimore, "Children's Institutions and the Accident Problem," ibid., p. 425.

35. Stephen S. Wise, "Justice to the Child," *AAAPSS* 35 (1910): 36.

36. Roy Lubove, *The Struggle for Social Security* (Cambridge, Mass.: Harvard University Press, 1968), pp. 43-65.

37. Paul Kellogg, "Occupational Standards," *Proceedings of the 37th NCCC*, 1908, p. 383.

38. Julia Lathrop, "Child Welfare Standards as a Test of Democracy," *Proceedings of the 46th NCSW*, 1919, p. 7.

39. Mary Richmond, "The Family and the Social Worker," *Proceedings of the 35th NCCC*, 1908, p. 78.

40. Bremner, *From the Depths*, pp. 213-43.

41. Cook County, Ill., Board of Commissioners, *Charity Service Report*, 1903, p. 6. Mary Richmond, *A Study of 985 Widows Known to Certain*

Charity Organization Societies in 1910 (New York: Russell Sage, 1913), p. 17.

42. David M. Schneider and Albert Deutsch, *A History of Public Welfare in New York State* (Chicago: University of Chicago Press, 1941), p. 185. Ruth Newberry, "Origin and Criticism of the Funds to Parents Act" (master's thesis, University of Chicago, 1912), p. 9.

43. Lubove, *The Struggle for Social Security*, p. 99. Alfred Fairbank, "Mothers' Pensions in Missouri," *Proceedings of the 41st NCCC*, 1914, pp. 442-42. L. A. Holber, "The Widows Allowance Act in Kansas City," in Edna E. Bullock, *Selected Articles on Mothers' Pensions* (New York: H. W. Wilson, 1915), pp. 11-12.

44. Mark Leff, "Consensus for Reform: The Mothers' Pension Movement in the Progressive Era," *Social Service Review* 47 (1973): 405-6. Schneider and Deutsch, *A History of Public Welfare in New York State*, pp. 185-86. Benjamin Barr Lindsey, "The Mothers' Compensation Law in Colorado," *Survey* 29 (1913): 714-16. Merritt W. Pinckney, "Public Pensions to Widows—Experiences and Observations Which Lead Me to Favor Such a Law," *Proceedings of the 39th NCCC*, 1912, pp. 473-75.

45. Homer Folks, statement in the discussion on mothers' pensions, *Proceedings of the 39th NCCC*, 1912, p. 487.

46. Lubove, *The Struggle for Social Security*, pp. 100-101.

47. Leff, "Consensus for Reform," p. 406.

48. William Hard, statement in the discussion on mothers' pensions in Bullock, *Selected Articles*, p. 186.

49. Commonwealth of Massachusetts, *Report of the Commission on the Support of Dependent Minor Children of Widowed Mothers* (Boston, 1913), p. 20.

50. New York State, *Report of the Commission on Relief for Widowed Mothers* (Albany, 1914), p. 7.

51. Commonwealth of Massachusetts, *Report of the Commission on . . . Widowed Mothers*, p. 14.

52. Lindsey, "The Mothers' Compensation Law in Colorado," p. 716.

53. William Hard, "The Moral Necessity of State Funds to Mothers," *Survey* 29 (1913): 773.

54. Julia Lathrop, statement in the discussion on mothers' pensions, *Proceedings of the 29th NCCC*, 1902, pp. 487-88.

55. Pinckney, "Public Pensions to Widows," p. 477.

56. Hard, statement in Bullock, *Selected Articles*, p. 184.

57. Schneider and Deutsch, *A History of Public Welfare in New York State*, pp. 181-82.

58. Bremner, *From the Depths*, pp. 46-50. For criticisms of outdoor relief see, for example, Josephine Russell Lowell, "The Economic and

Moral Effects of Public Outdoor Relief," *Proceedings of the 17th NCCC*, 1890, pp. 81-92.

59. Roy Lubove, *The Professional Altruist: The Emergence of Social Work as a Career, 1880-1930* (Cambridge, Mass.: Harvard University Press, 1965), pp. 1-24, quoted p. 6.

60. Edward T. Devine, "Pensions for Mothers," in Bullock, *Selected Articles*, pp. 177-78.

61. Carl Christian Carstens, "Public Pensions to Widows with Children," *Survey* 29 (1913): 462. Mary Richmond, "Motherhood and Pensions," ibid., p. 775.

62. Mary Wilcox Glenn, "The Relief of Needy Mothers in New York," *Proceedings of the 41st NCCC*, 1914, p. 453.

63. Frederick Almy, "Public Pensions to Widows—Experiences and Observations Which Lead Me to Propose Such a Law," *Proceedings of the 39th NCCC*, 1912, p. 492.

64. Carstens, "Public Pensions to Widows with Children," pp. 459-66.

65. Mary Richmond, statement, *Proceedings of the 39th NCCC*, 1912, p. 492.

66. Carstens, "Public Pensions to Widows with Children," p. 460.

67. Richmond, "Motherhood and Pensions," p. 774. Alice L. Higgins, statement in discussion on mothers' pensions, *Proceedings of the 39th NCCC*, 1912, p. 491.

68. Almy, "Public Pensions to Widows," p. 484.

69. Richmond, "Motherhood and Pensions," pp. 777-78.

70. U.S. Children's Bureau, *Laws Relating to Mothers' Pensions in the United States, Canada, Denmark and New Zealand*, Publication no. 63 (Washington, D.C.: Government Printing Office, 1919), pp. 8-11. House of Representatives of the 47th General Assembly of the State of Illinois, *Journal*, 1911, pp. 1436-37. Senate of the 47th General Assembly of the State of Illinois, *Journal*, 1911, p. 1045.

71. "Juvenile Courts—Funds to Parents," *Laws of Illinois* (Springfield, 1911), p. 127.

72. U.S. Children's Bureau, *Laws Relating to Mothers' Pensions*, pp. 12-13. *Annual Report of the Massachusetts State Board of Charities*, 1914, pp. 106-7, quoted p. 107. Robert H. Bremner, ed., *Childhood and Youth in America: A Documentary History* (Cambridge, Mass,: Harvard University Press, 1971), vol. 2, p. 395. "Administration of the Mothers' Aid Law in Massachusetts," in Bullock, *Selected Articles*, p. 75.

73. U.S. Children's Bureau, *Laws Relating to Mothers' Pensions*, pp. 13-14. Edith Abbott and Sophonisba P. Breckinridge, *The Administration of the Aid to Mothers Law in Illinois*, U.S. Children's Bureau

Publication no. 82 (Washington, D.C.: Government Printing Office, 1921), pp. 96-98.

74. David Tilley, "Adequate Relief to Dependent Mothers in Massachusetts," *Proceedings of the 41st NCCC*, 1914, pp. 455-56.

75. U.S. Children's Bureau, *Laws Relating to Mothers' Pensions*, p. 195.

76. Ibid., p. 122.

77. Ibid., p. 73.

78. Ibid., pp. 16-18.

79. Abbot and Breckinridge, *The Administration of the Aid to Mothers Law in Illinois*, pp. 19-26, 48-49, quoted p. 69. The average weekly wage for "lower-skilled" labor in 1911 was $10.13. U.S. Bureau of the Census, *Historical Statistics of the United States Colonial Times to 1970* (Washington, D.C.: Government Printing Office, 1971), vol. 1, p. 168.

80. W. M. Graham, "Mothers' Pensions and their Failure in Illinois," *Institution Quarterly* 7 (1916): 19. Emma O. Lundberg, "Aid to Mothers with Dependent Children," *AAAPSS* 98 (1921): 100.

81. Grace Abbott, *The Child and the State* (Chicago: University of Chicago Press, 1938), pp. 240-43. Social Security Act quoted p. 240.

82. Joel Handler and Ellen Hollingsworth, *The Deserving Poor: A Study of Welfare Administration* (Chicago: Markham, 1971), pp. ix, 1.

83. U.S. Children's Bureau, *Mothers' Aid, 1931*, Publication no. 220 (Washington, D.C.: Government Printing Office, 1933), pp. 8-9.

6

THE
CHILD,
THE PARENT,
AND THE LAW

As shown in the previous chapter, one element of child welfare reform in the Progressive era was increasing state support and control of the family unit. Public funds helped one-parent families to approximate the nuclear norm but these pensions were selective, strictly supervised, reformative and were too meagre to enable mothers to withdraw totally from the paid work force. A further area of reform concerned children's legal status with respect to their parents. Reformers campaigned for greater enforcement of parental duties. In particular they tackled what they considered one of the most urgent legal and welfare problems, the refusal of many parents to support their offspring. Their solution was to revise the laws forcing fathers to support their legitimate and illegitimate children. Legislation increased penalties for non-support, facilitated maintenance proceedings and tightened enforcement procedures. Often, however, a desire to deter or punish reluctant parents took precedence over the ostensible goal of guaranteeing children's economic welfare. In addition, the administration of such legislation revealed the impracticality of the laws which primarily affected working-class men with poor or irregular incomes and demonstrated the divisions between state apparatuses. Maintenance provisions were frequently translated by the courts into pittances and mothers were thrown back on kinship and community networks, private charity or public welfare.

THE CHILD UNDER COMMON LAW

Prior to the nineteenth century the legal relationship between parent and child largely followed the pattern of English common law. The child's rights were considered relatively unimportant. The law only guarded with enthusiasm the interests of those children who were heirs to property. In comparison, the father was given a virtually unlimited right to the custody, control, and earnings of a minor child. The mother was entitled to "no power but only reverence and respect." In any conflict with the father's sacred right over his own children, the legal interests of mother and child usually came off second best.[1]

The father's almost absolute power was granted in return for efficient performance of parental duties. These generally involved maintenance and protection of the child and provision of a suitable education. Common law regulations, however, were inadequate in many parts of the United States. The duty to support was often "merely a moral obligation creating no civil liability."[2] James Kent, in his commentaries written in 1826, expressed what appears to be the consensus of opinion: "The obligation of parental duty is so well secured by the strength of natural affection that it seldom requires to be enforced by human laws. . . . A father's house is always open to his children. The best feelings of our nature establish and consecrate this asylum."[3] Elsewhere, civil statutes that had been enacted demanding that the parent recompense individuals, institutions, and poor law authorities for necessaries furnished to a minor child, often operated unsuccessfully. Protection of the child was similarly sanctioned but rarely enforced. In 1765 William Blackstone, author of the highly influential eighteenth-century book *Commentaries on the Law of England*, had acknowledged that this duty was "rather permitted than enjoined by any municipal laws, nature in this respect working so strongly as to need a check rather than a spur."[4] In the case of education, although Massachusetts had passed a law requiring parents to send their children to school as early as 1642, the question of compulsory education and its enforcement was basically left unanswered until after the Civil War.

Parental, that is, paternal, legal dominance underwent only slight changes in the hundred years after the publication of Blackstone's commentaries. However, in the second half of the nineteenth century, significant moves were made toward restructuring the system of family law. Two basic principles were developed. The first was the equality of legal rights between mother and father, and the second was the paramount importance of the welfare of the child.[5] Describing the latter development, Florence Kelley argued in 1882 that the child's legal position was better than it had ever been. "Nowhere in the Commentaries," she wrote, "is there a hint that the common law regarded the child as an individual with a distinctive legal status." In contrast, the nineteenth century had witnessed a growing recognition of "the child's welfare as a direct object of legislation, apart from the family."[6]

THE CALL FOR STATE INTERVENTION

During the Progressive era this gradual elevation of the child's legal status continued. Part of the response to the problems arising from the growth of industrial captialism in late nineteenth-century America was increased state enforcement of parental responsibilities of maintenance, protection and education. Lawyer Sophonisba P. Breckinridge, speaking at the thirteenth Illinois Conference of Charities and Correction in 1908, described this shift in attitude. Analyzing the state's interest in children and the family, she isolated a number of areas of concern, the first being "the enforcement of the performance of parental duties where the parents are alive and capable both in intelligence and in economic ability." This interest was quite a new thing. "Speaking not pedantically as a lawyer, but basically as a historian," she declared, "it was an innovation of the present half century—almost, we may say, of the present generation."[7]

Reformers based their claims for state intervention on the doctrine of *parens patriae*, that is, that the public has a paramount interest in the welfare of its members. This was stated in two closely allied forms. First, parents were said to have a duty toward their children that the state should enforce because of the children's helplessness, their inability to distinguish right from wrong, and their extreme susceptibility to moral or bodily harm from influences they could neither avoid nor control. Second, the parents had a duty to the state, to create and maintain a high standard of citizenship. Bringing human beings into existence was, it was claimed, one of the most responsible acts of human life. For its own protection, society should demand that children be nurtured properly. While "the relation of the parent to child is to be sacredly guarded, . . . general welfare should be more sacredly guarded." Both these arguments rejected the ancient notion of God-given, inviolable parental rights. Increasingly the opinion was expressed that children had equal rights with their parents and that the family home was established for the child and not vice versa.[8]

THE RIGHT TO PUBLIC EDUCATION

The legal issue that was thought most relevant to the problems of dependency and neglect was that of maintenance. However, gains were made in other areas that may be mentioned briefly. Progressive social reformers defended children's right to public education and to protection against parental abuse of their labor. These topics cover a vast and complex territory, going far beyond the specific parent-child relationship and the problem of neglect. For this reason a detailed examination is unnecessary. Nevertheless, reformers in the fields of education and labor did bring into question the legal right of the child to protection from irresponsible parents.

At the turn of the twentieth century, school and employment records showed the presence in the work force of 1,750,000 youngsters between the ages of ten and fifteen. Critics of this situation singled out four major causes. In addition to the poor education system, the preference of employers for cheap labor, and the community's desire for cheap goods, they also pointed to "the indifference and equally selfish greed on the part of the parents" who wanted to increase the family income or provide themselves with cheap home help. Reformers saw acted out before them what Stephan Thernstrom describes as a pattern of property mobility whereby workers, particularly immigrants, compensated for their lack of occupational mobility by accumulating savings or property.

These workers often sacrificed their children's future by pushing them into the work force at an early age in order to make immediate gains. Alternatively, they kept their children at home to act as babysitters, interpreters, and general domestic help, allowing both parents to work if they needed to.[9]

Social workers such as Edith Abbott and Florence Kelley saw this as a largely unnecessary form of parental abuse. They denied that the child's earnings were normally required to keep a family from becoming dependent. Few widows, it was claimed, were being saved from the charity societies by their children's labor. Instead, parents who were poor but not destitute were perpetuating a practice that was harmful both to the child and to society at large. Reformers variously condemned premature employment and inadequate education for producing racial degeneracy, continued poverty, greater illiteracy, disintegration of the family, a rise in the crime rate, lowering of the wage scale, and an increase in the numbers of the unemployed.[10]

With an indomitable faith in the ability of education to eradicate antisocial attitudes, develop civic consciousness and promote Americanization, campaigners set out to force parents to give their offspring sufficient schooling. Believing that "an intimate relationship exists between child-labor and school attendance," they also supported the movement to control the intake of youngsters into the work force. To a considerable degree they achieved success.[11]

Legislation regulating school attendance and child labor was in existence prior to 1890. However, it was inconsistent and was ambiguously worded and carelessly enforced. As a result of awakened interest in compulsory schooling, new legislation was introduced, old laws expanded, and loopholes eliminated. By 1900, 32 states, mainly in the north and west, had passed laws demanding attendance, generally for the entire school session, fixing stiff penalties for parents who failed to comply and setting up facilities for inspection and prosecution. In 1918, with the enactment of the Mississippi school attendance law, compulsory education became universal. Similarly, although faced with strong opposition from industry, the child labor campaign, headed by the indefatigable members of the National Child Labor Committee, did provoke action at state and national levels. While varying from state to state, child labor laws raised the minimum working age, generally to 14, demanded proof of age and a suitable level of education, and frequently insisted upon certain basic conditions of health and physical development. Federal legislation introduced in 1916, however, was rescinded in the 1920s.[12]

THE RIGHT TO PROTECTION AGAINST ABUSE

Another area in which gradual gains were made was the legal protection of children against abuse, particularly physical abuse, by parents and guardians. The latter was a sensitive issue, since the principle that a parent may inflict punishment to discipline a child was part of America's heritage of common law. Parents had long had the privilege of battering, depriving, or otherwise ill-treating a child for the "benefit of his education." Criticisms of this position were frequently ignored on the basis that they undermined the successful working of the family. It is not surprising, therefore, that even in 1935, when Chester S. Vernier made his useful compilation of U.S. family law, only eighteen states and territories had statutes specifically regulating parental use of force. The majority of these stipulated that force was permissible provided it was "reasonable." In nine of these states it was expressly stated that homicide was excusable if caused by a parent in lawfully correcting his child, while a Louisiana law of 1922 made the curious exemption that "provisions for killing by stabbing do not apply to a person who, in chastising or correcting a child, chances to commit manslaughter without intending to do so." Why a parent should be disciplining a child with a knife or similar instrument is somewhat puzzling.[13]

If legislation directly limiting the parental power of control was not widespread, more general criminal statutes relating to offenses against children did, however, bring parents to account. It was mentioned in Chapter 2 that, beginning in New York in 1874, groups of concerned citizens had organized themselves into protective societies and begun to agitate for new and improved legislation defending children against physical abuse and moral neglect. These groups felt that "it would be monstrous to hold that under the pretense of sustaining parental authority children must be left without the protection of the law." In particular they denied that "parents have . . . more right to inflict cruel punishment upon their children than upon any other person." The reforms started in the 1880s were continued over the next three decades. By 1922, 27 states had passed laws forbidding any person to cruelly torture or punish juveniles, 22 states had made it illegal for adults to wilfully cause or permit the life or health of any child to be endangered, while 11 jurisdictions had made it an offense to unnecessarily expose children to the weather. Parents might also be brought to book for depriving a child of necessary food, clothing, and shelter. In addition to penalties of fines and imprisonment that might be imposed by the courts, provisions were also made to remove children from parents found to be unsuitable guardians.[14]

It is difficult to know whether judicial decisions took the question of the use of force against children more seriously in the 1920s than in the 1880s. There existed certain difficulties in procuring evidence against parents. The privilege of husbands and wives not to testify against each other was often an impediment, and judges were frequently loath to treat parents severely. Nevertheless, the decision as to whether punishment was moderate or not was increasingly felt to be one that parents themselves could not take but that had to be measured by an external standard.[15]

THE RIGHT TO SUPPORT

Finally, there was the question of nonsupport, particularly as it involved desertion. It has been noted that the apparent disintegration of family life was a subject of almost hysterical concern toward the end of the nineteenth century. The main stimulus to the collection and analysis of data on marital breakdown was the accelerating divorce rate. However, at that time divorce was a predominantly upper and middle-class solution to marriage problems.[16] The cost alone prohibited a large number of Americans from taking advantage of this legal option. The $50 required to obtain a divorce through the Chicago courts in the early 1900s was very expensive for a laborer earning an average of $12 a week. Also, working-class families were far less knowledgeable about their legal rights and were more easily cowed by complicated court procedures. Instead, many parents chose desertion as a viable alternative. Where a wealthy man was more likely to be bound to a locality or a profession and to be unwilling to sacrifice business opportunities and prestige in order to evade family responsibilities, a poor man had greater freedom to abscond. He might go so far as to leave one city for another and change his name or he might stay in his own neighborhood. Desertion also provided such men with a temporary escape from difficult circumstances. A survey conducted in New York in 1905 found that approximately one-half of the deserters studied had left home more than once. Other investigations showed an even higher percentage. All nationalities and racial groups experienced this phenomenon. Although the Jewish community, for example, was more sensitive to its desertion rate, there is no evidence that particular ethnic groups produced abnormally large numbers of defectors. Indeed, contemporary analyses of the incidence of nonsupport suggested to the investigators "that desertion is a failing common to the human race, not confined to any particular sections of it."[17]

In the large majority of cases, it was the husband who abandoned his wife and children. Women's greater responsibility for child care and poorer job opportunities made it less likely that they would leave their families. Frequently husbands' desertion forced them to seek aid from relief agencies and other charitable organizations. According to a survey of 54 charities, carried out under the auspices of the New York Charity Organization Society, between 7 and 13 percent of families under care had been deserted. Other organizations put the figures as high as 20 percent. Public authorities experienced similar demands for their services. For example, Cook County officials in 1909 reported 1,270 deserted families on their relief rolls, this being an estimated 14 percent of the total number of families in receipt of funds. Many agencies, such as the Minneapolis Associated Charities, were reluctant to give deserted wives financial aid at all, since they feared that this would encourage husbands to escape their responsibilities. Instead, they frequently preferred to split up the family and commit the children to institutions or foster homes until the mother could support them unaided. In the estimation of one prominent social worker, perhaps one-quarter of the juvenile commitments to New York institutions at the turn of the century were the result of abandonment and failure to support.[18]

INADEQUACY OF EXISTING STATUTES

There were a number of criminal statutes in existence in 1890 that made the refusal to maintain minor children an offense. Most made the crime a misdemeanor punishable by a fine of up to $100 or a short prison sentence. Despite these laws, the vast majority of parents who declined to support their families were virtually immune from arrest and prosecution. The lack of adequate agencies to track down deserters, the expense involved, public indifference, and bureaucratic red tape discouraged social workers from locating errant parents and bringing them to court if necessary. In the rare event that the father was ordered to pay a regular amount to maintain his dependents, there was little hope of enforcement. Often all that might be achieved was continued harrassment by the police and the charities involved, and this, as social workers attested, frequently encouraged the man to disappear again.[19]

It was toward the end of the century that the problems of non-support and abandonment really began to provoke cries of anxiety from welfare workers and their associates. In part, this new aware-ness was due to the nation's growing sensitivity to the fate of the American family. In part, it was a response to the obvious suffering involved. Charities and public authorities saw desertion and non-support "blighting the lives of thousands of children every year." The cases before them afforded many "pathetic examples of struggles to keep the home together," examples of mothers working them-selves into exhaustion and ill-health to avoid losing their children. More immediately, however, it was due to a realization of "the drain on the resources of . . . charitable agencies caused by the assumption of the deserter's burden." The primary motive for considering the problem was "not because of the religious social or moral questions involved, but that of dependency." The finan-cial reports of organizations throughout the country showed thousands of dollars being spent because parents were balking at their responsibilities. Furthermore, it was generally thought that desertion was on the increase, and social workers feared even greater demands in the future.[20]

In 1895 the issue became a national one when it was introduced for discussion at the 21st National Conference of Charities and

Correction. E. P. Savage, superintendent of the Children's Home of Minnesota, delivered a paper entitled "Desertion by Parents," in which he criticized the general ignorance and apathy of his colleagues in this area. He himself had dispatched questionnaires to associations throughout the country requesting information on the numbers of cases dealt with, the legal safeguards, and the efficiency of prosecutions. The response in 1895, and again two years later when he repeated his inquiries, indicated that few states had any idea of the extent of the problem nor any means of dealing with it satisfactorily. No national or state figures were available. Numbers gathered by one-quarter of the nation's children's agencies showed 7,334 youngsters in care as a direct result of desertion by their parents.[21]

Interest spread, gaining momentum after the turn of the century. From 1903 to 1914 social work's leading journal, *Charities* (later *Survey*), regularly published articles by welfare workers, judges, and lawyers on the effects of nonsupport and the inadequacy of existing legislation. Specific organizations held meetings with their fellow agencies to share information and propose remedies. In April 1903, for example, the New York Charity Organization Society's president, Edward T. Devine, called together workers from Philadelphia, Buffalo, Brooklyn, and New York City to discuss the desertion problem. As a result of this congress, a committee consisting of social workers Mary Richmond, W. H. Allen, and Paul Kellogg was elected to introduce a resolution at the next National Conference of Charities and Correction to petition governors of the various states to exercise their powers in extraditing deserting husbands. The conference subsequently supported the resolution.[22]

INVESTIGATIONS INTO THE CAUSES OF DESERTION

In addition to the National Conference of Charities and Correction, which continued sporadically to air the question of desertion until 1912, Catholic and Jewish conferences expressed their particular interest in the subject. At the second meeting of the National Conference of Catholic Charities in 1912, Patrick Mallon, a member of the Saint Vincent de Paul Society of Brooklyn, voiced the concern of his church for the large numbers of Catholics who deserted their families "in defiance of the natural law and their added obligation as the custodians of the immortal souls of their children."[23] Similarly, the Jewish community pronounced desertion a problem "of vital concern to our organized charities, particularly in the larger centers of population." Its anxiety was greater than that of other groups. Indeed, some Jews feared that the rate of desertion was proportionately higher among members of their faith than among those from other communities, although in fact there was no evidence to substantiate this. During the proceedings of the First National Conference of Jewish Charities held in 1900, a report was presented by the Committee on Desertions in which the authors discussed the pressures of immigration, discrimination, sickness, and poverty, which they felt encouraged Jewish fathers to abscond. Subsequent biennial conferences followed up the problem, analyzing case histories, presenting statistical information, and promoting the establishment of an agency that would centralize relevant data and act as a detective bureau.[24]

Jewish social workers were well aware that their knowledge of the causes of desertion was far from reliable. For that reason, Morris Waldman undertook a survey of the cases of desertion that had been dealt with by the United Hebrew Charities of New York between 1902 and 1903. Other agencies were also striving toward a better understanding of the phenomenon. In 1901 Zilpha Smith of the Associated Charities of Boston made a study of 234 wives who had been left without means of support. Philadelphia's Charity Organization Society followed suit in 1902. Three years later a more comprehensive investigation was completed by Lillian Brandt. Under the aegis of the New York Charity Organization Society, she had contacted all similar organizations in the United States and invited them to assist in gathering material by keeping special records during the year beginning on November 1, 1903. In all, 54 societies spread over 25 cities and 15 states agreed to the plan. Unfortunately, the number of satisfactory case histories gathered was far less than the three thousand that Brandt had expected. Most of the records were superficial. Nevertheless, details of some 591 instances of desertion were provided for analysis. Of these she rejected 17 in which the wife was the deserting party. Her interest, like that of her colleagues, was with the husband, who, as has been mentioned, was predominantly accountable for the upkeep of the family and who was responsible for the large majority of desertions.[25]

For the most part these early investigations agreed upon the basic causes of desertion. Like Frank Wade of the Buffalo Charity Organization Society, they tended to believe that "the real cause . . . is beyond all question, moral delinquency." An occasional denial was heard. One delegate to the first National Conference of Jewish Charities felt that "the moving cause of desertion, at least among Jews, is rather economic than social." Subsequent studies by Jewish charities, however, contradicted this assumption and placed the Jewish deserter squarely among deserters of all races and nationalities.[26] Economic problems were acknowledged as being responsible for a minority of cases of abandonment. It was conceded that unemployment and financial problems helped to break down family morale to the extent that the breadwinner fled to escape failure. Alternatively, unemployment forced him to seek work further afield, during which time he might gradually cut all contact with his family. One-quarter of the husbands studied by Brandt were unemployed at the time of their desertion. However, she, like many others, was inclined to be somewhat unsympathetic to them and tended to feel that "when lack of employment is the apparent cause of desertion it is probably only the occasion of it, and that the same characteristics which made a man desert when he is out of work are responsible for his not being steadily employed." Desertion was one area where moral explanations continued to be favored.[27]

Various "unsteady" habits were isolated as the major factors in the makeup of the typical deserter. Intemperance generally stood at the head of the list, followed by promiscuity, gambling, laziness, drug addiction, deceit, and a roving disposition. The wives' role in the family breakup was viewed more kindly. Only a few were thought to be so extravagant, slovenly, immoral, or obstreperous that the blame might be laid at their door. An even smaller number were accused of conspiring with their husbands to defraud charities of relief money. The majority, it was claimed, were good housekeepers and good mothers whose peculiarities of temperament were not enough to justify the man's failure to meet his obligations.

One contributor to *Charities* in May 1903 affirmed his faith in American womanhood by declaring that in cases of abandonment he did "not attach great weight to bad cookery."[28]

Later analyses of the problem presented a far more sophisticated picture of human relationships and the factors contributing to the breakup of a marriage. Joanna Colcord's monograph *Broken Homes*, published in 1919, is a more detailed account of desertion, taking into consideration a wider variety of problems such as differences in background, lack of education and vocational training, sexual and temperamental incompatibility, and the influence of relatives and acquaintances in addition to the more usually blamed bad habits. Her conclusions demonstrate a greater desire to understand than to accuse. This was not the case at the turn of the century, when the blame was quite definitely placed on the husband's shoulders and welfare reformers advocated remedies designed to bring him to account.[29]

NEW LAWS SUGGESTED

New legislation was to accomplish this. While reformers optimistically envisioned a gradual elevation of the moral tone of society that would reduce the incidence of desertion, they demanded immediate changes to keep the problem under control. In view of the legal confusion at the time on the subject of nonsupport and abandonment, they agreed with Carl Christian Carstens that "new laws must be placed upon our statute books to become the backbone of effort in family regeneration." It was the exact formula of these statutes that provoked debate.[30]

All agreed that both nonsupport and desertion should be made criminal offenses. A civil suit with its expense and delays was thought to be pointless in cases where the families were in the hands of charities and the husband's earnings were their main or only asset. Opinions differed, however, on the classification of the crime. Existing laws normally made the offense a misdemeanor, but some reformers thought this was inadequate. Taking a harsher, more punitive attitude toward deserting husbands, they advocated that the crime be upgraded to a felony. Frank E. Wade was representative of social workers who thought that the gravity of the crime warranted a reclassification. To him, desertion was "one of the most dastardly of human acts compelling the expenditure of large sums of public money and creating immeasurable vice and pauperism in the social order." It therefore deserved to be placed among society's more serious crimes. This change would act as a suitable deterrent, since most roaming husbands would "probably remain at home when they see before them the charge of felony and the possibility of imprisonment in a state prison." Wade's second argument in favor of making desertion a felony was that it would put greater pressure on district attorneys and governors to return deserters to their states of residence.[31]

The question of extradition was a vital one. Many charities and relief agencies had experienced difficulties in prosecuting parents who had fled across state lines. Governors had tended to be indifferent to the agencies' requests for aid, considering the expense and effort too great in view of the pettiness of the crime. Thus reformers felt it necessary to ensure that desertion be made an extraditable offense. But not all felt that it was essential to make desertion a felonious crime. William H. Baldwin, one of the most prominent figures in this area, argued the opposite.[32]

Baldwin, after pursuing a career in the steel industry for most of his life, had retired in 1901 to devote his remaining years to social work. Before his death in 1923, he contributed his energy and expertise to campaigning against tuberculosis and working for the Commission on Uniform State Laws, as well as pushing forward legislation on nonsupport and desertion. In his opinion the disadvantages of making desertion a felony were that the severity of the law would deter the wife from initiating legal proceedings and discourage juries from convicting such men. Baldwin also thought the move was unnecessary, since according to the U.S. Constitution, extraditions could be obtained for misdemeanors. He offered examples of states such as Kansas and Georgia that had honored requests from Illinois officials to return men to that state. Instead of upgrading laws, he thought it wiser and more profitable for public and private charities to petition governors to grant requests for extradition.[33]

Whatever the type of law advocated, it was agreed that stiff penalties should be provided. The desire to punish recreant husbands provoked some extreme suggestions, including the whipping post, "break(ing) stone for the rest of their days," and hanging. Amos

Barlow of the Children's Home Society of Michigan even went so far as to declare that "the father who abandons a helpless girl and her babe, or who abandons his wife and children without support should be made incapable of having more children." This, fortunately, was not the general response. Reformers wished to punish, certainly, but they also took into account the effect this would have on the children involved, at least the economic if not the emotional effect. Their solutions included imposition of a heavy fine and possibly the provision that this should go the the wife as guardian of the children. More importantly, they felt that an alternative penalty should be a substantial prison sentence, preferably with hard labor. This would, it was thought, act as an effective deterrent while also providing the means of support for the family if the man ignored the warning. A regular payment for each day's labor, over and above the cost of food and clothing, would be passed on by charitable and legal agencies to the wife and children. Imprisonment was rightly emphasized as a last resort. Baldwin and others realized the vital necessity of making legal provision for a suspension of sentence should the parent give a guarantee that he would support his family in the future.[34]

Other proposals were made with respect to initiation of proceedings, evidence for the prosecution, and court hearings. Since social workers had found difficulty in persuading wives to begin legal action for support, they suggested an amendment whereby it would be possible for anyone aware of the facts to make a complaint. Thus charities would no longer be dependent on the mood or emotional strength of the wife. To facilitate prosecution it was also suggested that the wife should be held a competent, compellable witness. In view of the fact that her evidence was crucial to the action, it was thought that the general exemption of husbands and wives from testifying against each other should be waived in this type of case. Another proposal was that proof of neglect should be *prima facie* evidence that such neglect was willful. Finally, those in favor of making desertion a misdemeanor recommended that the offense should be heard in the court of lowest rank within each jurisdiction so that the suit might proceed with least delay and expense. To keep a destitute family waiting month after month for a decision was rightly condemned as prolonging an already agonizing situation.[35]

LEGISLATION IS PASSED

Within individual states, leading social workers, philanthropists, judges, lawyers, and other reform-minded Americans congregated to campaign for enactment of new legislation or amendment of old. In New York, for example, the movement was spearheaded by the Charity Organization Society and the bill was drafted by a committee of nine representatives of leading charitable organizations at the conference of April 29, 1903. Up to that time desertion had been encompassed by Section 899 of the code of criminal procedure, which made the offense one of disorderly conduct, and Section 288 of the penal code, relating to cruelty to children. The whole quesion was debated extensively for over a year, there being a strong division of opinion as to the wisdom of including in the bill wives without children. The New York SPCC, conservative as ever, urged their exclusion on grounds of expediency, and the provision for wives alone was eventually struck out. The act, as passed, made it a felony for any parent or person charged with the care and custody of a child under 16 years of age to abandon it in destitute circumstances or to willfully omit to furnish necessary and proper food, clothing, and shelter. Such a crime was to be punishable by a fine not exceeding $1,000 or a prison sentence of not more than two years. In the case that a fine was imposed, it might be used at the discretion of the court to support the child. No reference was made to the profits of the parent's hard labor being passed on to the family.[36]

The exact formulas of nonsupport and desertion laws naturally varied between states. Most, like New York, acknowledged desertion and nonsupport as separate crimes in order that the breadwinner who stayed within the household yet refused to maintain his family in the proper manner should not escape the arm of the law. The majority also placed an age limit of 16 years on the children concerned, although some restricted themselves to infants under 3, while others stipulated only that the children be "minor." Unfortunately most states also agreed with New York in demanding that the child must be in "destitute or necessitous" circumstances before action could be taken. This, of course, stemmed from the preoccupation of social workers with children's problems that imposed a financial burden on the welfare system. The solution was largely aimed at removing the expense from charities and placing it back on parents' shoulders. [37]

Not all legislative reform groups had managed to see their way past the punishment of the offender to guarantee the welfare of the child. According to a survey made in 1922, under half of the nonsupport regulations in force at that time allowed for suspension of sentence and probation. Even more importantly, only 11 were reported as making provisions for a father's earnings in prison to be passed on to the family. The District of Columbia was among the minority; its act, drafted by William H. Baldwin himself and passed in March 1903, stipulated that during the father's commitment to the workhouse a sum of fifty cents per day would be collected on behalf of his wife and children. This, as might well be imagined, was hardly enough to keep a family above the bread line. Even Oregon's more generous allowance of $1.75 per day for families with three or more children might have been inadequate, depending on the size of the family and its place of residence. Nevertheless, states that did provide for such benefits were far ahead of the others in reducing the hardship arising from abandonment. One final notable variation in law concerned the person to be charged. By far the greater number of statutes referred to the perpetration of a crime by a "parent" or "person having the care of" a child. However, in 1935, five states still restricted the law to any "man" who should desert or fail to support his wife and children, and only six made express reference to the mother's duty to support. The principle of coguardianship was slow in evolving, and the problem of maintenance was still largely seen as part of the masculine domain. [38]

An attempt was made to bring about uniformity. The Commisioners on Uniform State Laws, after several years of study and deliberation, adopted a model law at a meeting in August 1910. Feeling that their work should not be too radical or rigid, the commissioners left the grade of the crime and the question of hard labor undecided, expecting individual jurisdictions to settle these points as they saw fit. The other provisions written into the Uniform Desertion Law encompassed all those reforms relating to penalties, instigation of proceedings, and relevant evidence that were mentioned earlier. Beginning with Massachusetts in 1911, one-third of the states chose to accept this format over the next two decades.[39]

By the end of the Progressive era, reformers in the majority of states had succeeded in passing and amending legislation, although not all of these were comprehensive statutes. In 1922, 44 jurisdictions had made desertion and abandonment a crime, while 43 had also declared nonsupport illegal. The remaining states and territories followed suit in the 1920s. Some had opted for making the offense a felony. Vernier's survey shows 14 states as having preferred the more severe legal option. In comparison, 23 jurisdictions had chosen to regard the offense as a misdemeanor, while the rest merely termed it a "crime" or a combination of felony and misdemeanor. In addition there was a motley array of cruelty laws, vagrancy statutes, and acts relating to adults' contribution to the delinquency and dependency of children.

If anything, the situation was unnecessarily confusing. It was often not clear how many of the older statutes had been implicitly repealed by later legislation. Also, in states where a number of different statutes covered the same legal territory but made different provisions, there was the danger that the child's welfare could depend on the preference of the prosecutor concerned. This was the case, for example, where suspension of sentence was expressly included in certain family desertion laws yet omitted in other relevant statutes. One parent, but not another, might be automatically incarcerated because of a lawyer's inclination toward one particular section of the criminal code.[40]

IMPLEMENTING THE LAWS

Despite their victories in the legislative field, many reformers felt that their efforts were being undermined by the absence of effective agencies capable of publicizing the crime and tracking down the offender. The onus of dealing with the majority of cases was left with children's protective societies like the Juvenile Protective Association of Chicago and the New York SPCC; to legal aid societies, to charity organization societies, and to other interested public and private agencies. They were aided, of course, to a large extent by the police force and the local judiciary. It was thought, however, that the situation demanded agencies and departments whose sole function would be the treatment and prosecution of offenders. The United Charities of Chicago, for example, promoted the idea of a desertion bureau, possibly connected to the Chicago Court of Domestic Relations, but nothing came of it at the time. One group of social workers, however, did put this idea into practice.[41]

As early as 1900, Jewish charities had advocated a central organization to deal with the problem. At that time they suggested that "a fund should be constituted and . . . placed in the hands of an executive committee to which all communications concerning desertion should be addressed and which should look after the extradition . . . of fugitives." Nothing came of this recommendation. Instead, individual agencies such as the Desertion Department of the United Hebrew Charities and the Legal Aid Bureau of the Educational Alliance assumed the task of locating and apprehending deserters in their particular regions. In 1906, deprecating the results of his colleagues' sporadic attempts to deal with the issue, Lee K. Frankel resurrected the question of the viability of a national desertion bureau. Four years later, at the National Conference of Jewish Charities held in St. Louis, it was eventually resolved by the executive committee that a bureau should be established to act as a clearing house for all Jewish societies in the country. The New York organizations proffered $5,000 to finance activities for the first 14 months, and that city, which housed over half of America's Jewish population, was chosen as a logical headquarters for the new agency.[42]

Upon the complaint of a wife, individual Jewish aid societies would submit a detailed account of the case and, if possible, a photograph of the missing husband to the central organization. In addition, the wife was also required to sign an affidavit authorizing the bureau to act on her behalf. The wheels were then set in motion. Publicity was the first instrument used in the process of tracking down the man. Yiddish newspapers in New York, Chicago, and other cities included in their pages a "Gallery of Missing Husbands" —photographs and descriptions of the "wanted" men. Descriptions were also forwarded to a large network of several hundred social agencies, which were urged to cooperate in discovering the whereabouts of offenders. Finally, the bureau had established a national body of correspondents and attorneys to deal with inquiries and to represent applicants before the courts whenever necessary. According to a report published in 1912, the success rate of the early period was somewhere in the region of 66 percent. Of 852 cases handled from February 1, 1911, to March 31, 1912, 561 men were located.[43] Presumably outside the concentrated, tightly knit Jewish community this figure, if accurate, was nowhere near the norm. In 574 cases surveyed by Brandt, the whereabouts of 223 were completely unknown.[44]

A significant number of the parents dealt with would be reconciled with their families or persuaded to support them without the necessity of resorting to court proceedings. Those parents who were considered uncooperative, however, were brought before the relevant authorities and charged. The type of court varied between jurisdictions. In the District of Columbia the juvenile court was chosen as a suitable legal structure, while in other areas cases of nonsupport and desertion were tried in municipal, county, and higher courts. During the second decade of the twentieth century a new type of tribunal was introduced, the court of domestic relations.

FAMILY COURTS

For some time reformers such as Baldwin had thought that cases involving desertion and other intrafamilial problems should be heard "in a court especially devoted to the subject of family relations rather than other crimes or property interests." It was also important that these cases be heard by judges particularly qualified in this area. In March 1909 the city of Buffalo, New York, introduced the first of these family courts. Brooklyn and Manhattan did the same in 1910, and Chicago established its court of domestic relations in 1911. From here the idea spread, until according to the *Social Work Year Book of 1929*, there were similar courts in operation in 13 states and the Territory of Hawaii. They varied considerably in their jurisdictions, some dealing with a comprehensive range of juvenile and adult problems including children's cases, bastardy, divorce, desertion and nonsupport, and contribution to delinquency and dependency. Others had a limited jurisdiction over adults or dealt with them exclusively. Whatever the types of problems dealt with, reformers were optimistic about the usefulness of such tribunals.[45] To Judge Charles N. Goodnow of Chicago, the domestic relations court stood "as a friend of the man or woman in trouble; a counsellor in time of need; a protector to the delinquent or homeless child; a doctor to the young girl who had unwittingly wronged; a mentor to both husband and wife when their misunderstandings have reached the breaking point."[46]

Of those men who could be located and who were later brought to court, often a large percentage were given a suspended sentence on the guarantee that they would contribute to the family's upkeep. If cases in the District of Columbia may be taken as an example, of 899 trials held in 1909, sentences were suspended in three quarters. Eleven percent of the men were committed to the local workhouse, and their meagre earnings of 50 cents per day were passed on by the juvenile court.[47] When orders for maintenance were stipulated, these were rarely more than supplements to income and aid received from charity. Reviewing 69 instances in which orders were given in 1905, Brandt found that judges awarded an average of $3 to $5 per week at a time when labourers earned $12 to $13 per week. In 17 of these 69 cases no payments were made and in 12 no data was available, indicating no payment. Thus, in only 40 had the courts any effect, and the majority of these only paid irregularly.[48] If men could not or would not contribute, state agencies did very little to enforce support. For most women with children desertion meant low-paid work, reliance on child labor, no support from their husbands and inadequate relief from private and public relief agencies.

Of course, these attempts to enforce parental support were largely confined to legitimate offspring. However, as will be shown in the following chapter, the Progressive period also witnessed significant changes in the status of the illegitimate.

NOTES

1. Ibid., pp. 85-87, 90-91. William Blackstone, *Commentaries on the Laws of England*, quoted in Grace Abbott, *The Child and the State* (Chicago: University of Chicago Press, 1938), vol. 1, p. 13. Chester S. Vernier, *American Family Law*, 5 vols., 1936 (reprint, Westport, Conn.: Greenwood

Press, 1971), vol. 4, pp. 17-23. Ivy Pinchbeck, *Children in English Society* (London: Routledge & Kegan Paul, 1973), vol. 2, pp. 362-85.

2. Vernier, *American Family Law*, vol. 4, pp. 55-65, quoted p. 4.

3. James Kent, *Commentaries on the Rights and Duties of Parents under the Common Law in the United States*, quoted in Abbott, *The Child and the State*, vol. 1, p. 49. Helen Clarke, *Social Legislation: American Laws Dealing with Family, Child and Dependent* (New York: Appleton-Century Co., 1940), pp. 225-40.

4. Blackstone, quoted in Abbott, *The Child and the State*, vol. 1, p. 11.

5. Ibid., pp. 49-76. Robert H. Bremner, *Children and Youth in America: A Documentary History* (Cambridge, Mass.: Harvard University Press, 1971), vol. 2, pp. 119-37.

6. Florence Kelley, "On Some Changes in the Legal Status of the Child Since Blackstone," *International Review* 13 (1882): 84.

7. Sophonisba P. Breckinridge, "The Treatment of Dependent Children by Public Agencies," *Proceedings of the 13th Illinois Conference of Charities and Correction*, 1908, pp. 53-54.

8. Byron C. Mathews, "The Duty of the State to Dependent Children," *Proceedings of the 25th NCCC*, quoted p. 368. Roger Baldwin, "How Shall We Frame a Consistent Public Policy?" *Proceedings of the 40th NCCC*, 1914, p. 190. Ray M. Connel, "The Ethics of State Interference in the Domestic Relations," *International Journal of Ethics* 18 (1908): 363-72.

9. "Report of the Committee on Child Labor," *Proceedings of the 30th NCCC*, quoted p. 152. Edith Abbott and Sophonisba P. Breckinridge, *Truancy and Non-Attendance in the Chicago Schools* (Chicago: University of Chicago Press, 1917), p. 276. Florence Kelley, *Some Ethical Gains through Legislation* (New York: Macmillan, 1905), pp. 58-59, 75. Graham Taylor, "Parental Responsibility for Child Labor," *AAAPSS* 27 (1906): 96-98. Stephan Thernstrom, *Poverty and Progress: Social Mobility in a Nineteenth Century City* (Cambridge, Mass.: Harvard University Press, 1968), pp. 115-37.

10. Kelley, *Some Ethical Gains*, p. 49. Florence Kelley and Alzina P. Stevens, "Wage-Earning Children," in Hull House Residents, *Hull House Maps and Papers: A Presentation of Nationalities and Wages in a Congested District of Chicago* (New York: Crowell, 1895), pp. 49-75. Abbott and Breckinridge, *Truancy and Non-Attendance*, pp. 128-46. See also Owen Lovejoy, "Child Labor and Philanthropy," *Proceedings of the 34th NCCC*, 1907, pp. 196-204; Alexander J. McKelway, "Child Labor and Citizenship," *Proceedings of the 35th NCCC*, 1908, p. 354; and Alexander J. McKelway, "Child Labor and the Home," *Proceedings of the 41st NCCC*, 1914, pp. 333.

11. E. N. Clopper, "Child Labor and School Attendance," *The American Child* 1 (1919): 100.

12. Lawrence Cremin, *The Transformation of the School: Progressivism in American Education* (New York: Alfred A. Knopf, 1974), pp. 88, 103, 127-28. Dana F. White, "Education in the Turn of the Century City," *Urban Education* 4 (1969): 169-81. Abbott and Breckinridge, *Truancy and Non-Attendance*, pp. 40-88. Walter I. Trattner, *Crusade for the Children* (Chicago: Quadrangle Books, 1970).

13. Vernier, *American Family Law*, vol. 4, pp. 19-20, 64-65. See also Monrad Paulsen, "The Legal Framework for Child Protection," *Columbia Law Review* 66 (1966): 682-87. Andrew J. Kleinfeld, "The Balance of Power among Infants, the Parents and the State," *Family Law Quarterly* 4 (1970): 425-33.

14. William J. Schultz, "The Humane Movement in the United States 1910-1922," *Columbia University Studies in History, Economics, and Public Law*, study no. 1 (New York: Columbia University Press, 1924), pp. 265-67.

15. Robert H. Bremner, ed., *Children and Youth in America: A Documentary History* (Cambridge, Mass.: Harvard University Press, 1971), vol. 2, pp. 119-24. Barbara Grumet, "The Plaintive Plaintiffs: Victims of the Battered Child Syndrome," *Family Law Quarterly* 4 (1970): 307-8.

16. William J. Goode, "Marital Satisfaction and Stability: A Cross Cultural Class Analysis," in Richard Bendix and Seymour M. Lipset, *Class, Status and Power: A Reader in Social Stratification* (London: Routledge & Kegan Paul, 1954), p. 379. Goode points out that in the twentieth century, lower-class families increasingly resorted to divorce until the balance of the nineteenth century was reversed.

17. Earle E. Eubank, *A Study of Family Desertion* (Chicago: City of Chicago Department of Public Welfare, 1916), pp. 19-20, 44-45, 64-67. Lillian Brandt, *574 Deserters and Their Families* (New York: Charity Organization Society, 1905), quoted p. 18. Kate Claghorn, "Immigration in Relation to Pauperism," *AAAPSS* 24 (1904): 192. Hugo E. Varga, "Desertion of Wives and Children by Emigrants to America," *Proceedings of the 39th NCCC*, 1912, p. 257.

18. Brandt, *574 Deserters*, p. 10. Eubank, *A Study of Family Desertion*, pp. 10, 25, 61-62. Cook County, Ill., *Charity Service Report*, 1909, p. 37.

19. E. P. Savage, "Desertion by Parents," *Proceedings of the 22nd NCCC*, 1895, pp. 213-15. E. P. Savage, "Desertion by Parents," *Proceedings of the 24th NCCC*, 1897, pp. 318-23. Mary Richmond, "Married Vagabonds," *Proceedings of the 22nd NCCC*, 1895, p. 515.

20. Joseph C. Logan, "A Social Policy for Dealing with the Recreant

Husband and Father," *Proceedings of the 38th NCCC*, 1911, quoted p. 405. Benjamin Tuska, statement in *Proceedings of the 1st National Conference of Jewish Charities*, 1900, quoted p. 86. "Family Desertion as a Pressing Social Problem," *Charities* 14 (1905): 657.

21. Savage, "Desertion by Parents," 1895, pp. 213-15; 1897, pp. 217-28.

22. Brandt, *574 Deserters*, p. 8. "Conference on Family Desertion," *Charities* 14 (1905): 483.

23. Patrick Mallon, "Desertion and Non-Support," *Proceedings of the 2nd National Conference of Catholic Charities*, 1912, p. 115.

24. "Report of the Committee on Desertions," *Proceedings of the 1st National Conference of Jewish Charities*, 1900, pp. 52-69, quoted pp. 52-53. "Report of the Committee on Family Desertion," *Proceedings of the 4th National Conference of Jewish Charities*, 1906, pp. 46-57. Morris D. Waldman, "Family Desertion," *Proceedings of the 6th National Conference of Jewish Charities*, 1910, pp. 54-84. "Report of the Committee on Family Desertion," *Proceedings of the 7th National Conference of Jewish Charities*, 1912, pp. 1-43.

25. Waldman, "Family Desertion," pp. 62-63. Brandt, *574 Deserters*, pp. 7-9. Eubank, *A Study of Family Desertion*, p. 6.

26. Frank E. Wade, quoted in "Conference on Family Desertions," p. 486. "Report of the Committee on Desertions," 1900, quoted p. 53.

27. Brandt, *574 Deserters*, pp. 24-25, 29-35, 41-42.

28. Ibid., pp. 11, 24-38. William H. Baldwin, "Family Desertion and Non-Support Laws," *Charities* 14 (1905): 660-61. "Conference on Family Desertions," pp. 485-86. William deLacy, "Family Desertion and Non-Support," *Survey* 23 (1910): 678-79. Helen Foss, "The Genus Deserter," *Charities* 10 (1903): 456. Frederick Bauer, statement in "Conference on Family Desertion," quoted p. 485.

29. Joanna Colcord, *Broken Homes: A Study of Family Desertion and Its Social Treatment* (New York: Russell Sage, 1919), pp. 17-49.

30. Carl Christian Carstens, "The Breaking Up of Families," *Proceedings of the 36th NCCC*, 1909, quoted p. 52. Savage, "Desertion by Parents," 1897, p. 324. Waldman, "Family Desertion," p. 71.

31. Frank E. Wade, "Family Desertion and Non-Support Laws," *Charities* 14 (1905): 682-86.

32. "Report of the Committee on Desertions," 1900, p. 54. Waldman, "Family Desertion," p. 80.

33. *Who Was Who in America*, vol. 1, 1897-1942 (Chicago: A. N. Marquis & Co., 1943), p. 51. For his main arguments see William H. Baldwin, "The Present Status of Family Desertion and Non-Support Laws," *Proceedings of the 38th NCCC*, 1911, pp. 410-11. See also William H. Baldwin, "The Inter-State Rules as Related to the Extradition of Deserters,"

Charities 16 (1906): 854-56. William H. Baldwin, "Child Desertion and Extradition in New York State," *Charities* 14 (1905): 1015-17.

34. Amos Barlow, quoted in Savage, "Desertion by Parents," 1897, p. 318. Logan, "A Social Policy," p. 405. Baldwin, "The Present Status," p. 411. Baldwin, "Family Desertion and Non-Support Laws," pp. 663-64.

35. Ibid., pp. 662-63. Baldwin, "The Present Status," p. 412.

36. Baldwin, "Child Desertion and Extradition," pp. 1016-17. Wade, "Family Desertion and Non-Support Laws," p. 682. Frank E. Wade, "Some Practical Results of New Family Desertion Laws," *Charities* 17 (1907): 708.

37. Vernier, *American Family Law*, vol. 4., pp. 66-68. Schultz, "The Humane Movement," pp. 267-69.

38. Ibid. William H. Baldwin, "Non-Support and Its Remedies in Massachusetts," *Journal of Criminal Law and Criminology* 8 (1917): 1-9. William H. Baldwin, "Making the Deserter Pay the Piper," *Survey* 22 (1909): 249-52.

39. Baldwin, "The Present Status," p. 412.

40. Vernier, *American Family Law*, vol. 4, pp. 62, 66-68. Schultz, "The Humane Movement," pp. 267-69.

41. Wade, "Some Practical Results," p. 711. *Annual Report of the United Charities of Chicago*, 1915-1916, p. 15.

42. "Report of the Committee on Desertions," 1900, quoted p. 56. "Report of the Committee on Family Desertion," 1906, pp. 51-52; 1912, pp. 1-2. Boris D. Bogen, *Jewish Philanthropy* (New York: Macmillan, 1917), pp. 174-77. Charles Zunser, "The National Desertion Bureau: Its Functions, New Problems and Relations to Other Agencies," *Proceedings of the National Conference of Jewish Social Service*, 1923, pp. 386-404.

43. Ibid. Bogen, *Jewish Philanthropy*, pp. 176-77. "Report of the Committee on Family Desertion," 1912, pp. 7-43.

44. Brandt, *574 Deserters*, p. 49.

45. Baldwin, "The Present Status," pp. 408-9, quoted p. 411. "Report of the Committee of the National Probation Association," *Proceedings of the 46th NCSW*, 1919, pp. 124-32. *Social Work Year Book*, 1929 (New York: Russell Sage, 1930), p. 43.

46. Charles N. Goodnow, "The Chicago Court of Domestic Relations," in Sophonisba P. Breckinridge, ed., *The Child in the City* (London: P. S. King and Sons, 1911), pp. 330-40, quoted p. 333.

47. Wade, "Some Practical Results," pp. 709-11.

48. Brandt, *574 Deserters*, p. 49.

7

THE ILLEGITIMATE CHILD

According to the commentaries of William Blackstone, children were "of two sorts, legitimate . . . or bastards."[1] A long history of social and religious prejudice had divided infants into two separate species, with correspondingly different legal rights. Or rather, the legitimate child was accorded certain rights with respect to his parents, while the child unfortunate enough to be born out of wedlock was left unprotected. The legal burden of illegitimacy continued to blight the lives of millions of American children until in the twentieth century it was tempered by reform activity designed to bring about equal care and protection for all children. The welfare reformers of the Progressive era were late in acknowledging the injustice of this legal distinction. As will be discussed in this chapter, it was not until the beginning of World War I that they recognized the extent of the problem, the amount of suffering involved, and the increasing cost to welfare agencies. Their championship of the cause of the illegitimate was also diluted and circumscribed by the general public's sensitivity to the fate of the family unit. Nevertheless, they were able to make the first steps toward reforming stagnant and blatantly unfair legislation, particularly in the area of maintenance and support.

THE SITUATION FOR THE CHILD

In nineteenth-century America, bastardy was viewed as an offense against God's law and the institution of marriage. When, as frequently was the case, the mother and child became dependent on the community, it was seen as a threat to society's well-being. The usual response, therefore, was either punitive or was concerned with relieving poor law authorities of the liability to support. Although the persecution of women with illegitimate children was no longer as severe as that portrayed in Hawthorne's *Scarlet Letter*, and women were no longer whipped for their sins, the unmarried mothers were still ostracized and humiliated, while their children often carried the stigma of illegitimacy with them for the rest of their lives.

The child born out of wedlock was neglected in family law. English common law recognized no legal relationship between that child and either parent. The child was looked upon as *filius nullius*, the son of nobody. The child could therefore neither inherit from mother and father nor transmit property to them. Neither could the illegitimate child be legitimized by the parents' subsequent marriage. The legal duties of the parents of such a disadvantaged child were basically limited to the stipulations of the poor laws. The United States had essentially followed the discriminatory English pattern, although some states had later alleviated some of the worst features. For example, provisions were made declaring the children of certain annulled marriages legitimate, allowing for legitimation by subsequent matrimony, and creating rights of inheritance between the mother and the child. From an early date American legislatures, like the English, saw fit to impose the duty to support on both parents in order to relieve the local community of the burden. Laws were introduced permitting unwed mothers to institute bastardy proceedings, whereby a warrant was issued for the man's apprehension, followed by a preliminary hearing and possibly a trial. Should the putative father be found guilty, he might be ordered to pay a small sum for the child's maintenance. These bastardy laws, which were largely civil actions with a quasi-criminal procedure, remained unchanged for decades.

In Massachusetts, for example, until the new act of 1913, the law in force was one passed in 1785. By the 1890s, reforms in this area were long overdue.[2]

In the late nineteenth century, single American women were legally denied the means of contraception and essential birth control information.[3] If they became pregnant and were unable to secure an abortion, they were forced to give birth to their illegitimate children. No one knows just how many infants were born out of wedlock at this time. Birth registration laws differed between states, and in only a few were the figures reliable. When the U.S. Children's Bureau made an attempt to gather nationwide information in 1915, it found that only one-third of the states and large cities could provide accurate numbers. On the basis of these figures it was estimated that approximately 32,400 illegitimate children had been born during that year, this representing 1.8 percent of all live births. This was the first assessment of the extent of the illegitimacy problem and undoubtedly a gross underestimate.[4]

Daughters of wealthy families were presumably able to deal with an illegitimate child discreetly if not always easily, but an unwanted pregnancy often forced less fortunate women to seek aid from charities and other welfare agencies. These mothers were generally young. Almost half of those studied by the Juvenile Protective Association of Chicago in 1914 were under the age of 21. They represented a wide range of nationalities and religions. Most were working-class. The large majority of mothers studied were domestic servants or factory workers, while a smaller number were clerks, seamstresses, laundresses, and so on. Few had any special training. Given their occupational backgrounds, it is not surprising that they experienced great financial difficulty in coping with a child. The average weekly wage of the Chicago group was $6.75, while over three-quarters earned less than $9.00.[5] In the same year the average wage of "lower skilled" labor was $10.78 per week.[6]

Apart from the general relief agencies and children's organizatons who offered help to unmarried mothers and their infants, there were a variety of societies and maternity homes who specialized in caring for this group of women. Typical of such organizations was the Boston Society for Destitute Mothers and Infants, established in 1873 to take care of "the country girl bewildered and led

astray by life in the great city" as well as other mothers in distress.[7]
More famous were the Florence Crittendon Missions, founded in
the following decade by Charles N. Crittendon, a wealthy New
York druggist, for the reclamation of fallen women. By 1900 there
were 59 Florence Crittendon Missions throughout the country. They
took in pregnant women, supported them, trained them in basic
domestic skills, found them positions if possible, and tried to
teach them "the beauty and necessity of perfect obedience, the
requisite of a perfect character." Obviously moralistic criteria
guided the running of the homes and their selection of suitable
women. They were largely interested in helping mothers who
intended to keep their children and were morally "fit." Often they
refused to help those who had previously had illegitimate children,
however sorry their plight. These were diverted to other, less
particular, maternity homes, hospitals, and midwives.[8]

Naturally, many women did not try to keep their children.
Social and economic pressure encouraged thousands to dispose of
their infants as soon as possible. This produced many tragedies.
Jacob Riis vividly portrayed the fate of babies abandoned in New
York's streets. After a night spent at police headquarters each
child travelled "up to the Infants Hospital on Randall's Island
in the morning, fitted out with a number and a bottle, that seldom
see much wear before they are laid aside for a fresh recruit."[9]
Alternatively the children might be placed in the baskets or on the
turnstiles of foundling homes, which accepted them all without
question. Some disposed of their unfortunate youngsters through
midwives, maternity homes, or hospitals, which were only too keen
to give the children away for a suitable fee. Many of the infants
were lost sight of altogether. Of 3,000 illegitimate children born
in Chicago during 1914, one-third subsequently disappeared without
trace. In the opinion of the Juvenile Protective Association, this
method of getting rid of a child was "like opening the window
and hurling him out into the vortex of the world and no-one knows
where he has been whirled or what his fate."[10]

If a mother chose to support her child, she had many obstacles
to overcome. In general she received little help from the child's
father. In only a small number of cases did the two later marry and
so provide a legally recognized home for the child. Just as in-

frequently was maintenance provided for the child. The mother's only legal option was to take the man to court, but few mothers were sufficiently strong-minded or knowledgeable to do so. Fear of publicity or of the judge's questions, fear of revenge and violence discouraged many from instituting proceedings. Ignorance of the law or the disappearance of the father prevented many more. In the Children's Bureau survey of Boston's illegitimacy cases for 1914, only 13 percent were taken to court, and in only 7 percent was any financial provision made for the child's support and education. Rarely was there a uniform and organized method for investigating and prosecuting such cases. If a judgment was made against the father, the amount given was usually insufficient, a small lump sum or a weekly payment of, in Illinois for example, $2 a week for the first year and $1 a week after that.[11]

So often the mother, pressured by the need to work and look after her child, unable to obtain a job where she could keep her baby with her, unsupported by the child's father, and sensitive to the scorn of much of society, eventually gave up and turned her infant over to child-caring organizations. Of illegitimate children born in Boston during 1914, more than three-fifths would reach welfare agencies in the first year of their lives.[12]

ILLEGITIMACY BECOMES A SEPARATE MATTER

It was not until the second decade of the twentieth century that reformers interested in child welfare isolated illegitimate children as a group requiring urgent attention. They had tended to treat them as merely one part of the motley array of dependent and neglected children who demanded public or private care and supervision. However, with increasing knowledge of the factors detrimentally affecting the health and welfare of the nation's children, social workers and philanthropists were forced to recognize the peculiar handicaps of children born out of wedlock. Investigations into infant mortality, for example, illuminated the hazards that faced them. Although exact figures were not available, it was estimated that the mortality rate of illegitimates was approximately three times that of children born in wedlock. It was awareness of the appalling death rate of illegitimate children that caused the Massachusetts SPCC in 1909 to declare that the "whole question of illegitimacy is one that should have careful study on the part of some competent group."[13] Similarly, surveys of the conditions in unregulated private institutions and boarding homes indicated the problems of survival for this class of youngsters. Disreputable homes could mistreat illegitimate children without fearing that irate parents would intervene. The surge of interest in desertion and nonsupport that has already been discussed, also served to focus attention on the illegitimate, whose dependency was often the result of parental refusal to take responsibility for their maintenance. A further stimulus was given by analyses by children's institutions and agencies of the reasons for the admission of children. Illegitimacy was a common cause and hence was seen as a significant drain on public and private funds.[14]

To some extent this new sensitivity to the fate of illegitimate children was part of the then current attempt to strengthen family life. While the normal family unit was considered ideal and reformers had no intention of undermining this structure by encouraging illegitimacy, they came to feel that it was possible to approximate the family unit by keeping mothers and babies together. Just as they encouraged widows and deserted wives to keep their families intact, so they suggested that unmarried mothers should not give up their children. This, it was claimed, would benefit both the children, who needed mother love, and the women, who would be helped to become respectable, responsible people. Kate Waller Barrett, president of the Florence Crittendon Mission and a prominent defender of the unmarried mother, declared that "if we cannot have that trinity which God intended—husband, wife, child—we can have the other trinity—mother, child, home—that has a mighty potency in it for good."[15] Children's agencies increasingly adopted policies of finding positions for mothers where they could take their infants with them or encouraging others to board their children while they worked.[16]

The unwed mother was no longer seen as irretrievably immoral. As social workers became more aware of why girls became pregnant, they emphasized the environmental factors involved. Some of the mothers were still labeled vicious. Another significant number were claimed to be mentally defective. However, the majority of the women studied were found to be average people whose main problems were abnormal family backgrounds, lack of training, ignorance, and the absence of recreation facilities. Thus they were treated more sympathetically and were given the opportunity to keep their children if possible.[17] The old idea that illegitimate children inherited the sins of the parents was also discredited. Now it was strongly advanced that "illegitimate children are as good as the legitimate. . . . As to mental ability and potentiality for general useful citizenship, they are at least on a par with those who start life regularly."[18]

Concern for the illegitimate was also given a boost by the outbreak of World War I. This event focused attention on children in general by demonstrating the poor physical and mental quality of the American citizens being sent to fight overseas. It was hoped that better specimens would be produced in the future. More immediately, it posed the threat of an increased number of illegitimate children. American social workers were informed that the ratio of illegitimate to legitimate births in Europe was rising due to the "mobility" of its thousands of soldiers. This trend was forcing European nations to extend state aid to the children of soldiers and to question the existing support laws. Although it was recognized that the illegitimacy rate in the United States was much lower than that in Europe, social agencies were extremely sensitive to this issue. Moves were made to prevent any increase in illegitimacy. The U.S. Secretary of War, for example, organized a Commission on Training Camp Activities to provide recreational facilities and opportunities for a relatively normal social life for the men in the camps. In the event that these attempts at moral protection failed, social workers were advised to prepare themselves for the boom. Judge Harry M. Fisher of the Chicago Municipal Court warned his colleagues that "unless we prepare now to care for them they will become a serious burden to the community."[19]

Regardless of whether the numbers were in fact increasing, reformers had come to the conclusion that the illegitimate child deserved particular attention. Carl Christian Carstens, speaking at the New York Conference on Illegitimacy in 1920, attested to this change in attitude. He condemned the carelessness with which this problem had been viewed since the beginning of history and admitted that in the United States "the child born out of wedlock has not had a square deal." However, he pointed hopefully to a well-defined tendency among his fellow social workers to improve this situation, to modify laws and social customs in order to guarantee the illegitimate child physical, mental, and moral well-being.[20] Others agreed. They criticized the stigma of illegitimacy as an "unjust, ungodlike, un-American discrimination" against an innocent child, deplored the poor welfare provisions, and more importantly for this chapter, demanded reform of the laws affecting the child born out of wedlock.[21]

NATIONWIDE DEBATE

The development of this nationwide interest in the problems of illegitimacy followed a familiar pattern. This time, however, the leading role was taken by the newly created U.S. Children's Bureau.

A brief mention of the issue can be found in the proceedings of the 1909 White House Conference on Dependent Children. Delegates expressed their fears of "a rising tide of illegitimacy," as was "evidenced by the rapidly increasing number of maternity homes, baby farms and kindred agencies for the care of infants."[22] Recognizing their ignorance in this area, they supported collection of birth statistics. Concern about illegitimacy gradually gained momentum in the second decade of the twentieth century, until by 1917 it was the subject of regular debate. Throughout the decade the annual reports of the more advanced children's organizations, such as the Boston Children's Aid Society and the Massachusetts SPCC, frequently touched on the question. Certain societies, like the Juvenile Protective Association of Chicago, made their own studies of bastardy cases. During 1912 and 1914 two major surveys were conducted by the Juvenile Protective Association, the first being an investigation of the fate of the city's illegitimates and the second being a study of the backgrounds of 600 unmarried mothers. From 1914 onwards, *Survey*, the *American Journal of Sociology*, the *National Humane Review*, and other periodicals also demonstrated their growing interest.[23]

Naturally, the various charitable conferences speculated on the problem. Between 1910 and 1920 the National Conference of Charities and Correction heard 19 papers on relevant topics, ranging from the mentality of the unmarried mother to the necessity for legal reform. Although the Catholic and Jewish conferences showed little interest in this area, various state conferences considered the issue sufficiently important to warrant discussion. A further boost to reform was given by the Children's Code Commission, which by 1920 had been established in 17 states to study and codify the wide variety of laws relating to child welfare. These analyses and investigations necessarily provided a wealth of information on the legal handicaps of children born out of wedlock.[24]

Nevertheless, it was the Children's Bureau under the directorship of Julia Lathrop that provided the major stimulus to reform. As early as March 1915, Lathrop had come to the conclusion that "the question [of illegitimacy] is a very big one and not yet being dealt with satisfactorily."[25] In the same month a study of illegitimacy in Boston was approved, the results of which were published in 1920 as the second section of a three-part volume entitled *Illegitimacy as a Child Welfare Problem*. The first part of this inquiry, a brief survey of available statistics, of the rights and disabilities of illegitimate children, and of the protection provided by public and private agencies, was printed a few months earlier. At the insistence of Ernst Freund, professor of law at the University of Chicago, the Children's Bureau also sponsored a very valuable survey of the bastardy laws in operation throughout the United States and in a number of foreign countries. In conjunction, it published and distributed translations of the progressive Norwegian legislation. Finally, by means of conferences, the Children's Bureau brought the best minds together to consider necessary reforms. While the subject of illegitimacy was not greatly discussed at the eight regional and Washington, D.C., conferences held in May and June of 1919, social workers throughout the country did touch upon the legal handicaps of this group of children, the advantages of keeping mothers and babies together, and the urgent necessity of new legislation. More important were the Conferences on Illegitimacy held in Chicago and New York during February of 1920. Sixty prominent social workers, judges, lawyers, probation officers, and so on, representing 21 states, Washington, D.C., and Canada, gathered to hear formal papers and local reports. These dealt with the broad principles of legislation on behalf of children born out of wedlock.[26]

The consensus of opinion among child welfare reformers was that existing legislation in this area was "rotten." Like Fisher, the majority felt that "while the law in general is slowly making progress, this particular branch has remained almost stationary for centuries."[27] Changes were urgently needed. The difficult question to be decided was how far reforms could go without injuring the status of the family or arousing the hostility and antagonism of legislatures and the general public.

Reformers had before them the Norwegian example of progressive illegitimacy legislation. Copies of the Castberg law of 1915, named after Norway's minister for social welfare, who had guided its development, were widely distributed and discussed within social work and legal circles. This act made a number of radical changes in the status of the illegitimate child, among them the right, after paternity is established, to inherit from the father and to take his name. It also improved provisions and procedures relating to the child's maintenance and made it compulsory for the state to institute paternity proceedings in every case. American reformers debated whether it was necessary or advisable to attempt similarly radical alterations in family law.[28]

The more progressive social workers and legal personnel agreed that the ideal was to give children born out of wedlock all the rights with respect to their parents that legitimate children already had, to obliterate the distinction completely. This seemed both just and socially sound. These workers did not want to see marriage downgraded or an increase in illegitimacy. As might be expected, they in no way condoned sexual relationships outside marriage. They certainly did not share feminist Ellen Key's hope that a time would come when society would look upon the "love relation" as the private affair of responsible adults. Nevertheless, they acknowledged that to handicap a child for the indiscretion of the parents was totally unjust.[29]

There were, however, recognizable diffculties in passing such legislation, given the prevailing moralistic attitude toward illegitimacy. Freund was one reformer who admitted that "whether resting upon fancied or upon real grounds, the objections to legislation of the most advanced type are for the moment insuperable." He felt that if immediate results were to be achieved, he and his colleagues could not afford to set their sights too high.[30] In consequence, many reform-minded groups chose to devote their energies to one urgent and uncontroversial issue, that of maintenance. They did advocate changes in the status of illegitimate children, however. As a result of the Chicago and New York conferences in 1920, a syllabus of propositions was drawn up to serve as a basis for future legislation. These recommendations supported the legitimation of an unlawful child by the marriage of the parents or by an appropriate act or declaration. They also supported the right of the child to inherit from the father even though not legitimated and the right to the name of the father once paternity had been determined. However, by far the greater volume of discussion and activity centered upon the parents' duty to support.[31]

There was general agreement that the outdated bastardy proceedings should be replaced by paternity support legislation that would establish humane and efficient procedures, adequate sums of maintenance, and realistic means of enforcing the court's orders. It was thought that fathers had escaped their responsibilities for too many years, that the state could no longer sanction "paternal selfishness in its crudest and most brutal form." To correct this, legislation was required that would "compel the father to share responsibility for his child no matter how embarrassing to him." A number of amendments were suggested.[32]

The first issue taken up concerned the person responsible for instigating the paternity suit. As was mentioned earlier, the burden had previously fallen upon the mother, who was often too frightened or ignorant to take advantage of her rights. It was now recommended that the state should be a party to the case. Since, it was argued, illegitimacy was a subject of public concern, proceedings should be started by public authorities if necessary. Equipped with trained officials and backed by public resources, the state could ensure action in all cases that came to its notice. There was less agreement on the nature of the suit. Some believed that it was beneficial to keep it a civil action, since paternity could then be established without burdening the man with the stigma of a criminal record. Others pointed to the law of Massachusetts, where criminal proceedings secured the use of the probation system and made extradition possible. Since both alternatives had their advantages, a third group concluded that it was "desirable to provide for the use of either form of proceedings as the exigencies of the case or the local conditions may demand."[33]

The problem of extradition was one that disturbed many legal minds. If a particular state retained its civil procedure, how could its authorities prevent a man from freely absconding? For some the answer lay in extending the provisions of the family desertion and nonsupport acts to cover the parents of illegitimate children. William H. Baldwin, the dynamic force behind much desertion legislation, was wholeheartedly in favor of including children born out of wedlock. Twelve states did in fact expressly nominate illegitimate children in their legislation. Freund, on the other hand, felt that since the offenses of deserting a family and failing to support an unlawful child were very different, to cover them indiscriminately by one provision would tend to confuse different kinds and grades of obligation. Freund's solution was that a complainant should be able to sue a man not only in the residential state of the mother but wherever he might be found. A uniform law enacted by all states would, it was argued, make the benefits reciprocal.[34]

Further recommendations for reform involved the time limit placed on the institution of proceedings and the evidence that might be used against the mother. According to most bastardy laws, a mother could only bring a suit against the putative father of her child within a certain fixed period. This was normally up to two years from the birth of the child. There was an obvious flaw in this stipulation. If a father agreed to pay maintenance for that short period and then refused to offer further support, the mother was left without recourse to legal action. As a remedy it was put forward that the time limit should apply from the moment of birth *or* from the date of the last payment.[35] Another loophole that was detected and condemned was the principle of *exceptio plurum concubentium*. Under this ruling, if a man could prove that the mother of an illegitimate child had had sexual relations with more than one man during the period when conception might have occurred, the case against him might be dismissed. Arguing that "it is the right of the child and not that of the mother which furnishes the primary consideration in allowing a course of action," they advocated that this harsh principle be removed from the paternity support laws. Instead, if more than one man was suspected of being the child's father and insufficient evidence could be brought against any one of them, it was thought that they should all contribute toward the child's support.[36]

Once a man was adjudged to be the father of an illegitimate child, the major concerns were, of course, the amount payable toward the child's upkeep and the method of enforcement. There was overwhelming discontent with the paltry sums that were being meted out by the courts. George Mangold, author of *Children Born out of Wedlock* (1921) was one who felt that "one of the most unsatisfactory phases of the enforcement of our bastardy laws is the amount of compensation allowed." Unlike supporters of the Norwegian law, most American reformers did not agree that the amount of maintenance should be in proportion to the parents' wealth. Instead they demanded a lump sum or weekly payment sufficient to provide adequate food, clothing, shelter, and education. The exact amount would preferably be made at the discretion of the judge, although it should not fall below a certain minimum. It was also thought essential that the sum be regularly reviewed at future dates and that maintenance payments should be subtractable from a man's estate in the event of his death. Furthermore, in order that a mother should not be inveigled into accepting an inadequate private settlement, reformers suggested that new legislation should make the condition that this should not be less than a set minimum figure.[37]

The value of providing adequate support naturally depended on efficient enforcement of the court's orders. The common method was to require a security from the father. If he failed to provide this he could be sent to jail for a limited period. This was obviously a remnant of older punitive attitudes towards bastardy and was of no benefit to the child, who was left without support while his father languished in jail. Influenced by the provisions made for deserters, reformers suggested the adoption of a system of probation or, for the persistent defaulter, hard labor where the prisoner's earnings would be passed on to the mother and child.[38]

STRUGGLE FOR IMPROVED LEGISLATION

Having discussed the blatant shortcomings of antiquated legislation, individuals and reform groups were faced with the more difficult task of gathering support and inducing legislatures to pass more liberal statutes. The struggles lasted for years. The Illinois Committee for Social Legislation, for example, spent four years trying to change the bastardy law of that state. This committee had first been organized in 1912 under the directorship of James Tufts, professor of philosophy at the University of Chicago. In subsequent years it acted as an unofficial coordinating body for all important pieces of social legislation. Freund took charge of the drafting of the bills. From 1915, he and a small group of dedicated reformers pressed for a legal amendment to raise the maximum payment from $550 to $3,000 and to transfer proceedings from the criminal courts to the chancery courts, where the rules of evidence were less severe.

A bill was subsequently drafted by Fisher, proposing that after the determination of a man's paternity, his illegal child "would be to all legal intents and purposes his child" and making changes in the amount of maintenance and type of legal proceedings. This was widely distributed throughout the state to women's clubs, social service organizations, and the press. However, there was some dissension, particularly among the women's groups. Some thought that bastardy should be kept a crime in order to maintain the moral sanction against conceiving children out of wedlock. Other organizations, feeling that the Fisher bill was not sufficiently progressive, chose not to support a program of legislation at that time. They preferred to circulate the Castberg law, sponsor lectures by such speakers as feminist author Katherine Anthony, and produce educational propaganda.

The Fisher bill encountered further opposition in the legislature, where many members felt that it went too far. The chief objection was the bill's failure to set upper limits to the sum a father might be ordered to pay. Country members, in particular, were disturbed by visions of women blackmailing wealthy men to support their unlawful offspring. The Illinois legislature did agree to raise the maintenance payments by $50 in the first year and $25 in succeeding years. Their self-applauded magnanimity was to no avail, however. Although the Fisher bill passed both the House and the Senate, it was not in time to secure House concurrence in the Senate amendments.[39]

By 1919 child welfare reformers in Illinois had sufficiently reconciled their differences and educated public opinion that a new illegitimacy statute was placed on the books. This act made paternity support proceedings a civil action, doubled the maintenance payments to $200 for the first year of the child's life and $100 for nine successive years, and prohibited the complainant from making a private settlement with the father for less than $800. The word "bastard" was eliminated from the law, an indication of the new spirit that was slowly infiltrating welfare circles.[40]

Progress was indeed slow. Illinois was one of the very few states that succeeded in making substantial changes before 1920. North Dakota introduced the most radical illegitimacy law. This act, passed in 1917, declared that every child "was the legitimate child of its natural parents." The child was therefore to be supported by both parents and had the right to inherit from its mother and father and their collateral and lineal kin. Unfortunately this brave stance was somewhat undermined by rather narrow limits on the time within which the mother might bring a suit and by the rejection of the mother as a competent witness if the putative father died.[41]

In the same year Minnesota passed what was probably the most comprehensive legislation relating to illegitimacy, covering legal status, support, transfer of guardianship, supervision of maternity homes, and birth registration. Social workers in Minnesota had petitioned from 1913 for a commission to be appointed to study and revise the laws relating to children. In August 1916 the state government was finally convinced that a child welfare commission was necessary. As a result of the commission's activities, 41 bills were presented to the 1917 legislature; 33 of these passed, among them a new illegitimacy law.

With respect to support, the Minnesota law was intended "to safeguard the interests of illegitimate children and secure for them the nearest possible approximation to the care, support and education that they would be entitled to if born of lawful marriage." The State Board of Control was given authority to instigate action where necessary. The proceedings would be analogous to those followed in a criminal case, and the trial would be held before a jury. One welcome improvement in the Minnesota law was that it was now held to be no defense that the complainant had had sexual contact with other men during the period when the child might have been conceived. If found guilty, the man was henceforth to "be subject to all the obligations for the care, maintenance and education of such child and to all the penalties for failure to perform the same, which are or shall be imposed by law upon the father of a legitimate child of like age and capacity." His obligations continued until the child was 16 years of age. No definite sum was stipulated; rather the amount was left to the judge's discretion. The mother could also sue for her confinement expenses. Failure to pay the required maintenance was punishable by a jail sentence of a minimum of 90 days. Finally, after paternity was established, the father's name was added to the child's birth certificate.[42]

As seemed to be inevitable, the value of the new Minnesota illegitimacy legislation was seriously diminished by its administration. The provisions often went unenforced. For example, according to a study of illegitimacy in 1921, paternity actions were instituted in only one-third of the cases coming to the attention of the State Board of Control, and court orders for support were given in one-sixth. Of the fathers found guilty, approximately half later defaulted in their payments. The amounts themselves were frequently below the sums considered adequate by the state board. Although the fundamental idea of the law was to keep the illegitimate children in their mothers' custody, only 35 percent of the children studied in 1921 were still with their mothers at two years of age. A subsequent survey by the U.S. Children's Bureau, in 1932, indicated that only slight improvements had been made during the decade. Dorothy Puttee's investigation of *The Illegitimate Child in Illinois* (1937) shows that these administrative failings were not confined to Minnesota.[43]

The achievements of reformers in the area of illegitimacy were certainly not spectacular. As Mangold admitted in his monograph on children born out of wedlock, "Progressive thought [was] far ahead of legislative enactment."[44] Faced with widespread conservatism, these reformers often sacrificed the ideal of equal rights for the easier goal of relieving public and private charity of the burden of a large number of dependent children. Despite an ostensible commitment to helping unwed mothers support their children, the courts, faced with putative fathers on low incomes and probably influenced by a double standard which condoned male extramarital sex, rarely granted women sufficient allowances to make them financially self-supporting. Unmarried mothers, like deserted wives, had to fall back on other resources.

Nonetheless, the legal reformers of the period did begin to rid America of her old attitude towards the "bastard." They declared the name obnoxious, the stigma unjust, and the laws unfair. In the 1920s more states succeeded in amending their medieval statutes, and a Uniform Illegitimacy Act was drafted and later adopted by seven states.[45] That we have not yet actualized the potential of progressive ideas may be seen in recent legal battles to provide for the support and inheritance rights of children born out of wedlock.[46]

NOTES

1. William Blackstone, *Commentaries on the Laws of England*, quoted in Grace Abbott, *The Child and the State* (Chicago: University of Chicago Press, 1938), vol. 1., p. 9.

2. Ibid., vol. 2, pp. 493-95, 507-8. Chester S. Vernier, *American Family Law*, 5 vols., 1936 (reprint, Westport, Conn.: Greenwood Press, 1971), vol. 4, pp. 189-208. Helen Clarke, *Social Legislation: American Laws Dealing with Family, Child and Dependent* (New York: Appleton-Century Co., 1940), pp. 315-23. Robert H. Bremner, ed., *Children and Youth in America: A Documentary History* (Cambridge, Mass.: Harvard University Press, 1970-1), vol. 1, pp. 49-53; vol. 2, pp. 170-78.

3. See Linda Gordon, *Woman's Body—Woman's Right* (Harmondsworth, England: Penguin, 1977).

4. Emma O. Lundberg and Katharine Lenroot, *Illegitimacy as a Child Welfare Problem*, Part I, U.S. Children's Bureau Publication no. 66 (Washington, D.C.: Government Printing Office, 1920), pp. 10-27, figures given p. 26.

5. Lundberg and Lenroot, *Illegitimacy as a Child Welfare Problem*, Part II, pp. 38-39, 46-47. Percy Kammerer, *The Unmarried Mother* (Montclair, N.J.: Patterson Smith, 1969, first printed Boston: Little, Brown, 1918), pp. 328-29. Louise de Koven Bowen, *A Study in Bastardy Cases* (Chicago: Juvenile Protective Association, 1914), pp. 9-10. This study of 419 unmarried mothers showed the following occupational distribution:

	Percent
Houseworkers	32.0
Factory workers	19.0
Hotel workers	10.8
Tailoresses, seamstresses, or milliners	10.0
Laundresses	6.0
Stenographers	1.2
Other office occupations	4.0
Miscellaneous	18.0

6. U.S. Bureau of the Census, *Historical Statistics of the United States, Colonial Times to the Present* (Washington, D.C.: Government Printing Office, 1975), Part I, p. 168.

7. *Annual Report of the Boston Society for Destitute Mothers and Infants*, 1917-1918, p. 5.

8. Kate Waller Barrett, "History of the Florence Crittendon Mission," *National Florence Crittendon Magazine* 2 (1900): 59-60, quoted p. 59.

9. Jacob A. Riis, *How the Other Half Lives* (New York: Hill & Wang, 1957, first printed New York: Scribner's, 1890), p. 142.

10. Juvenile Protective Association of Chicago, *The Care of Illegitimate Children in Chicago* (Chicago: the Association, 1913), pp. 4-12, quoted p. 12. Louise de Koven Bowen, "Birth Registration and the Establishment of Paternity," in U.S. Children's Bureau, *Standards of Legal Protection for Children Born out of Wedlock*, Publication no. 77 (Washington, D.C.: Government Printing Office, 1921), p. 54.

11. Lundberg and Lenroot, *Illegitmacy as a Child Welfare Problem*, Part II, pp. 47-48. Illinois Committee for Social Legislation, *Social Legislation in Illinois* (Chicago: the Committee, 1917), p. 8.

12. Lundberg and Lenroot, *Illegitimacy as a Child Welfare Problem*, Part II, p. 50.

13. Ibid., Part I, p. 35; Part II, quoted p. 41.

14. Ibid., Part II, p. 51. Of Boston's public child caring agency, 11 percent of the inmates were illegitimate. Of those in the private agencies, 17 percent were illegitimate, and of the children receiving care from the Division of State Minor Wards, 23 percent. The cost of this care of Boston's illegitimate children was estimated at $124,000 for 1914.

15. Kate Waller Barrett, "Motherhood as a Means of Regeneration" (Washington, D.C.: National Florence Crittendon Mission, 1910), p. 11. Mrs. Frank D. Watson, "The Attitude of Married Parents and Social Workers toward Unmarried Parents," *Proceedings of the 45th NCSW*, 1918, p. 105. A. Madorah Donahue, "The Case of an Unmarried Mother Who Has Cared for Her Child and Succeeded," *Proceedings of the 44th NCSW*, 1917, pp. 282-84.

16. For example, *Annual Report of the Boston Children's Aid Society*, 1914, p. 16.

17. Kammerer, *The Unmarried Mother*, pp. 320-25. George Mangold, *Children Born out of Wedlock* (Columbia, Mo.: University of Missouri Press, 1921), pp. 41-44. Jean Weidensall, "The Mentality of the Unmarried Mother," *Proceedings of the 44th NCSW*, 1917, p. 288. Emma O. Lundberg, "The Child Mother as a Delinquency Problem," *Proceedings of the 47th NCSW*, 1920, p. 299.

18. Juvenile Protective Association, *The Care of Illegitimate Children*, p. 15.

19. Emma O. Lundberg, "Illegitimacy in Europe As Affected by the War," *Proceedings of the 45th NCSW*, 1918, pp. 299-300. Harry M. Fisher, "The Legal Aspects of Illegitimacy," ibid., p. 299.

20. Carl Christian Carstens, "What is the Practical Ideal of Protection and Care for Children Born out of Wedlock?" *Standards of Legal Protection*, pp. 95-96.

21. Kate Waller Barrett, "How We Conduct Our Rescue Home," *National Florence Crittendon Magazine* 2 (1900): 185. Ada E. Sheffield, "The Nature of the Stigma upon the Unmarried Mother and Her Child," *Proceedings of the 47th NCSW*, 1920, pp. 119-22.

22. Resolution, *Proceedings of the [1909] Conference on the Care of Dependent Children*, p. 164.

23. *Annual Report of the Boston Children's Aid Society*, 1912, p. 9. *Annual Reports of the Massachusetts Society for the Prevention of Cruelty to Children*, 1911, pp. 35-36; 1912, p. 22; 1913, p. 29. Juvenile Protective Association, *The Care of Illegitimate Children in Chicago*. Bowen, *A Study of Bastardy Cases*.

24. Lundberg and Lenroot, *Illegitimacy as a Child Welfare Problem*, Part I, pp. 88-90. Emma O. Lundberg, "Progress toward Better Laws for the Protection of Children Born out of Wedlock," *Proceedings of the 47th NCSW*, 1920, p. 112.

25. Julia Lathrop to Emma Lundberg, March 19, 1915. United States Children's Bureau Papers, Box 59, Washington, D.C., National Archives.

26. Lundberg and Lenroot, *Illegitimacy as a Child Welfare Problem*, Parts I and II. Ernst Freund, *Illegitimacy Laws in the United States and Foreign Countries*, U.S. Children's Bureau Publication no. 42 (Washington, D.C.: Government Printing Office, 1919). U.S. Children's Bureau, *Norwegian Laws Concerning Illegitimate Children*, Publication no. 31 (Washington, D.C.: Government Printing Office, 1918). U.S. Children's Bureau, *Standards of Legal Protection*.

27. Fisher, "The Legal Aspects," pp. 294-95.

28. U.S. Children's Bureau, *Norwegian Laws*, pp. 1-37. Ernst Freund, "The Present Law Concerning Children Born out of Wedlock and Possible Changes in Legislation," in *Standards of Legal Protection*, p. 27.

29. Carstens, "What is the Practical Ideal?" p. 96. Ada E. Sheffield, "Report of the Committee on Illegitimacy," *Proceedings of the 46th NCSW*, 1919, p. 81. Cheyney C. Jones, "A Tentative Outline for a Study of Illegitimacy," *Proceedings of the 45th NCSW*, 1918, p. 91.

30. Freund, "The Present Law," p. 27.

31. "A Syllabus of Propositions to Serve as a Basis for a Program for Illegitimacy Legislation," in *Standards of Protection*, p. 20.

32. Robert F. Keegan, "Policies of Public and Private Agencies in Dealing with Illegitimacy," *Proceedings of the 5th National Conference of Catholic Charities*, 1918, quoted p. 160. Juvenile Protective Association, *The Care of Illegitimate Children in Chicago*, quoted p. 26. Kate W. Barrett, "The Unmarried Mother and her Child," *Proceedings of the 37th NCCC*, 1910, p. 98.

33. Mangold, *Children Born out of Wedlock*, pp. 153-55. Freund, *Illegitimacy Laws*, pp. 36-37. "Resolutions of the Chicago Conference," U.S. Children's Bureau, *Standards of Protection*, quoted p. 14. Louise de Koven Bowen, *Some Legislative Needs in Illinois* (Chicago: Juvenile Protective Association, 1914), p. 5.

34. William H. Baldwin, letter to Ernst Freund, June 25, 1910. Ernst Freund papers, University of Chicago Library, Box 1. Baldwin, "The Present Status of Family Desertion and Non-Support Laws," p. 412. Freund, *Illegitimacy Laws*, pp. 26, 46-52. Mangold, *Children Born out of Wedlock*, pp. 170-71.

35. Freund, *Illegitimacy Laws*, pp. 35-36.

36. Ibid., quoted p. 37. Mangold, *Children Born out of Wedlock*, p. 161.

37. Ibid., quoted p. 155. Freund, *Illegitimacy Laws*, pp. 41-42, 52-53. Bowen, *Some Legislative Needs*, p. 72.

38. Ibid., p. 7. "Resolutions of the Chicago Conference," p. 14. Freund, *Illegitimacy Laws*, pp. 43-45.

39. Illinois Committee for Social Legislation, *Social Legislation in Illinois*, pp. 8-10. Ernst Freund, letter to James Tufts, Nov. 25, 1914, James Tufts papers, University of Chicago Library, Box 3.

40. An Act to Amend Sections 1, 3, 4, 8, 11, 16, and 18 of an Act Entitled, "An Act Concerning Bastardy," *Laws of Illinois*, 1919, pp. 422-24.

41. Freund, *Illegitimacy Laws*, p. 25.

42. The provisions of the Minnesota act are given in Grace Abbott, *The Child and the State* (Chicago: University of Chicago Press, 1938),

vol. 2, pp. 552-67. See also Otto Davis, "Children of Unmarried and of Illegitimate Parents: Recent Legislation in Minnesota and Elsewhere," *Proceedings of the 45th NCSW*, 1918, pp. 96-101. W. Hodson, "The Scope and Purpose of the Minnesota Law," in U.S. Children's Bureau, *Standards of Legal Protection*, pp. 40-48.

43. Mildred B. Mudgett, *Results of Minnesota's Laws for the Protection of Children Born out of Wedlock*, U.S. Children's Bureau Publication no. 28 (Washington, D.C.: Government Printing Office, 1924), pp. 217-20. Unpublished report by the U.S. Children's Bureau on the Minnesota law in Abbott, *The Child and the State*, vol. 2, pp. 570-71. Dorothy Puttee, *The Illegitimate Child in Illinois* (Chicago: University of Chicago Press, 1937), pp. 66-69.

44. Mangold, *Children Born out of Wedlock*, p. 182.

45. After the conferences in Chicago and New York, the Children's Bureau appointed a committee headed by Ernst Freund to consider illegitimacy legislation and to draw up a model bill. Choosing not to make any suggestions concerning the status of unlawful children, the committee drew up a model support law, which was approved by the Commissioners on Uniform State Laws in 1922. This law reaffirmed the idea that both parents were responsible for the maintenance of an illegitimate child until he or she reached the age of 16. Claims might be made against the father's estate if he died before that time. Failure to support was to be regarded as an offense. The Uniform Illegitimacy Act also provided that fathers who could not produce the required security would not be sent to jail but would be put in the custody of a probation officer under the condition that they pay maintenance regularly. Clarke, *Social Legislation*, p. 331. Abbott, *The Child and the State*, vol. 2, p. 501.

46. For example, see Harry D. Krause, "The Non-marital Child—New Conceptions for the Law of Unlawfulness," *Family Law Quarterly* 1 (1967): 1-9. Krause pointed out that in 1967 fathers in Texas and Idaho were still under no obligation to support, while in only four states did a judgment in a paternity suit give the child the right to inherit from the father.

8

PUBLIC REGULATION

Previous chapters have examined the mothers' pension movement and the changing legal status of children. These developments were merely two manifestations of a wider public involvement in the field of child care and protection. While the government had always acknowledged a certain responsibility for the support of the country's dependent and neglected children, it had never assumed exclusive control. Indeed, throughout the nineteenth century, private philanthropy, staffed by innumerable enthusiastic volunteers, had taken a major part in rescuing, maintaining, and shaping the values of America's disadvantaged children. As the century closed, however, a disillusionment with private charity was discernible among many leading welfare figures. The problems of an increasingly urban and industrialized society had convinced them of the limitations of isolated, uncontrolled, and financially restricted associations. The threat of social disorder prompted agitation for greater government participation, particularly at the state level. As a result, the government extended its activities in the direct care of children, in regulation of children's agencies, and in the overall direction of child welfare. This trend was not without opposition. Private charities, church bodies, and other conservative forces delayed and diverted the course of this impulse toward public welfare. Nevertheless, as will be shown in the following two chapters, the Progressive era witnessed a significant movement toward that interrelated structure of local, state, and federal services that, for good or ill, comprises the present child welfare system in America.

LIMITATIONS OF THE PUBLIC SECTOR
IN THE NINETEENTH CENTURY

Throughout the nineteenth century, the public sector played a distinctly minor role in the battle to alleviate and cure problems of dependency and distress. Private philanthropy prospered, nourished by a complex interplay of social, economic, political, and intellectual factors that exalted the individual and voluntary association with others.

The urge to collective action permeated nineteenth-century American society. Alexis de Tocqueville, casting a discerning eye over the new republic, observed that "wherever at the head of some new undertaking you see the government in France, or a man of rank in England, in the United States you will be sure to find an association." This national characteristic de Tocqueville attributed to the democratic nature of American society. The dynamic of an aristocracy resulted from the strength of individual men. In America, citizens were independent and feeble, powerless to achieve their ends unless they chose to act in concert.[1]

Certainly, egalitarianism, mobility, and the absence of a rigid class structure made the status of the individual vague and ambiguous. They created anxieties and tensions that might be relieved by coordinated activity. Charitable and philanthropic associations provided one source of communal strength and a means of winning social recognition. The nation's heterogeneity further promoted the organizing instinct. The disestablishment of churches after the American Revolution, the consequent multiplication of sects and the influx of Catholicism ensured the increase of church activity in the realm of welfare. The periodic waves of immigrants deposited on America's shores during the nineteenth century similarly resulted in the creation of innumerable benevolent societies. Organizations such as the Charitable Irish Society of Boston and the German Society of New York acted as buffers between individual newcomers and their alien environment while serving to reinforce their sense of ethnic identity.[2]

Self-help gathered an intellectual armory to justify and advance its position. Faith in the nation's abundant resources helped to exalt the idea of self-sufficiency and reject the notion that poverty was a necessity. God's will was no longer seen as a satisfactory explanation for want, and most people had come to accept the view that "in our highly favored country, where labor is so much demanded and so liberally rewarded and the means of subsistence so easily and cheaply obtained, poverty need not and ought not to exist."³ Individual failure, intemperance, immorality, and idleness were seen as the causes of most distress. A Protestant ethic that emphasized salvation through hard work, piety, and frugality bolstered this general analysis. Obviously if problems of need were essentially moral in nature, then their solution demanded the personal influence of the nation's more fortunate and hence more virtuous citizens.⁴

To this home-grown emphasis on private aid was added the imported creed of the classical economists. In England and France, followers of Adam Smith and the Physiocrats proclaimed the existence of a natural economic order whereby each man, in pursuing his own interests, incidentally brought about the welfare of the entire community. Any interference with the individual endangered the whole. Public poor relief, for example, was to be condemned as promoting the proliferation of the unfit. As Richard Hofstadter demonstrates in his book *Social Darwinism in American Thought* (1959), Americans grasped the concept of laissez faire and applied it even more rigidly than the Europeans to their own situation. Further encouraged by Herbert Spencer, who placed these ideas on a scientific basis and extended them to all spheres of human experience, many Americans regarded any extension of government activity with suspicion. Spencer saw governments as merely committees of management, established to protect rights that had already been developed among individuals in a social state. Governments should therefore confine themselves to such elementary tasks as administration of justice and protection of citizens from external and internal aggression. The majority of the tasks necessary for the smooth working of society should be done by voluntary groups.⁵

According to Sidney Fine, while few took Spencer's extreme stance on the value of a "negative" state, most Americans exhibited a cautious attitude toward government activity. They also expressed little faith in the capacities of elected representatives and their appointed henchmen. The political scandals of the Gilded Age confirmed theoretical analyses of the limitations of government control. E. L. Godkin, the moving spirit behind the *Nation*, was not alone in believing that there was no legislature in his time that was "controlled by scientific methods or by the opinions of experts in jurisprudence or political economy."[6] The low reputation of the government extended to the welfare arena, where there was a distinct trend away from the use of public outdoor relief. There was also a noticeable tendency to view public institutions as distinctly different from, and inferior to, private institutions. Charles Loring Brace expressed a conviction common to the nineteenth century that, in comparison with private asylums, the country's "public institutions are dull and lifeless. They have not the individual enthusiasm working through them, with its ardor and power. They are more like machines."[7] This attitude flourished despite the fact that many private organizations had become large-scale bureaucratic systems hardly distinguishable from their public counterparts in size, hierarchical structure, specialization, and routinization.

The care and protection of children exemplified this preference for voluntarism. Private organizations dominated. According to statistics compiled for the U.S. Bureau of the Census at the turn of the twentieth century, 956 out of 1,075 institutions for children were managed by a wide variety of ethnic, ecclesiastical, and other private groups. They catered to approximately 90 percent of the children under care at that time. Similarly, all SPCCs and most child-placing agencies were privately controlled.[8]

EXISTING PUBLIC PROVISIONS

The limited public provisions for the dependent and neglected that did exist assumed a number of forms. The almshouse, once the foremost repository for homeless children, still housed a significant number of youngsters. In 1890, 5,629 children under the age of 15 were reported to be among the inmates of the country's poorhouses.[9] This, however, was increasingly considered to be little better than consenting to their death. Partly as a result of this disillusionment, the states, in the second half of the nineteenth century, founded various specific institutions for destitute and ill-treated children.

Such was the case in Ohio, for example, where the presence of two thousand children in infirmaries immediately after the Civil War helped to bring about the creation of county homes. These asylums, supported by the counties and controlled by four trustees appointed by the county commissioner, were originally designed to be temporary shelters. However, due largely to inadequate foster-care facilities, the county institutions became the permanent home of many hundreds of children. By 1890 homes had been established in 38 of Ohio's 88 counties and the numbers of inmates were increasing rapidly.[10]

Similar conditions influenced the foundation of another institutional variant, the state school. In 1871 Michigan relief authorities discovered that many children "yet suffered for an agency strong enough to supply means and wise enough to devise methods to guarantee to all dependent and ill-treated children, their natural right to protection and education." The result of these authorities' concern was the establishment of the Michigan State Public School, a central institution that acted as an agency for the reception of children and their distribution to families. Accepting children aged from 6 months to 12 years committed to it by the probate court, the school provided medical and educational aid and placed them in homes selected by a county agent. This formula for reaching all dependent children throughout a state was subsequently adopted by Minnesota, Wisconsin, and Rhode Island before 1890.[11]

A fourth, though somewhat restricted, avenue for government child care was asylums for the dependents of soldiers and sailors active in the Civil War. In the wake of that crisis, children's homes sprang up in Pennsylvania, Illinois, Kansas, Minnesota, Ohio, Indiana, Iowa, and Wisconsin. Their original function was of course modified as the years passed, but most survived into the twentieth century by extending their facilities to grandchildren of war victims, to the families of veterans of the Spanish-American War, or to unrelated destitute children. On January 1, 1904, there were ten asylums of this type, catering to almost 3,700 waifs.[12]

Finally, in accordance with the general trend in child care, initial inroads had been made into the area of state foster care. Massa-

chusetts pioneered this field when, in 1882, the then current State
Board of Charities was given permission to board dependent children
with individual families without preliminary institutional training.
This state of affairs was the climax of a slow process of change
that, beginning in the 1850s, had seen undifferentiated almshouse
care give way to segregated treatment at the Monson Primary
School in 1866. In turn, this institution was transformed by the
state board into a temporary asylum and eventually replaced by
five temporary boarding homes. From this establishment infants
and older children were boarded with suitable families for sums
that, in the 1890s, varied from $1.50 to $2.75 weekly, according to
age.[13]

STATE SUBSIDIZATION OF THE PRIVATE SECTOR

The above facilities comprised the spectrum of public child care
at the beginning of the Progressive era. For the most part the
state was content to allow private individuals and associations to
take upon themselves the greater burden of responsibility. Where
governments were unwilling or felt themselves unable to furnish
aid, they frequently chose to subsidize private and sectarian
organizations. From 1806, when the New York City Orphanage
first received an appropriation, the practice had spread in an
unintentional and haphazard manner. Payments, in the form of
either lump sums or per capita grants, seemed to make available
the specialized treatment needed while requiring little effort on the
part of the authorities and making minimal demands on the taxpayers. The system did not go unchallenged.

In many states there were attempts to prohibit government
allowances, particularly to religious organizations. However, where,
as in New York, the state legislature was specifically forbidden
to authorize payments to children's agencies, such aid was consequently dispensed by municipal and county bodies. By 1904 over
50 percent of the maintenance of that state's children's institutions
was provided in the form of government subsidies.[14]

On the national scale, subsidies comprised 21.7 percent of the
total running costs of children's institutions.[15] The incentive given
to the formation of private associations was clearly evident. According
to Amos Warner, author of *American Charities* (1894), between

1885 and 1894 there were a significant number of institutions in the United States that received in excess of their maintenance costs. Child care could be a profitable business.[16]

A LACK OF STATE REGULATION

Private child-care organizations came into being, flourished, and died. Prior to 1890 the states rarely controlled their formation nor called them to account for their activities. A few licensing regulations did exist, however. In Pennsylvania, for example, an act of 1865 made it a misdemeanor for any persons other than a duly incorporated institution to receive and care for more than two children under three years of age. Likewise, the Michigan legislature, in 1887, made it necessary for every association to obtain a written certificate of approval from the county superintendent of the poor or from the county agent of the State Board of Charities. Such provisions, however, were scarce and hardly comprehensive. Regulation of the treatment provided was little better. Although there were in existence, by 1890, ten state boards of charities and correction, their function was largely limited to the supervision, coordination, and improvement of public charities. When, as was the case in New York from 1871, the supervisory board was empowered to investigate the activities of certain private associations, the actual amount of regulation was often insignificant. William Rheinlander Stewart, president of the state board of New York in the first decade of the twentieth century, claimed that his predecessors had, for many years, averaged one investigation per annum.[17]

This indifference to the nature and workings of the country's numerous homes, institutions, and placing agencies resulted in various limitations and abuses. In states where there was no check on the need for incorporation, the outcome was often a duplication of facilities in certain areas and a virtual absence in others. Idiosyncratic admission policies with regard to the age, sex, race, religion, or physical, mental, and moral condition of children frequently left groups outside the private charity system.

Since the plight of children exerted an overwhelming appeal, child care attracted both the less scrupulous, desiring to serve their own interests, and the genuinely enthusiastic but ignorant. The Ladies' Deborah Nursery and Child Protectory of New York was one example of both unintentional and purposeful abuse. This particular organization, largely supported by per capita grants from the city, was found by an investigative committee appointed in 1896, to be managed by people who were personally gaining from their position. The directors were not only renting their own property to the nursery but were also supplying all the institution's provisions. The records demonstrated financial ignorance and irregularities in the disposition of funds. Inadequate amounts were being spent on the children themselves, in terms of food, clothing, and education, while the salaries of employees and the maintenance of buildings received liberal amounts.[18]

Worse abuses occurred among the myriads of unlicensed homes that flourished in every city. Many were "baby farms," accepting unwanted, often illegitimate, children for a stipulated sum. The survival of infants in these homes often depended on sheer chance. As various investigations by the Juvenile Protective Association of Chicago demonstrated, the conditions were frequently so unsanitary as to endanger the children's health. Medical attention was nonexistent, and cases of tuberculosis, venereal disease, and rickets were common. Nourishment was inadequate, training negligible, and the suitability of the women in charge more than questionable. The following record was made of a visit to a Chicago "baby farm" of the period.

> Another home where eight children were boarded was filthy and unsanitary. The visitor called at 10:30 a.m. and found two of the older boys in a basement room, eating canned beans for breakfast. The other six children were still in bed, in a room on the second floor. Three children occupied one bed, two occupied another bed and one child was lying in a broken baby carriage. The bedding was wet and foul beyond description; the floor was littered with rags, scraps of paper, whiskey bottles and dirt that had apparently been accumulating for weeks. At 1:30 in the afternoon of the same day, the visitor returned to the home. The caretaker was dressing the six small children, none of whom had had anything to eat up to that time. Six of the children were physically defective; four of them had rickets; one had a skin disease; and one, a subnormal boy, nine years of age, who had never attended school, was almost blind.[19]

These uncontrolled homes accepted children for a fee, so they often disposed of them for a further sum. Infants were handed over to individuals with no investigation of their character nor record of the transaction. The newspaper advertisements found in city dailies offering or requesting attractive, amiable babies and strong, healthy children illustrated the market for children who might be "adopted" for $50 or more. A typical notice offered a "beautiful girl, 4 years of age; blue eyes and auburn hair, excellent health and charming disposition, legitimate parentage. HIGH COST OF LIVING reason for selling."[20] Being a child broker offered ample reward.

DISILLUSIONMENT WITH LAISSEZ-FAIRE

A growing awareness of the extent to which the welfare of the nation's children was dependent on the efficiency and integrity of unregulated private organizations was one factor contributing to a reevaluation of the role of the government in child care. The magnitude of the child problem created by rapidly increasing industrialization, urbanization, and immigration encouraged a similar reassessment. Reformers and welfare workers interested in children shared in the spreading nationwide disillusionment with laissez-faire ideas.

Faced with large-scale unemployment, poverty, and crime, economists, sociologists, and political scientists such as Richard Ely, Edmund Ross, and Woodrow Wilson strongly denied the viability of a doctrine of noninterference. They saw it as not only unethical and unscientific, but also as unnecessary in a democracy, where the government was not an entity apart from the people but merely its agent. Laissez-faire ideology was condemned as dangerous in a complex, industrial society. Like H. C. Adams, many came to believe that "as countries become more complex, the functions of government must necessarily extend to continuously new objects."[21] The state, instead of confining itself to a limited protective function, would promote the public welfare by appropriate positive action. It would be "an efficient agency for the political betterment of social and economic conditions throughout the land."[22]

Discussions on behalf of dependent and neglected children reflected this change in thought. Support for increased government activity came from public and private agencies alike. Men such as Hugh Fox, president of the New Jersey Children's Protective

Alliance, and Ernest Bicknell, general superintendent of the Chicago
Bureau of Charities, joined Homer Folks, Hastings Hornell Hart,
Carl Christian Carstens, and other executives of private charities
in advancing new programs of state activity. Many of these later
took up positions on public boards of charity or in state children's
organizations. Their opinions were echoed by figures already
prominent in the public service, officers such as Stewart and
Robert W. Kelso, Secretary of the Massachusetts State Board of
Charities. They argued that thousands of children, particularly in
the mushrooming cities, were suffering because the once dynamic
force of private philanthropy had failed to response to post-Civil
War needs. Radically changed conditions demanded a drastic
revision of thought on the role of voluntarism in the American
social system.

In an address to the Illinois State Conference of Charities in
1914, W. E. Hotchkiss of Chicago advised his colleagues that the
growing complexities and difficulties of current industrial-urban
life made it "inevitable that the state should assume an increasingly
important role in safeguarding the welfare of children."[23] Others
expressed similar beliefs. They pointed to state interference in the
fields of banking, insurance, factory inspection, building regulations, and so on, and supported "any process of government which
increased the dynamic force of the machinery for social order or
added to the common sum of social energy."[24] The unfortunate
condition of dependent and neglected children was seen as an obvious
area in which the state could promote social order. The time had
come, it was declared, when the state should know how many of its
children were destitute or maltreated, what became of these youngsters, and how it might best guarantee their care and protection.[25]

The crux of the debate, of course, was where to draw the line between public and private effort. Leading welfare reformers were in
agreement that the welfare pendulum should not swing too far
toward socialism. "To attempt to make of the State a Universal
Providence" was to invite "absolute and speedy ruin."[26] They
argued that private philanthropy still had much to offer, that the
principle of voluntary association was still legitimate in a rapidly
changing society. Socialist Charles R. Henderson, himself a forceful proponent of social insurance, still considered voluntary organ-

izations, at their best, to be "the indispensable means of innocent and wholesome gratification, the pioneers of progress, the guardians of dearly bought agencies of research and culture."[27] Similarly, Carstens felt the necessity in the child welfare sphere for a group of interested citizens who could discover new areas of need and secure and maintain good standards of work.[28]

Nevertheless, the trend of opinion was in favor of a changed and somewhat reduced role for private children's agencies. Four areas were isolated as being in need of revision. Reformers advocated (1) greater direct care of dependent and neglected children by public agencies, (2) financial separation of the public treasury and private charity, (3) state supervision of private organizations, and (4) creation of a public body for research and education. The first three of these will be examined in this chapter. The agency for research and education, the U.S. Children's Bureau, will be discussed in Chapter 9.

DIRECT CARE BY PUBLIC AGENCIES

The first area touched upon was the state's role in the reception and treatment of children. Ideas varied as to the exact function to be allowed private associations, but in general their role was seen as involving experimentation, temporary care, and the treatment of specific child problems.

Private agencies were praised as invaluable in the initiation of new methods, the establishment of certain standards of care, and the stimulation of local interest. But, Carstens suggested, when they had clearly demonstrated the value of a local experiment, it was in the community's interest that such services be taken over by the state. The greater resources of the government could, it was argued, ensure that beneficial methods and systems be given a much wider application.[29] Another possible functional division depended on the permanence of the care given. Folks, in his book, *Care of Destitute, Neglected and Delinquent Children* (1900), saw the transfer of guardianship to the state as affording a logical division in the field of child care. When children were permanently removed from their families, they should be maintained by the state. It was felt that private organizations were more suited to the care and protection of youngsters in need of temporary aid and to the rehabilitation of the family unit.[30] Finally, welfare workers suggested that private associations were better equipped to tackle specific problems. Children with physical or mental handicaps that demanded exceptional care or those with peculiar family situations might be treated more effectively by private charity. The state, on the other hand, having far greater authority, could reach out to all types of dependents. Where private agencies were unable to intervene because of legal restrictions or had neglected a particular group of children, public organizations could act effectively.[31]

Whatever the respective roles to be allotted to public and private agencies, most reformers were agreed that there should be an increase in direct care by government bodies. The exact formula would naturally depend on a state's particular needs. Social workers with experience of the state school system pressed their own solution on their colleagues, insisting that "it would be a great blessing to the dependent child life of every state if there were one state-wide institutional home for children, strong in resources, wise in its foundations and organized in manner to increase its guardians' benefits."[32] They pointed to its economy, its broad scope, and most significantly its success in reducing the incidence of child dependence. Others rejected the single institution idea and propounded their own variants, whether local institutions, specific boards of child welfare, or children's divisions within the existing structure of public welfare.

AN END TO SUBSIDIZATION

The second area of reform involved separation of the public treasury and private agencies. The history of subsidization had demonstrated to social workers and philanthropists the financial disadvantages of the practice, together with its detrimental effect on inmates and its retardation of a unified public welfare program.

Whereas public authorities had originally approved appropriations on the assumption that "private institutions invariably manage at much less cost than public institutions,"[33] they now criticized the snowballing expense. They now reasoned that by giving institutions an unregulated pecuniary incentive, the government had unwittingly encouraged the creation and perpetuation of many unnecessary organizations. Subsidies were, according to Folks, responsible to a large extent for the increase in the number of dependent children being raised in New York's institutions. He was acutely aware of the temptations facing a manager who, by discharging an inmate or placing him in a family home, was losing $75 to $110 per annum. Money unnessarily diverted to private agencies was also believed to be preventing the development of an efficient and comprehensive system of child welfare. On the one hand, less funds were available for public institutions, which were consequently forced to use inadequate equipment and employ poorly trained staffs. On the other hands, subsidies created a body of vested interest that, by political lobbying, the use of special influence, and obstructive tactics, sought its own prosperity at the expense of progressive social work.[34] To men such as Warner the situation appeared disastrous. It was "as though the city should try to get its streets paved by announcing that any regularly incorporated association that should pave a given number of square yards of street—location, time and method to be decided by itself—should receive a given amount from the public treasury."[35] The end result would be chaos.

At the same time that they attacked private philanthropy for its selfishness, reformers also cajoled their colleagues. The withdrawal of aid would, they claimed, also be in the best interests of private charity, since public grants discouraged individuals from financing their local associations. Even when the aid received was extremely small, declared one prominent Catholic social worker, people got the impression that the state was supporting private institutions and so felt disinclined to donate.[36]

Some supporters of increased public welfare was so disillusioned by the pitfalls of subsidization that they envisaged total abolition as the best solution. If private citizens wished to help their fellow human beings they should, it was thought, be prepared to bear the financial burden alone. This viewpoint was unrealistic in the face of the firm entrenchment of the practice and the incapacity of private funds to meet many community needs. Not all reformers were so intransigent on this issue; some took a more practical stance. They suggested that where subsidies had not yet been introduced they should be avoided. However, in states such as Pennsylvania where the practice was widespread, an efficient system of regulation would minimize the evils inherent in the subsidization.[37]

REGULATION OF PRIVATE CHARITIES

Supervision was the third topic in the debate on pubic policy. It was a key issue. Private agencies and public subsidies were obviously firmly established and would continue to be necessary for a long time to come. Immediate problems seemed to demand "extension of the functions of government on its regulative side rather than its administrative power."[38] Throughout the 1890s and the first decade of the twentieth century, the National Conference of Charities and Correction (after 1917 the National Conference of Social Work) heard a variety of papers on the subject of state supervision. For several years after the turn of the century a regular committee was appointed to evaluate developments in this area. At the White House Conference of 1909 and at individual state conferences, the question of the regulation of private charities was debated extensively.

Those in favor of state supervision stressed three main benefits to be achieved: eradication of abuses, uniformity of methods, and improved direction of child-caring activity as a whole. Critics claimed that the magnificent work done by many private agencies could not obviate the positive evils within the system. Hugh Fox informed delegates to the National Conference of 1899 that they would easily draw upon "a common fund of experience for hundreds of instances to illustrate the gross abuse of the more or less irresponsible power which is placed in private hands."[39] Others argued that the state's duty was to ensure that funds appropriated from the public treasury or received from individual citizens were properly and economically used. All donations were given in trust, and the trustee should be accountable by some rational method to the general public. More important, to many reform-minded social workers, was the protection of the health and life of those under care. Children were helpless beneficiaries, often exploited and ill-treated. State supervision by an official body would ensure the elimination of instances in which children were "herded together in unventilated rooms, cared for by ignorant nurses, fed with improper food . . . [and] died by the hundreds when they ought to have lived."[40]

Naturally, only a minority of agencies were guilty of abuse. All organizations, however, were thought to be in need of a "clearing house of information" to help raise standards of children's care.

Representatives at the National Conference rightly recognized that hundreds of smaller agencies had no access to a "stimulus of intelligent, disinterested criticism—eternal to and independent of the institution."[41] Such organizations were failing to readjust to a changing environment and were pursuing haphazard policies to the detriment of their inmates. What was needed, in the opinion of Folks and others, was "some means of making the experience of each available for many or all, somebody from whom any institution which purposes to establish a placing-out department or something along the line of industrial training, can learn what other institutions have successfully undertaken."[42] A state supervisory body could provide that service.

The accumulation of factual information concerning all agencies would provide the basis for a third benefit, the overall direction of child welfare. Social workers were becoming increasingly aware of the duplication and uneven distribution of private facilities. There was therefore felt to be an urgent need for "somebody who is thinking not only as to how to do the best for a given number of children, but about the tendency and development of child-caring work as a whole."[43] This somebody would sound the alarm if excessive zeal compromised the goals of child welfare or if areas were being neglected.

To achieve the degree of supervision required, a number of legislative moves were suggested. Public control was to be exercised from the beginning of an organization's existence. In order to ensure that only suitable, financially viable groups entered the field, it was thought necessary to require the approval of a state board of charities or similar body for the incorporation of all child-caring agencies. The charter thus granted might be suspended if the institution or agency persistently refused to carry out its work in a proper manner. Closely allied to this principle was the granting of a periodic license. Preferably renewed on an annual basis, this certificate would guarantee continued maintenance of adequate results. Failure to achieve such standards would result in its withdrawal.[44]

A further method of keeping associations up to scratch was the stipulation that they report at regular intervals to the state board concerned. The information required would allow the government to know the whereabouts of each child, the reason for admission, the progress and condition of the ward, and the final disposition. Finally, advocates of an expanded public welfare system demanded periodic visitation and inspection of all agencies dealing with children. They insisted that only by regular examinations of the work being undertaken could the government be sure of the elimination of abuses and the maintenance of suitable standards. The need was thought to be particularly pressing in the case of placing agencies, whose charges were sometimes distributed carelessly and subsequently ignored. Hart and Folks were two professionals who enthusiastically supported "State visitation of children placed in homes." To placate the managers of the various institutions and placing agencies, reformers stressed that moderation and a spirit of helpful cooperation would infuse official intervention. Persuasion rather than coercion was to be the ultimate aim.[45]

The more radical supporters of state supervision wanted to extend government regulation to all private charities, regardless of whether the government contributed financially to their upkeep. Executives of the more progressive nondenominational private agencies joined with members of state boards in denying the right of certain children's charities to exemption. All charity, it was claimed, was essentially a work of public concern and hence it was the duty of the state to see that such work was properly conducted.[46] Liberal Catholics such as David Tilley, president of the Saint Vincent de Paul Society of Boston, concurred. They attemped to persuade their fellow workers that, as Catholics, they could not "afford to stand in the way of progress but must be in the vanguard, eager to adopt and perfect what is found good."[47] However, many remained unconvinced and resisted what they considered unwarranted interference.

As might be expected, opposition came from the country's sectarian organiations and their supporting religious bodies. The protests of such agencies as the Catholic Protectory of New York and the German Orphan House of Indianapolis joined those of nondenominational associations like the New York SPCC, which continued to pursue a conservative line. Representatives of dissenting agencies saw the new growth in public welfare activity as a direct threat to their survival. They felt that, ideally, the government should restrict itself to the enactment of legislation designed to enable private institutions and charities to continue to expand. Since this appeared to be against the current trend of opinion, the best that private charity might hope for was the careful limitation of state power.

Private children's agencies voiced their opposition to certain government-sponsored projects. In New York, for example, Commissioner of Charities John A. Kingsbury set up a municipal children's bureau in 1916 to place out many of the city's institutionalized children. It was vehemently attacked by Catholic institutions. They feared that it would "tend to lessen in proportion to the extent of its success the utility of our own various homes and orphanages," while also presenting the threat of proselytization.[48]

Likewise, associations under private control jealously guarded their financial aid against any government attempts to withdraw or reduce it. Perhaps one of the best examples of the defense of subsidies is that of Illinois. Here, from 1879, the legislature had authorized per capita grants to the state's two Protestant and two Catholic industrial training schools. Between 1882 and 1917, nine attempts were made to nullify the practice by various county and state authorities, generally on the question of the validity of aid to sectarian organizations. Other efforts were made by the Cook County Board of Commissioners to limit their liability for payment to a fixed amount per month.

These challenges were consistently defeated. The courts regularly brought down a decision that, in religious institutions, it was "contrary to fact and reason to say that paying less than the actual cost of clothing, medical care and attention, education and training . . . is aiding the institution where such things are furnished." In addition, an investigation in 1911 into charities in the state of Illinois questioned the legality of the county's attempt to limit the total amount of subsidies paid.

Rather than restricting the incidence of subsidies in Illinois, the publicity and an increase in per capita grants from 1911 onward led to the formation of 14 more training schools before 1920. Expenditures increased from approximately $62,000 in 1910 to $271,000 in 1920. Furthermore, by an amendment to the juvenile court law in 1923, counties were authorized to appropriate funds for child-placing agencies as well as industrial training schools. Subsidization, in Illinois at least, was hardly a dying practice.[49]

Not surprisingly, the subject of state supervision provoked a considerable amount of critical comment. At conferences and through the media, private charities demonstrated their obvious fear that the state would trespass too far into the management and internal discipline of the organizations concerned. Questions of interagency cooperation and the overall development of child welfare paled into insignificance when the associations' autonomy was apparently threatened.

It was put forward that "the charity which is real and also strictly private should not be under an a priori supervision and inspection on the part of the state." Scrutiny before incorporation was allowed to be a reasonable safeguard against fraudulence and ignorance. Similarly, it was considered acceptable that "ex posteriori the state may inspect and must inspect . . . when a complaint of criminal neglect is made." However, any more than this was generally thought to be an "unnecessary and almost insulting infringement of private, personal liberty." To demand regular examinations was, critics claimed, tantamount to presuming guilt before sufficient proof was given. From the churches' point of view, supervision was also unwarranted interference with the religious liberty guaranteed by the Constitution, that is, the principle of absolute separation of church and state. The charitable affairs of churches should, in their opinion, be totally free from government "meddling."[50] Many institution directors and managers were adamant that whatever constructive criticism was needed to ensure the continued health and welfare of dependents could easily be provided by the agencies themselves.

It was this spirit of anxious insularity that led the New York SPCC to challenge New York State's ruling on supervision. At the New York Constitutional Convention of 1894, an amendment was adopted providing for supervision by the State Board of Charities over all charitable, correctional, and reformatory institutions. Subsequently, state agents began inspecting and investigating children's institutions and agencies. The SPCC, traditionally aloof from other children's societies and dominated by the attitudes of its president, refused to accept the value of this innovation. In Elbridge Gerry's opinion, such interference would cripple associations while producing no practical benefit. In the case of his own organization, one that was totally supported by private means, supervision would "absolutely obstruct its entire business besides making public no end of confidential communications received by it." As a consequence, in 1898 the SPCC refused to admit the public inspector and took the case to the state Court of Appeals. It denied that it was a charitable institution within the meaning of the Constitution of 1894 but rather "an arm of the law." The care, clothing, food, and medical attendance furnished to children temporarily in its custody were claimed to be incidental to the SPCC's real work.[51]

The Court of Appeals found in favor of the SPCC and, in addition, restricted the legitimate supervision of the state to those charities in receipt of public funds. The state board was thus compelled to relinquish jurisdiction over more than one-half of the private charities in New York State. Welfare figures such as Stewart saw its effect as destroying the system of state inspection, "built stone by stone in a series of clearly expressed statutes." It was "a public calamity."[52] Not until the 1930s was supervision of all private charities largely restored.

THE STATE TAKES A GREATER ROLE

Despite objections, diversions, and challenges, welfare reformers in many states made headway toward their goals of greater public participation in the care and protection of dependent and neglected children. Governments extended their facilities for the direct care and placement of the states' wards. By 1923, according to figures in a special census report entitled *Children under Institutional Care*, there were 138 public institutions and 82 public child-placing agencies in existence. Of these, 44 were run by the states; 156 were controlled by various counties; and 20 were managed by municipalities. At first glance this seems only a slight increase, being 11.7 percent of the total number of facilities as opposed to 10 percent in 1904. However, in terms of the number of children involved it represented a virtual doubling. While exact figures are not available, it is estimated that somewhere between 18.4 and 21 percent of the country's dependent and neglected children were under government control, as compared with 10 percent at the turn of the century.[53]

The expanded child-care system encompassed a wide variety of institutions and agencies. The state-controlled home and school remained popular. Montana, Colorado, Nebraska, and Alabama established orphanages for dependent children during this period, bringing the total number of state homes of all kinds to 32. Far greater advances, however, were made in the area of child placement by government bodies. Massachusetts continued to forge ahead. On November 30, 1921, the Division of Child Guardianship of the Massachusetts State Department of Public Welfare had under its care, in free or boarding homes, approximately 5,280 children. Other states, like Alabama, followed suit by setting up child welfare divisions within their own welfare systems, while yet another group of states, including New Jersey, and the District of Columbia established boards of children's guardians. In 1897, largely as a result of the efforts of the New Jersey State Charities Aid Association, a campaign was set in motion for the creation of a state board that would place out all children who became public charges and conduct its own supervision of them. In March of 1899 a State Board of Children's Guardians, consisting of seven unpaid members, was set up. Under its auspices children were placed immediately upon reception in homes of the same religious faith.[54]

Although many new developments on behalf of dependent and neglected children occurred at the state level, there was also a greater appreciation of the need for county child welfare agencies. Previously thought to be somewhat inefficient, the county came to be thought of by many social workers "as on the whole the most feasible administrative unit."[55] The realization that child problems in rural areas had been largely ignored in favor of more pressing urban crises, focused new attention on the county. The number of county homes increased, as did county boards of children's guardians. First introduced in Indiana in 1891 under the control of the county commissioners, county boards were responsible for cooperating with the State Board of Charities in the care of dependent children. They subsequently proved themselves invaluable. By 1923 there were 65 such boards operating in Indiana, and these had 1,561 children under care during that year. Even municipalities recognized the utility of this structure, as evidenced by the institution of a board of children's guardians in Portland, Oregon, in 1919.[56]

Although not so pronounced as the movement for public care of dependent and neglected children, there was also a trend toward government participation in work for the protection of neglected children. Executives such as Carstens of the Massachusetts SPCC came to the conclusion that the state should take over much of the work of the existing SPCCs. He saw private associations as being necessary in the early development of protective work but believed that, because the basic principles had since been established, it was fitting for the government to intervene, thus allowing cruelty societies to pursue more educational work.[57] In the second decade of the century, several government bodies came to agree. West Virginia, for example, decided in 1919 to replace its humane society by a State Board of Children's Guardians. Unlike boards in other states, this agency took an active, prosecuting role in cases involving mistreated youngsters. A similar transfer occurred in Minnesota in 1917, this time through the existing county child welfare structure. In other counties and cities throughout America, juvenile courts began to take on themselves some of the functions of protective associations. By 1920 this development was still embryonic, yet the direction was already obvious.[58]

Less success was achieved in the area of subsidies. As was seen in the example of Illinois, pressure by church institutions and non-sectarian organizations, together with the urgent need for facilities to house and place children, combined to ensure the continuance of public allowances. The solutions offered by reformers had been vague, especially as to the ways in which elimination might be achieved. Indeed, many came to see the impracticalities involved in their opposition to subsidies. Thus, as late as 1933, 52.1 percent of U.S. children's institutions were still receiving grants. Improvements were more realistically brought about by a beneficial swing away from general lump sum appropriations to direct payments for specific children and more efficient regulation of the disposition of public monies.[59]

More comprehensive state supervision gradually came into being during this period. Arlien Johnson's study of *Public Policy and Private Charity* in the late 1920s demonstrates this movement. By 1929 the majority of states had passed legislation regulating the activities of children's institutions and placing agencies. Twenty-five states had enacted regulations concerning the periodic visitation and examination of various types of children's agencies. Similarly, the issuance of licenses became an integral part of the welfare systems of 29 states, although, only 13 states demanded regular certification of all children's agencies. The others specified particular kinds of institutions, foster care agencies, boarding homes, and maternity hospitals. Reporting at intervals to the respective supervisory authorities was made compulsory in 22 states. Of the four remedies suggested by progressive social workers, the need for approval of incorporation received least attention. By the end of the 1920s only 13 states had insisted that children's organizations acquire an approved charter from the state authority.[60]

Events in Illinois illustrate the way in which the state increased its surveillance of private philanthropy. Prior to 1890, the sole reference to the duty of the government to supervise private charities was contained in an act of 1869 that created the Board of State Commissioners of Public Charities. One section of this legislation authorized visitation and inspection of all charitable and correction institutions receiving aid from the state. This later applied to the four industrial training schools that had catered to dependent children before 1890.

In 1899 the juvenile court law, brought about by some of America's most renowned welfare figures, marked the beginning of a new stage in the public welfare system of Illinois. By the terms of the original act, no court could order the commitment of a dependent child to an association that had not filed an annual report with the state commissioners in the preceding financial year. This implied the necessity of procuring the annual approval of the board of commissioners of Public Charities. One section of this legislation authorized visitation and inspection of all charitable and correction indent, neglected, or delinquent children. Six years later, child-placing agencies were specifically made subject to state supervision. The relevant act of 1905 required not only that placing organizations report quarterly on all children placed in families and the State Board keep a record of such wards, but also that the state appoint an agent and two visitors to visit children in their new homes. Although limited by insufficient funds and inadequate staff, as usual, Illinois authorities did manage to reach many thousands of children in subsequent years.

This supervisory power remained unchanged by the administrative reorganization in 1909 whereby the Board of State Commissioners was replaced by a double-headed authority, the Board of Administration and the State Charity Commission. Additional duties placed upon the new Board of Administration were those of licensing home-finding associations and inspection of lying-in hospitals. The gross abuses found in maternity homes produced considerable agitation for stricter control. Hence, in 1915, the new Maternity Hospitals Act required the board to license hospitals caring for maternity patients and to eliminate those whose standards were not adequate. This the board did. Of 75 such hospitals inspected in 1918, for example, only 44 were allowed to continue in existence.

One further extension of public supervision brought boarding homes under equal surveillance with their fellow children's agencies. In 1917, largely as a result of the horrifying revelations of conditions in Chicago's "baby farms," a committee of Chicago social workers drew up a bill for the licensing and inspection of boarding homes caring for two or more children under the age of sixteen. While this was defeated in 1917, a similar act was successfully passed two years later.[61]

Of course, the efficiency of such provisions depended on the commitment of the state boards in question. Kingsbury, the commissioner of New York charities, discovered to his dismay certain authorities were loathe to exercise their supervisory duties. Appointed by New York's mayor, John Mitchell, in 1914, Kingsbury had immediately set out to assess the quality of the care given to children by private institutions and to determine the agencies' right to public funds. He established a committee of prominent child welfare workers to conduct an independent investigation into 42 children's institutions. The result was a report that vehemently criticized the low standards required for approval by the State Board of Charities. Malnutrition, overwork, unclean and vermin-ridden conditions, antiquated methods of punishment, little recreation, and poor education were the charges brought against the directors of certain agencies. In May 1915, Kingsbury and William Doherty, the second deputy commissioner, launched an attack on the state board through the press and the forum of the National Conference of Charities and Correction. Investigations had indicated, Doherty claimed, that "either the inspectors of the State board of Charities . . . are not thoroughly posted and alive to the changes constantly being

made in progressive child-caring institutions or else they have failed⁓
to grasp any proper concept of the modern acceptation of what is
adequate institutional care of dependent children."⁶² New York's
newspapers echoed the complaints.

The result of the publication of these findings was a furor in which
charges and countercharges were hurled from one public authority
to another. Sectarian organizations also joined the fray, with accusations of religious prejudice, conspiracy, and perjury. The city
officials refused to be deterred by their opposition. Consequently, in
January 1916, Charles H. Strong was appointed by Governor Charles
S. Whitman to conduct an investigation into the State Board of
Charities and its place in the entire welfare system. The final report
of this commission substantiated Kingsbury's claims. It condemned
the board's consistent failure to withhold licenses from poor-quality
agencies and to compel necessary improvements. The state inspection service had fallen far short of the goals of the Constitution of 1894.
Concluding that "the state must always dominate the partnership
between it and the private institutions," the Strong Commission
advocated tougher measures, greater publicity, and a revision of
the board's function, methods, and personnel. While there was an
improvement in the supervision carried out by the board, bills
aimed at drastic reorganization were conveniently lost in committees.
A complete change in board membership was the only positive
outcome of the legislative attempt to strengthen the government's
supervisory power at this time.⁶³

Battles were lost and won in the fight for an expanded public
child welfare system. Reformers were often thwarted by opposing
interests and the bureaucratic red tape, delaying tactics, and political hassles within the government structures responsible for child
care and protection. To a significant extent, however, they achieved
their goals. By the end of the Progressive era they had taken significant steps towards greater state care of dependent children and state
regulation of children's agencies. In the next chapter, two further
extensions of public influence in child welfare will be examined.

NOTES

1. Alexis de Tocqueville, *Democracy in America* (New York: Mentor,
1956, first printed 1835–1840), pp. 192–202, quoted p. 198.

2. Walter I. Trattner, *From Poor Law to Welfare State* (New York: Free
Press, 1974), pp. 29–42.

3. *Annual Report of the New York Almshouse Commissioners*, 1847, quoted in David M. Rothman, *The Discovery of the Asylum: Social Order and Disorder in the New Republic* (Boston: Little, Brown, 1971), p. 157.

4. Robert H. Bremner, *From the Depths: The Discovery of Poverty in the United States* (New York University Press, 1967), pp. 16-21.

5. Richard Hofstadter, *Social Darwinism in American Thought* (Boston: Beacon Press, 1968), pp. 31-49.

6. Sidney Fine, *Laissez Faire and the General Welfare State* (Ann Arbor: University of Michigan Press, 1964), pp. 5-9, 29-45, E. L. Godkin quoted p. 58.

7. Charles Loring Brace, *The Dangerous Classes of New York and Twenty Years Work among Them* (New York: Winkoop and Hallenbeck, 1872), p. 28.

8. U.S. Bureau of the Census, *Benevolent Institutions, 1904* (Washington, D.C.: Government Printing Office, 1924), p. 26.

9. U.S. Bureau of the Census, *Paupers in Almshouses, 1923* (Washington, D.C.: Government Printing Office, 1923), p. 10.

10. Grace Abbott, *The Child and the State* (Chicago: University of Chicago Press, 1938), vol. 2, pp. 14-15, 44-50. Joseph P. Byers, "The County Homes of Ohio," *Proceedings of the 28th NCCC*, 1901, pp. 236-38.

11. C. D. Randall, "The Progress of State Care for Dependent Children," *Proceedings of the 29th NCCC*, 1902, quoted p. 243. C. D. Randall, "The Michigan System of Child Saving," *American Journal of Sociology* 1 (1896): 710-24.

12. Robert H. Bremner, ed., *Children and Youth in America: A Documentary History* (Cambridge, Mass.: Harvard University Press, 1971), vol. 2, pp. 259-63. U.S. Bureau of the Census, *Benevolent Institutions, 1904*, pp. 46-127.

13. R. W. Kelso, *The History of Public Poor Relief in Massachusetts* (Boston: Houghton Mifflin, 1922), pp. 164-88.

14. Abbott, *The Child and the State*, vol. 2, pp. 10-12, 15-17, 73-112. Arlien Johnson, *Public Policy and Private Charity* (Chicago: University of Chicago Press, 1931), pp. 1-16.

15. U.S. Bureau of the Census, *Benevolent Institutions, 1904*, pp. 29-30.

16. Amos Warner, *American Charities* (New York: Thomas Crowell, 1894), p. 404.

17. Frank J. Bruno, *Trends in Social Work, 1874-1956: A History Based on the Proceedings of the National Conference of Social Work* (New York: Columbia University Press, 1957), pp. 31-36. Gladys Fraser, *The Licensing of Boarding Homes, Maternity Homes and Child Welfare Agencies* (Chicago: University of Chicago Press, 1937), p. 9. William Rheinlander Stewart, "The Necessary and Reasonable Powers of a State Board of Charities," *Proceedings of the 34th NCCC*, 1907, p. 32.

18. New York State Board of Charities, "Report of an Investigation of the Affairs of the Ladies,' Deborah Nursery and Child's Protectory by a Special Committee" (Albany, 1896) in Bremner, *Children and Youth in America,* vol. 2, pp. 333-34.

19. Arthur Guild, *Baby Farms in Chicago* (Chicago: Juvenile Protective Association, 1917), pp. 8-9.

20. *Annual Reports of the Chicago Juvenile Protective Association,* 1917-1918, p. 14; 1919-1920, p. 23, adoption notice p. 25.

21. Fine, *Laissez Faire and the General Welfare State,* Chapter 6-8, Adams quoted p. 202.

22. Theodore Roosevelt, quoted ibid., p. 338.

23. W. E. Hotchkiss, "Child Welfare," *Institution Quarterly* 4 (1914): 214.

24. Hugh Fox, "The Relation of a State Board of Charities to Child Caring Societies and Institutions," *Proceedings of the 16th NCCC,* 1899, pp. 384-85, quoted p. 385.

25. "Report of the Committee on Child Saving," *Proceedings of the 24th NCCC,* 1897, pp. 87-88. Ernest Bicknell, "Interference of a Municipality on Behalf of Its Wards," pp. 375-78.

26. "Report of the Committee on Children," *Proceedings of the 35th NCCC,* 1908, p. 21.

27. Charles R. Henderson, "The Place and Function of Voluntary Associations," *American Journal of Sociology* 1 (1896): 334.

28. Carl Christian Carstens, "Report of the Committee on Children," *Proceedings of the 42nd NCCC,* 1915, p. 98.

29. Ibid., p. 95.

30. Homer Folks, *Care of Destitute, Neglected and Delinquent Children* (New York: J. B. Lyon, 1900), p. 95.

31. Galen Merrill, "Some Recent Developments in Child Saving," *Proceedings of the 27th NCCC,* 1900, p. 228. S. C. Griffin, "Relative Functions of the State and Private Charities in the Care of Dependent and Neglected Children," *Proceedings of the 36th NCCC,* 1909, pp. 55-57.

32. Charles E. Faulkner, "Institution Care for Dependent Children," *Proceedings of the 31st NCCC, 1904,* p. 342.

33. R. Prendergast, "State Aid to Private Institutions," *Proceedings of the 13th NCCC,* 1886, p. 165.

34. Folks, *Care of Destitute, Neglected and Delinquent Children,* pp. 97, 116, 145-47. See also Robert D. Dripps, "The Policy of State Aid to Private Charities," *Proceedings of the 42nd NCCC,* 1915, pp. 465-73. Bird S. Coler, "The Subsidy Problem in New York City," *Proceedings of the 28th NCCC,* 1901, pp. 132-35.

35. Warner, *American Charities,* p. 417.

36. David Tilley, "The State and Private Institutions," *Proceedings*

of the 1st National Conference of Catholic Charities, 1910, p. 76.

37. For example, Dripps, "The Policy of State Aid," pp. 458, 471-73.

38. Fox, "The Relation of a State Board of Charities," p. 388.

39. Ibid., p. 385.

40. Hastings Hornell Hart, "State Supervision of Private Charities," *Proceedings of the 29th NCCC*, 1902, quoted p. 131. Homer Folks, "State Supervision of Child-Caring Agencies," *Proceedings of the 22nd NCCC*, 1895, pp. 209-10. Robert W. Kelso, "Supervision and Licensing of Private Charities," *Proceedings of the 44th NCSW*, 1917, p. 368.

41. Carstens, "Report of the Committee on Children," p. 96. William J. White, "State Supervision of Private Charitable Institutions," *Proceedings of the 34th NCCC*, 1907, p. 83.

42. Folks, "State Supervision of Child-Caring Agencies," p. 209.

43. Ibid.

44. R. W. Hebberd, statement, *Proceedings of the [1909] Conference on the Care of Dependent Children*, p. 61. Hugh Fox, statement, p. 60. Conclusions, ibid., p. 194.

45. Folks, "State Supervision of Child-Caring Agencies," pp. 209-10. Kelso, "Supervision and Licensing of Private Charities," pp. 366-68. Hastings Hornell Hart, "State Visitation of Children," *Proceedings of the 7th Illinois Conference of Charities and Correction*, 1902, pp. 309-10, quoted p. 309, J. J. Kelso, "State Supervision of Children in Foster Homes," *Charities* 7 (1901): 526-28.

46. For example, R. W. Hebberd, "Report of the Committee on State Supervision and Administration," *Proceedings of the 29th NCCC*, 1902, p. 21. White, "State Supervision of Private Charitable Institutions," pp. 79-83.

47. Tilley, "The State and Private Institutions," p. 79.

48. Arthur Rosenberg, "John Adams Kingsbury and the Struggle for Social Justice in New York, 1914-1918" (Ph.D.diss., New York University, 1968), pp. 189, 198-99. Catholic opposition quoted p. 199.

49. Johnson, *Public Policy and Private Charity*, pp. 80-108, 132-78, quoted p. 108.

50. Richard D. Biedermann, "State Supervision of Private Charities," *Proceedings of the 38th NCCC*, 1911, pp. 42-43. See also D. J. McMahon, "Private Institutions and Public Supervision," *Proceedings of the 29th NCCC*, 1902, pp. 136-40.

51. *Annual Reports of the New York Society for the Prevention of Cruelty to Children*, 1897, pp. 8-9; pp. 6-12, quoted p. 11. Bremner, *Children and Youth in America*, vol. 2, pp. 398-410.

52. William Rheinlander Stewart, "State Inspection of Private Charitable Institutions, Societies and Associations," *Annual Report of the New York State Board of Charities*, 1900, pp. 219-20.

53. U.S. Bureau of the Census, *Children under Institutional Care, 1923* (Washington, D.C.: Government Printing Office, 1927), pp. 25, 170-201. The reason that accurate percentages cannot be given is that several agencies included delinquents in the figure returned. If we exclude these altogether, the percentage of dependents under public care is 184. If we include them, the percentage is 21.0.

54. Hastings Hornell Hart, "The Development of Child Placing in the United States," in U.S. Children's Bureau, *Foster Home Care for Dependent Children*, p. 8. Hugh Fox, "Boards of Children's Guardians," *Proceedings of the 31st NCCC*, 1904, pp. 311-16.

55. Carstens, "Report of the Committee on Children," p. 102.

56. Evans Woolen, "The Indiana Boards of Children's Guardians Act," *Proceedings of the 28th NCCC*, 1901, pp. 234-36. T. E. Ellison, "Child Saving under State Supervision without a State School," ibid., pp. 230-33. U.S. Bureau of the Census, *Children under Institutional Care, 1923*, pp. 48-139.

57. Carl Christian Carstens, "The Development of Social Work for Child Protection," in U.S. Children's Bureau, *Standards of Child Welfare: A Report of the Children's Bureau Conference, 1919*, Publication no. 60 (Washington, D.C.: Government Printing Office, 1919), p. 141.

58. William J. Schultz, "The Humane Movement in the United States 1910-1922," *Columbia University Studies in History, Economics, and Public Law*, Study no. 1 (New York: Columbia University Press, 1924), pp. 218-20, 223-28.

59. U.S. Bureau of the Census, *Children under Institutional Care, 1933* (Washington, D.C.: Government Printing Office, 1935), p. 60. No figures for subsidies were collected for the 1923 report, as it was felt that methods of financial reporting were too unstandardized to be worth considering.

60. Johnson, *Public Policy and Private Charity*, pp. 29-35. Fraser, *The Licensing of Boarding Homes*, pp. 11-57.

61. Johnson, *Public Policy and Private Charity*, pp. 52-55, 66-67. *Biennial Report of the Illinois Board of State Commissioners of Charities*, 1906-08, p. 30.

62. Rosenberg, "John Adams Kingsbury," pp. 239-40. William Doherty, "A Study of the Results of Institutional Care," *Proceedings of the 40th NCCC*, 1913, pp. 1902. "Report of the Commissioner," *Annual Report of the New York City Department of Public Charities*, 1914, pp. 14-15.

63. Rosenberg, "John Adams Kingsbury," pp. 242-43. Charles H. Strong, "Report of the Commission to Examine into the Management and Affairs of the State Board of Charities," in Abbott, *The Child and the State*, vol. 2, pp. 116-22.

9

THE JUVENILE COURT AND THE CHILDREN'S BUREAU

In the development of public child welfare during the Progressive era, two institutional innovations stand out in relief. The creation of the juvenile court at the end of the nineteenth century was hailed as perhaps the nation's greatest achievement on behalf of its youth. Lavish praise was showered on this new tribunal for its treatment of a wide variety of children's problems completely separately from adult cases, for its use of new methods, and for its employment of specially qualified personnel. Similarly, the establishment of the U.S. Children's Bureau in 1912, to act as an agency for research and the dissemination of information, was acclaimed as a triumph in welfare circles. Neither agency was predominantly interested in the affairs of dependent and neglected children. Delinquency was the main concern of the courts, while the Children's Bureau directed its attention to a broad spectrum of health, education, and welfare questions. Nevertheless, both involved themselves with problems of dependency and neglect, with various beneficial and detrimental results.

THE JUVENILE COURTS

America's juvenile court system was the confluence of a number of intellectual and institutional developments, some of which have already been touched upon. One tributary was the growing loss of confidence in the effectiveness of private philanthropy and the corresponding support for an assumption of greater public responsibility in welfare matters. Private elements joined public officials in championing the organization of the new courts and, in some instances, took part in their operation until the government could assume total control. Another stimulus came from the increase of specialized services and institutions for dependent, neglected, and delinquent children. Children's aid societies, protective associations, houses of refuge, and so on, were part of the separation of the treatment of children's problems from those of adults. The courts and the legal system had not yet felt the impact of this specialization.

Throughout the nineteenth century, dependent, neglected, and delinquent children were made public wards by a wide variety of courts and social agencies that were often incapable of understanding and dealing with their situations. The courts were frequently restricted in the ways they might dispose of children or forced by monetary conditions and institutional deficiencies to return children to the same detrimental environments from which they had come. Juvenile lawbreakers were particularly unfortunate. In most states, common criminal law did not greatly differentiate between the adult and the minor who had reached the age of criminal responsibility. This varied between seven and twelve years. A child who was caught breaking the law might be arrested by a police officer, deposited in the local cells along with adult offenders, tried in the regular criminal courts, and subsequently fined or committed to the county jail, workhouse, or reformatory. Sporadic attempts had been made to improve these conditions. As early as the 1870s Massachusetts had introduced provision for special court procedures for juveniles. An agent of the State Board of Charities was authorized to attend trials and find homes for those whose behavior did not warrant institutionalization. This incipient probation system slowly gained popularity and, by the 1890s, had become mandatory. In general, however, the criminal courts had failed to deal satisfactorily with juvenile offenders, and more relevant machinery was thought necessary.[1]

Attitudes toward juvenile delinquency at the turn of the century were changing rapidly. The new emphasis on environmental factors in character development made old methods of treatment seem effete. Professional correctional workers and administrators could no longer accept the monolithic explanations of criminal behavior, which attributed delinquent tendencies to biological defects. Cesare Lombroso's theories were losing favor, and more penologists and welfare workers were moving toward the viewpoints of William James, Adolph Meyer, and William A. White. Accepting the fact that deficiencies in character could often be traced to a child's early environment, many came to feel that "the way is open for an attempt to prevent such undesirable traits by an understanding of the child and a modification or elimination of those environmental factors which produce such results." New methods and new machinery were required if this preventive treatment was to succeed policies of retribution and punishment.[2]

A further area in which important changes had taken place was in the courts of equity. As we have seen in Chapter 6, decisions regarding custody of children, guardianship, and administration of the property of minors were reinforcing the idea of *parens patriae*, the belief that the state was responsible for the welfare of the infirm and the helpless. The state's duty toward dependent and neglected children was not a novel idea. Its application to the juvenile offender, however, was a totally new concept. The offender was now looked upon not as a criminal but as a child in need of care. The extension of the parental arm to delinquents, whether valid or not, provided the theoretical foundation for the nonpunitive treatment reformers were seeking.[3]

ESTABLISHMENT

The nation's first juvenile court was established in Cook County, Illinois, in 1899. The story is too well known to need any great elaboration here. Anthony M. Platt and Joseph M. Hawes have presented detailed pictures of its inception.[4] It is only necessary to briefly relate the circumstances surrounding its creation. Although one of the leading agitators admitted that it was "very difficult to say who originated this idea or that,"[5] certain groups may be given credit for creating a consensus in favor of a new law. The Chicago Women's Club provided a consistent impetus for reform throughout the 1890s and, in 1895, drew up a bill providing for a separate children's court with probation facilities. Unfortunately the bill

was later shelved because of doubts as to the constitutionality of
creating a new tribunal with a jurisdiction already assigned to other
courts.[6] The dissatisfaction of the Chicago Women's Club was
echoed by the discontent of the Illinois Board of Public Charities,
whose members condemned the "demoralizing irresponsibility with
which juvenile offenders were treated" by the police, the courts,
and the reformatories.[7]

The issue was taken to a wider audience when, at the meeting of
the Illinois Conference of Charities and Correction in November
1898, papers were presented on the need for reform. Feeling that
"all children are children of the state or none are," speakers advocated the creation of "an entirely separate system of courts for
children . . . [and] a children's judge who should attend to no
other business."[8] Subsequently, the Chicago Bar Association was
approached to draft an acceptable bill. A committee of prominent
lawyers and executives of charitable organizations, under the chair-
manship of Judge Harvey B. Hurd, produced a bill that circum-
vented earlier problems of unconstitutionality. The proposed
legislation conferred jurisdiction on courts already in existence
and permitted rather than compelled them to transfer cases to
the juvenile court. The act "to regulate the treatment and control
of dependent, neglected and delinquent children" was introduced
in the Illinois House of Representatives in February 1899 and,
despite the reservations of the House Judiciary Committee, was
approved. It passed through the Senate in July of the same year.[9]

Other states had reached similar conclusions as to the need for
a specifically juvenile court system. In Denver, Colorado, Judge
Benjamin Barr Lindsey had independently agitated for a new court
and achieved his goal in 1901. Word spread rapidly. Lindsey himself maintained a secretary to answer the thousands of inquiries
that came to him from all parts of the globe. Illinois authorities
were besieged with requests for copies of their law, and they themselves sent circulars to daily newspapers and journals advocating
adoption of their system. The National Conference of Charities
and Correction and state conferences took up the question. By 1909
ten states and the District of Columbia had authorized localities to
establish juvenile courts. Twelve states followed suit in the next
three years. By 1925 only Maine and Wyoming had not made pro-

visions for a children's court. In some states a special court was created to deal with juvenile cases. The majority, however, gave special jurisdiction to courts already in existence.[10]

SCOPE

Confidence in the benevolence of the state and the absence of other far-reaching public child welfare agencies encouraged the creation of a juvenile court of very broad scope. This sociolegal innovation was given jurisdiction over a wide variety of children's cases. The close connection between dependency, neglect, and delinquency in the minds of reformers had a similar effect. For many welfare workers and philanthropists, there was a definite relationship between the unfortunate, the ill-treated, and the criminal. It was commonly thought that "a child who today is simply neglected may be dependent tomorrow, truant the next day and delinquent the day after that.[11] Wishing to reach children before they had actually committed an offense, they sought to control the behavior of children whose circumstances seemed morally detrimental. Accordingly, they framed laws in which the distinctions between dependency, neglect, and delinquency were conveniently vague and that encompassed all types of youthful misbehavior. In Illinois the definition of delinquency of 1899, which referred to lawbreakers, was later broadened to include nebulous groups of children classified as "incorrigible" or "ungovernable." Their offenses were purely juvenile and often trivial. This loose definition of delinquency, together with definitions of dependency and neglect, gave the court power over a large number of children. The potentially dangerous nature of this power will be discussed later.[12]

Although delinquency was the court's major concern, it did handle a significant number of dependent and neglected children. Social workers such as Hastings Hornell Hart felt that it was "a great mistake to overlook what can be done by the court for the dependent child."[13] The proportion of children in these categories naturally varied from state to state. In most they comprised an important part of the clientele. In 1915, for example, the Cook County Juvenile Court handled 1,886 cases of dependency, as compared with 3,202 charges of delinquency.[14] All manner of problems were dealt with. Cases of cruelty, failure to protect, desertion, illegitimacy, orphanage, and adoption were regularly brought to court. Problems stemming from destitution of the parents were also handled. Often parents voluntarily came to the court to surrender their children because they were financially unable to cope. In the early days of the court, many hundreds of families were subsequently separated. Following the introduction of mothers' pension legislation in the second decade of the twentieth century, courts were handed another means of confronting the question of poverty. Before 1920, 18 courts were authorized to administer these funds to suitably qualified parents. The scope of the juvenile courts did not stop here. In some states, like Colorado, the juvenile court could bring negligent parents to account under laws prosecuting adults for contributing to the dependency or delinquency of their children. In cities such as Baltimore, an additional service was offered whereby any person might seek aid from the court's probation officers.[15]

Reformers were optimistic that this catch-all legal innovation would solve many youthful problems. It was lauded as "the wisest method yet devised for the care of delinquent and dependent children."[16] Even Theodore Roosevelt, in a message to the U.S. Congress in December 1906, praised the juvenile court for compelling the home to do its duty, for helping unfortunate families, and for building juvenile character.[17]

The guiding principle of this new piece of government apparatus was supposedly the approximation of parental care for children in need of discipline and protection. It was thought that "the juvenile judge has simply the parental and human problem of trying to do just what the child needs to have done for him."[18] For the dependent and neglected, the juvenile court was to offer humane understanding of their misfortunes. A full knowledge of the facts concerning each child's physical, mental, and moral condition and familial and social environment would allow the court to act in that child's best interests. To the parents the court might be a friend or foe. It they were adjudged morally fit and willing to cooperate, it would be "an elder brother, offering encouragement and helpful advice as to how the home may be improved and the environment of the children and of the family generally sweetened and purified." If it was proven that they had neglected the child, the court would be a stern reckoner.[19]

THE JUDGES

A crucial part of this individualized treatment was thought to be the personality and ability of the juvenile court judge. Because of the responsibility that rested upon this person, it was felt that he or she should be specially equipped. In the opinion of corporate lawyer Bernard Flexner, the judge should be not only a trained lawyer but also "a student of and deeply interested in the problems of philanthropy and child life. . . . He should be able to understand the child's point of view and his idea of justice."[20] This faith was shared by many of those who were the first to accept positions in the new tribunals. While in some courts the presiding judge was merely one rostered from another court to serve for a few months, in others the judges chose to serve on the juvenile court bench for a longer period. Such was the case with Judge Richard Tuthill, the first appointee to the Chicago court. His attitude was avowedly paternal. Faced with a delinquent boy, his policy was to "talk with the boy, give him a good talk just as I would my own boy."[21] His successor, Merritt W. Pinckney, a serious, determined man, took his role as paternal overseer just as seriously. The most well-known juvenile court judge was Lindsey, guiding light of the Denver court from 1901 to 1927. A devout pragmatist who was afraid of "consulting and studying any sociological works for fear [he] might embibe [sic] some theory," Lindsey attempted to bring the personal touch to his new creation. He established a rapport with delinquents that became almost legendary in welfare circles. Among the local gangs of Denver and the unfortunate children brought before him, he managed to inspire affection and loyalty.[22]

Not all judges were as confident of the ability of one man to control the reformation, reeducation, and rehabilitation of the children brought to court. Julian Mack, who served on the bench of the Cook County Juvenile Court from 1905 to 1907, berated his comrades for endowing juvenile court judges with innate genius. While giving men such as Lindsey their due, he nevertheless believed that "few judges are really temperamentally fitted, and few are so eminently endowed as to be able to do the juvenile court work and the probation work and all the other work that must be done if the court is to be really successful." He preferred the court to rely more on an efficient, trained staff of probation officers.[23]

PROBATION

Probation was to be one of the foundation stones of the juvenile court. If the court was not to punish but to place children in improved surroundings, preferably in their own homes, it needed an expert supervisory staff. Homer Folks, chairman of the New York State Probation Commission from 1905 to 1906, explained the usefulness of probation to his fellow delegates at the 1906 National Conference of Charities and Correction. Probation, Folks stressed, was by no means a simple act of clemency on the part of the judge, nor a special relationship between the judge and the probationer. Instead it was a way of dealing with moral delinquency. As applied specifically to neglected children, it was, in effect, an effort to reach the parents and change their attitude toward their children. Folks and his colleagues saw probation as a method that recognized the part of the environment in creating and rectifying children's problems. In the eyes of these reformers, it was the only way in which individualized treatment could be carried out. Ideally, the probation officer would be a friend to the child and the family, going into the home, studying the surroundings, and remedying detrimental influences. Men and women with special qualities and training were needed. Chicago social worker Louise de Koven Bowen envisaged them as "endowed with the strength of a Samson and the delicacy of an Ariel," as being "tactful, skillful, firm and patient." Folks preferred to emphasize the need for adequate training, artful selection, and supervision of probation work by an executive officer other than the judge. Folks and Bowen and their fellow social workers were enthusiastic about the possibilities of development. Probation was, to them, "the cord upon which all the pearls of the juvenile court are strung."[24]

PROCEDURES

Untroubled by doubts as to the benefits of the new system, social workers and legal personnel began the process of inquiring into and treating a host of juvenile problems. For many children the machinery was set in motion when petitions were filed by social agencies, parents, relatives, or other individuals to have them declared dependent or neglected. In Chicago these petitions were received by the Complaint Division of the Cook County Probation Department, which attempted to sift out those cases that did not warrant court action. Anonymous complaints were ignored completely, with perhaps unfortunate consequences for some of the children involved. Others were referred to more appropriate welfare agencies. In 1918, of 3,012 petitions considered by the Complaint Division, some 1,282 were adjusted without the cases being brought to court. Those cases thought to be sufficiently serious were investigated by the Probation Department, which tried to assemble a factual account of the child's history and present social environment. If it was thought necessary, the child in question might be removed from his or her home and taken to the court's detention center. Here the child might stay for two to three weeks before a decision on his or her future was made. The number of dependent children who were kept in the detention home was always smaller than the number of delinquents; nevertheless, in 1905 for example, 579 dependent children were admitted to the Detention Home at 625 W. Adams Street. Here they were examined, washed, given new clothing, fed, and taught by teachers provided by the Chicago Board of Education.[25]

In the early years of the Chicago court, dependency and neglect cases were heard on two mornings per week. The staff tried to make the proceedings as informal as possible and to minimize the child's contact with the court. In general the child would be brought before the bench at the beginning of the hearing and then dismissed unless his or her physical condition was to be introduced as evidence. The youngster's own feelings about the situation were not seen as really relevant to the problem; his or her fate was to be decided by "experts." Much attention was given to the creation of a less austere, more intimate atmosphere. A small chamber without any of the legal trappings of adult courts was thought to be more conducive to the solution of children's problems. The clerk would call each case in order, and the probation officer would come forward with the child, the parents, and witnesses. Grouped around the desk, they would listen to the probation officer's statement and give their own testimony.

DISPOSITIONS

After hearing the evidence given by the parties involved, the juvenile court judge decided the disposition of the child before him.

Normally the judge accepted the recommendation of the probation officer, since there was little time to devote to each case. Reformers might have envisaged a close, friendly relationship between judge and juvenile, but the large number of cases ruled this out. In Chicago, for instance, 25 cases might be heard in one morning, allowing each one perhaps 10 or 15 minutes of the judge's time.

Having decided upon the status of the child before him, the judge had various options. The case might be dismissed or continued for a definite period. If the child were to be permanently removed from the family or had no family, a guardian might be appointed who would later consent to that child's adoption or placement. A more common alternative in Chicago was to commit the boy or girl to one of the four industrial training schools that served the area. Between 1915 and 1919, 40 percent of children coming before the court were sent to these institutions. It is difficult to know whether this large percentage of commitments was warranted. If, as was claimed, most of the less serious cases were handled externally and only the most grievous instances of neglect and the most clear-cut cases of dependency were brought to court, then this figure might be justified.

Unfortunately, the early case records afford little information except for the age of the child, the number of times in court, and the disposition. When causes were listed they were generally simplified to such classifications as "drunkenness of mother" or "immorality of father." Certainly, the industrial training schools remained a popular receptacle for dependent and neglected children throughout the Progressive era.[27]

A smaller number of dependent children were put on probation. During the years between 1915 and 1919, just over one quarter of all dependent children were returned to their own homes under the supervision of the court.[28] Social workers were confident of beneficial results. Hart, for example, was convinced of "the value of the probation system as applied to the dependent child." In the Cook County Court, "the use of the probation officer to guard the interests of the child brought in as dependent and allowed to remain with the parents is just as valuable for the dependent as it is for the delinquent child."[29] Probation officers visited their charges and the families regularly and attempted to remedy the problems they found there. While this rehabilitation was supposedly carried out through a relationship of trust and understanding, it is obvious that coercion was part of the probation officer's armory. Timothy Hurley could advise probation officers to enter a family almost as one member of it and immediately follow this by urging them to use threats if parents refused to cooperate. Probation officers were backed up the authority of the court, which had the power to remove children from their families. They did not hesitate to use this weapon to force parents to conform to the behavioral norms they themselves accepted.[30]

DEFECTS

Although the creation of the juvenile court system was greeted with enthusiasm, it was not long before critics arose to tone down this roseate picture. After two decades of experience, social workers and members of the bar began to point out the serious limitations of the system and the inadequacy of its services. More importantly, they challenged the scope of the juvenile court, its assumption of an administrative role that might have been better given to another agency, and its detrimental confusion of the various types of children.

In June 1921 a conference on juvenile court standards was held at Milwaukee under the auspices of the U.S. Children's Bureau and the National Probation Association, at which prominent welfare and legal personnel reviewed 21 years of juvenile court work. In her introductory statement, Julia Lathrop expressed the feeling of many of her fellow delegates that in this area "our performance lags behind our laws." Edward Schoen, judge of the Juvenile Court of Essex County, New Jersey, went further. "Our juvenile court machine has been improved and altered as new light has come," he told his colleagues, "but it is still in a formative state and is not yet fully recognized as the great social agency for good" that reformers had hoped it would be.[31]

There was considerable disappointment over the limited spread of the juvenile court concept. Surveying its importance, welfare workers realized that it had been largely confined to the major urban areas and that only a small number of children were receiving its benefits. According to a Children's Bureau study conducted by Evelina Belden in 1918, there were 321 courts with separate hearings for juveniles and regular probation services. Of these, 56 were cities with populations over 100,000; 118 in towns and cities of between 25,000 and 100,000; and 105 in towns of between 5,000 and 25,000. Only 42 served predominantly rural areas.[32] Children's Bureau Director Grace Abbott spelled out the deficiency: "Since approximately fifty percent of our population lives in rural areas and the proportion of children in the rural population is greater than that in the urban, the failure to make the juvenile courts available to these children is very serious."[33] Blame was attributed to a continuing and widespread lack of understanding as to the real significance and purpose of the juvenile court on the part of social workers, members of the bar, and the general public.

Even where juvenile courts had been firmly established, their performance had not always come up to scratch. There were many juvenile courts, it was claimed, where the staff was totally inadequate both in number and in quality, where investigations were superficial, and where results were obtained mainly by trial and error rather than according to casework methods. The institutions to which children were sent were often overcrowded and retained punitive attitudes. Furthermore, it was declared, few studies had been made to assess the effectiveness of the different types of treatment meted out by the court.[34]

Far more fundamental than this denigration of the court's personnel and facilities was a questioning of the court's expansive jurisdiction. To fill a void in the public child welfare system, the children's court had exerted its influence in all directions. It had set itself up as the premier child-saving institution. Some social workers and members of the legal profession still had faith in the original concept. At the National Conference of Social Work held in 1920, several speakers voiced their preference for a social agency with extensive powers. They gave their support to a court with jurisdiction "broad enough to bring within the state's protection, any child in need of such special care, no matter what the cause— dependents as well as others." The juvenile court alone, it was felt, could coerce relatives, keep a check on the working of other welfare agencies, and give the child the treatment required.[35]

The trend of opinion, however, was in favor of a contraction of the court's jurisdiction. Carl Christian Carstens, speaking at the

Conference on Juvenile Court Standards in 1921, criticized the court for considering itself "the only children's agency of any importance in the community." It attempted to do everything but did nothing particularly well. Carstens blamed ambition on the part of the judge and probation officers for these "excursions into the general field of welfare." The answer, in his opinion, was to transfer some of the court's authority to other agencies.[36] Many of his colleagues had reached a similar conclusion. They condemned the excessive numbers of children being brought to court, the consequent delays in hearing cases, and the insufficient time the judge allotted to each case. Whereas at the time of the court's inception, there had been no other agencies to share the responsibility, now they existed. It was thought that some cases might be better handled by a family court. Other problems might be settled outside the court by nonjudicial agencies. The administration of mothers' pensions was one task that was seen as out of place in court proceedings. In Chicago one valuable morning per week was taken up handling pension applications. Gradually social workers became convinced that "whenever possible, such administrative duties as . . . relief should not . . . be required of the juvenile court but should be administered by agencies organized for that purpose."[37] Poverty was not thought reason enough for a child to be involved with the court. In their study *Juvenile Court and Probation*, published in 1914, social worker Roger N. Baldwin and lawyer Flexner expressed their belief that "the jurisdiction of the court insofar as it applies to the dependent and destitute child, unaccompanied by any act of parental omission, is really misplaced." They thought the court should confine itself to matters of custody, guardianship, neglect, and cases in which parents were diseased or infirm.[38] Some social workers even suggested that neglect charges should not be heard in the juvenile court. This type of action, it was claimed, conferred an unnecessary stigma upon the persons involved. Instead, parents could be dealt with through other nonjudicial agencies or, if they proved intractable, might be prosecuted through other courts.[39]

Although most of the arguments for a contraction of the courts' jurisdiction were concerned with inadequacy of facilities, overloaded calendars and availability of other agencies, there was also some recognition that the vague definitions of delinquency, dependency, and neglect and the unclear lines between them might have unfortunate consequences for the children. In 1921 Edith Abbott and Sophonisba Breckinridge published a study of the early days of the juvenile court for the Russell Sage Foundation. The survey was undertaken with the hope of getting a better understanding of the needs of the youngsters involved and a "more intelligent judgement of the juvenile court's usefulness in child-saving." Among the problems they discovered was the lack of a hard and fast line between the various categories of children. The list of offenses for which delinquents were brought to court sometimes included truancy and dependency as if they were delinquency charges. The two social workers revealed the confusion in the treatment of the different groups. They found that "children are sometimes committed to a delinquent institution and therefore treated as if they were in fact delinquent when the charge in the court record may be only 'lack of care,' 'death of a mother and drunken father,' 'desertion of father and drunkenness of mother' or some similar charge against the home."[40] However, these investigators went no further in exploring the potential for unjust treatment inherent in a view that saw dependency, neglect, and delinquency as different phases of one social phenomenon. Abbott and Breckinridge partly excused the confusion because of the need to treat children according to their needs. Individualized care demanded that there be no rigid classification. While their emphasis on flexibility can be commended, it does not alter the fact that the lack of distinction between the groups of children often allowed the state's interests to triumph over the child's.

It has been left to modern historians and lawyers, such as Anthony Platt and Margaret K. Rosenheim, to spell out the dangers involved. Both writers are well acquainted with the flaws in the present-day juvenile court system and see many of these problems as being of long standing. Platt's examination of the Illinois child-saving system is an important attempt to show the way in which crime control and childsaving were intimately bound together. He demonstrates how the juvenile court law was expanded to include large numbers of predelinquent children whose behavior was seen as sufficiently threatening to warrant legal interference. The judge and the probation officers were frequently influenced in their decisions less by what the child had done or suffered than by what the child might possibly do in the future if left unchecked. An adult would not have been treated in such a way. "Granted the benign motives of the child savers," Platt claims, "the programs they enthusiastically supported diminished the civil liberties and privacy of youth."[41] Rosenheim, in her work on the present-day juvenile justice system, shows that the tension between the desire to protect society and the desire to protect the child still troubles the law's treatment of the child. Pleas for stricter definitions of delinquency, dependency, and neglect heard in 1921 are still being heard in legal circles today, as concerned individuals and organizations try to improve the lot of the child who comes into contact with the law.[42]

The creation of America's juvenile court system was thus not the glorious event prophesied by reformers. It had serious faults that were eventually identified. Nevertheless, it did serve a very valuable purpose. There were many thousands of cases where dependent and neglected children were urgently in need of legal intervention in their lives. Where there were questions of parental custody, deprivation of freedom, or institutional commitment to be decided, the juvenile court offered more hope for constructive treatment than the previous legal structure had done. If not the ultimate in child saving, the juvenile court was one of the more important welfare innovations of the Progressive era.

THE U.S. CHILDREN'S BUREAU

At the same time that the juvenile court was being fitted into America's child welfare jigsaw, another element of state involvement was coalescing in the minds of leading reformers. Once it had been enough to spur local groups, municipal authorities, and state legislatures to correct specific problems. Now, as the century witnessed an epidemic of activity on behalf of children, it seemed imperative to have a national overview. The acceptance of common goals and standards by welfare agencies and the coordination of activities were considered necessary if good will, effort, and expertise were not to result in confusion. The education of a national public seemed a prerequisite for further improvements in welfare. Reformers turned to the federal government as the best agency for achieving these aims.

Throughout the 1890s, a steady stream of complaints could be heard concerning the fragmented nature of child-saving work. Arguments for an increase in state supervision, it will be remembered, condemned the insularity of many associations and agencies, their ignorance of advanced methods of care, and the lack of information available on relevant subjects. The annual meeting of the National Conference of Charities and Correction was often the only oppor- tunity for social workers and philanthropists to find out what was happening in other parts of the country. These few days were precious, but they were hardly enough to provide the delegates with the information they needed. Individual researchers seeking nationwide statistics had to rely on the mail and the cooperation of their fellow social workers. The response was rarely adequate. State boards of charities and correction were increasing their store of knowledge concerning children, but progress was painfully slow. At the national level, government departments incidentally collected factors relating to children but seldom analyzed them for the bene- fit of child welfare agencies. It was not until 1904, for example, that the U.S. Bureau of the Census provided its first reports on the in- mates of benevolent institutions and gave the number of children being housed by them. Welfare workers had to wait a further six years before the Census Bureau gave an estimate of the extent of foster care.[43] What was needed was a national organization to ask and attempt to answer the most important questions relating to children's lives, an organization that would determine the best methods of child-rearing, the minimum necessary period of formal education, the optimum safeguards against exploitation of child labor, and the conditions under which the state might intervene in children's lives for their care and protection.

THE NATIONAL CHILD LABOR COMMITTEE

After 1900 the complaints became more strident and a solution was put forward. The first formulations of a plan for a national fact- finding agency are generally attributed to Florence Kelley and Lillian Wald. Both women had had extensive experience in settle- ment houses, part of the function of which was to act as clearing houses of information on health and welfare problems. Kelley had spent part of her apprenticeship at Hull House in Chicago before moving on to the Henry Street Settlement in New York, where she had met Wald, who was then in charge of public health nursing. They were both acutely aware of the factual void in all areas of child welfare and the limitations this placed on their own work. Deluged by requests for advice, they were forced to admit that there were so many questions of enormous national importance concerning some of which reliable information was "wholly lacking."[44] Settlement house work also taught both women the need for a multiple approach in solving child welfare problems. Everything was related to everything else. A solution to the infant mortality rate could not be pursued independently of family welfare, which in turn was dependent on community welfare. This flexible, multi-faceted approach would later become one of the hallmarks of the U.S. Children's Bureau.

The deficiency of information about children's lives and the need for a wide-ranging attack on welfare problems were made even more obvious when the two women stepped outside the confines of the settlement house to support campaigns against abuses by the industrial system, particularly the exploitation of child labor. When Kelley investigated children's working conditions, she rapidly became aware that to ensure productive, healthy working lives for juveniles it was necessary to reform the compulsory education laws, provide mothers' pensions, put through factory safety legislation, and make minimum wage and maximum hours provisions. Such reform depended on the facts being well known. In a series of lectures delivered in 1900 and later published as *Some Ethical Gains in Legislation*, Kelley outlined a U.S. commission that would "correlate, make available and interpret the facts concerning the physical, mental and moral condition and prospects of the children of the United States, native and immigrant." This new body would tackle the most pressing problems of infant mortality, birth registration, mental defectiveness, delinquency, orphanage, desertion, illegitimacy, illiteracy, offenses against children, and child labor.[45] Wald's thoughts followed a similar path. During a breakfast conversation at the Henry Street Settlement, the two women angrily discussed that day's newpaper account of congressional financing of a campaign to fight the boll weevil. It seemed blatantly unjust to them that children should not have a greater claim on the federal government's funds.[46]

Initial moves toward a Children's Bureau were made under the auspices of the anti-child-labor organizations. Kelley and Wald took the lead in the creation of a child labor committee within the Association of Neighborhood Workers. This embryonic organization later became the New York Child Labor Committee, which in turn joined with other reform-minded groups throughout the country in April 1904 to become the National Child Labor Committee (NCLC). The Committee's prime goal was the amendment of state legislation to protect youngsters from too-early labor and ensure educational opportunities. Its immediate task was to collect information. Only then could reformers begin to educate public opinion and convince opponents. Much of the legwork had to be done by the committee members themselves. As Assistant Secretary Owen Lovejoy recollected, it seemed to the committee "that very much of the time and strength expended . . . could be done much better and much more appropriately by the government than by any private organization." The members felt that it was not their duty but the state's to know how many children were employed and under what conditions. "What are [government] departments for if they are not to furnish to the people information concerning the working children at a time when it can be used?" The same paucity of data crippled other areas of child welfare reform. Consequently, at a meeting of the committee's Board of Trustees (previously the Executive Committee) on April 22, 1905, the concept of a federal children's bureau was formally endorsed.[47]

THE CHILDREN'S BUREAU BILL

Having received the support of President Theodore Roosevelt and a number of government officials, the committee drew up a bill for a federal agency, the duty of which would be "the collection of information and the dissemination of the results of the latest scientific work on the care and protection of children, then furnishing to the several states the basis for wise legislation and to the officers of states' boards the information necessary to efficient administration of laws relating to the welfare of children."[48] While it is clear that initially the proponents of the bill fully intended the children's bureau to be a spearhead of reform, the bill was later redrafted to emphasize the less controversial task of information collection.

The Federation of Women's Clubs and the National Consumers' League added their support to the NCLC campaign by petitioning their representatives. Unfortunately, their efforts were in vain. The bill introduced into the U.S. Senate in January 1906 and into the House in May of that year was met with polite indifference and was never reported out of committee.

After this rebuff, the NCLC temporarily shelved the idea of a children's bureau and turned its attention to the possibility of a federal child labor law. When this also failed, it reverted to the fight for the bureau. This time the campaign was more extensive and more efficiently organized. Thousands of pamphlets and letters were distributed to influential individuals and groups, with encouraging results. Clergymen, lawyers, social workers, journalists, and other professionals voiced their approval, as did organizations like the American Medical Association and the American Federation of Labor.

In January 1909 the White House Conference on the Care of Dependent Children brought the issue to the attention of leaders in the child welfare field. In a wise move, the need for a federal bureau was closely linked to the problems of dependent children, thus partially removing it from its potentially controversial connection with child labor regulation. The support from the delegates was overwhelming, although some, like Folks and James West (secretary of the National Child Rescue League), expressed a strong preference for a private fact-finding agency. West's anxieties concerning increasing state control of child-rearing mores and the possible conflicts between state and federal jurisdictions prefigured later hostile responses to the children's bureau bill. The majority were clearly in favor of a government organization, but acknowledging the arguments of the minority, they also accepted a resolution for the establishment of a private agency—a desire fulfilled in 1920 by the creation of the Child Welfare League of America.[49]

At the time of the conference a bill to establish the bureau was pending in Congress. As a result of the White House meeting, Roosevelt was persuaded to send a personal message to Congress arguing that "it is not only discreditable to us as a people that there is no recognized and authoritative source of information upon these subjects relating to child life, but in the absence of such information as should be supplied by the Federal Government many abuses have gone unchecked, for public sentiment, with its great corrective power, can only be aroused by full knowledge of the facts."[50]

Additional pressure was created by the establishment of an NCLC office in Washington early in 1909 to lobby politicians, answer queries, and sway the opposition. Presbyterian minister Alexander J. McKelway, the committee's assistant secretary for the southern states, was given the unenviable task of lobbyist. He engineered House and Senate committee hearings on the children's bureau bills, at which an impressive array of experts gave evidence in favor of such legislation. These prominent social workers, judges, and philanthropists reiterated arguments that had already been widely publicized. They berated the U.S. government for its apathy toward children, for its ignorance of how many were born and died and how they were cared for. Folks put forward the case for the dependent child. There was, he claimed, "no authoritative statement of the total amount of such work [for dependent children] and far less any authoritative interpretation of the work, of the results of the experience; of what becomes of these children; of what kinds of citizens they are making." It was thought that social workers, given the right information, might not only tackle the immediate problem of dependency more successfully but might work toward the "obliteration of the dependent child as a class." The work of the children's bureau, it was emphasized, would not duplicate that done by the existing U.S. Bureau of the Census, Department of Labor, or Bureau of Education. Furthermore, by confining itself to research and investigation, it would not infringe upon the liberties of the states.[51]

Despite the broadened support for the children's bureau bill and the NCLC's more effective lobbying tactics, the proposed legislation made slow progress against congressional inertia and the opposition of conservative organizations and defenders of child labor. It was delayed, diverted, and dismissed through session after session of Congress. As might have been expected, the New York SPCC made its presence felt, waging a constant campaign against the bill. Elbridge Gerry's successor, John W. Lindsay, repeatedly expressed his disdain for "academic" research that, he believed, would interfere with the immediate treatment of abuse and neglect. Government activity in this area would "inevitably lead to confusion, friction of authority and the serious derangement of our work."[52] It would gobble up private bequests that might more profitably go to his organization. Lindsay and Gerry were also among critics of the centralizing tendency of recent welfare legislation. To Gerry, the scheme for a children's bureau was "a dangerous one." Practically, it created "an additional department of the United States Government for the purpose of dictating to states the laws they should pass for their own government on the subject of children."[53] In a minority statement attached to a House report on the proposed bureau, opponents of the bill similarly claimed this particular field of interest to be "specifically the work of the states." It was felt that the entrance of the national government would lead to a cessation of interest on the part of the states. Ignoring the claim that the work of the bureau was sanctioned by the general welfare clause of the Constitution, critics condemned it as an invalid aggrandizement of federal power.[54]

Besides being unconstitutional, the new legislation was also seen as a threat to the sacred privacy of American family life. Senator Weldon B. Heyburn of Idaho, speaking at the second session of the 62nd Congress in 1912, brought up this objection. Assuring his fellow congressmen of his sympathy for the needs of youth, he nevertheless condemned the bill for its attack on the rights of parents. Child labor regulation was also part of this sinister trend in legislation. Heyburn was adamant that "while upon the face of the measure it merely provides for the taking of statistics, the accumulation of knowledge, yet we know from other measures which have been introduced, some from the same source, that it contemplates the establishment of a control, through the agencies of government, over the rearing of children." To quell this complaint, reformers were forced to insert a clause in the original bill stating that no official of the bureau would enter a house against the wishes of the head of the family.[55]

A further challenge to the children's bureau came from those who felt that the necessary research and investigation could more effectively be carried out by an existing government department. Throughout the debate, various suggestions were made to incorporate the new work into the Bureau of the Census or the Department of Commerce and Labor. However, the respective heads of these departments, S.N.D. North and C. P. Neill, had resisted this move and had given their opinions in favor of a separate agency. In 1910 the idea of child welfare being incorporated into a new bureau of health was tossed around. President William Howard Taft was keenly promoting increased efficiency and economy in government and found this solution far more palatable. Reformers strongly rejected the suggestions.

Finally, in 1911, the Bureau of Education sought to swallow up the proposed children's bureau. Unlike his predecessor, the new commissioner of education, Philander P. Claxton, denied the need for a separate agency. "All the items specified with one possible exception (child labor) are," he claimed, "either direct or indirect problems of education." With a larger appropriation from the federal government, Claxton felt that he could adequately investigate a wide variety of children's problems. Wald and Lovejoy politely tried to convince him of the mutuality of their interests but refused to consider this alternative at such a late date. They pressed on with their campaign.[56]

Hostility and indifference were gradually worn down, and success eventually came. On January 31, 1912, the bill passed the Senate, on April 2 the House of Representatives, and seven days later President Taft put his signature to it. The new act placed the Children's Bureau in the Department of Commerce and Labor. The United States now had an agency to investigate and report "upon all matters pertaining to the welfare of children and child life among all classes of our people."

STAFFING THE BUREAU

The main decision that remained concerned the appointment of a chief. Jane Addams and Wald were favorites for the position, but both immediately declined. Samuel McClune Lindsay, professor of social legislation at Columbia University and one of the key members of the NCLC, also rejected the offer. As a result, Lathrop found herself at the helm of this important controversial organization and faced with the task of proving its worth.[57]

The federal Children's Bureau was the first government agency to have a female head. Addams, considering possible candidates for the job, thought that it would be a pity "not to have a woman and a very able woman in the position." In many ways, as Nancy Weiss has argued, the history of the Children's Bureau is inseperable from the history of a group of strong, ambitious women— Addams, Lathrop, Kelley, Grace Abbott, and Wald. The bureau would be "a focal point of the newly emerging career woman and for the professional and social leverage for which women were striving." These women came from similar backgrounds. With the exception of Wald their families were middle class and reform-oriented; they had fathers who supported female education, and strong female role models in their immediate families, to provide them with greater options than the domestic future of most of their contemporaries. College had given them an intellectual armory and a determination to use their knowledge in a practical and humanitarian manner. It had also provided them with a sense of community among women, a familial alternative that they were to recreate in the settlement houses after graduation and in their lifelong friendships. These women, like many of their generation, needed to create a place for themselves in society where their talents and ambition might be given rein. Activity on behalf of children and the family was a socially acceptable outlet for their considerable intelligence and energy. The Children's Bureau was merely one, though a very important, aspect of their work on behalf of America's children.[58]

NEW ROLE FOR THE FEDERAL GOVERNMENT

The creation of the Children's Bureau signaled the entry of the federal government into the child welfare arena. Until the twentieth century the strength of voluntarism and the sensitivity of state governments had allowed the federal government only a negligible part to play in providing welfare services. The fleeting experiment of the Freedman's Bureau, occasional donations of land to institutions, and the release of public lands in the Northwest Territory for the support of schools had been its major sallies into this area. Dorothea Dix's hard won battle for aid to house and maintain the nation's mentally ill had achieved short-lived results. Passed by

Congress in 1854, the bill to appropriate land to help pay for the construction of mental hospitals was brought down by President Franklin Pierce's veto. Declaring that he could not "find any authority in the Constitution for making the Federal Government the great almoner of public charity throughout the United States," Pierce returned welfare responsibility back to the states. The Children's Bureau was thus an adventurous move, the first stirrings of a leviathan, which would gradually gain momentum through the following decades.[59]

THE BUREAU STARTS WORK

The bureau began operations in a very modest fashion. Despite pleas for an appropriation of $164,640, it was allotted a miserly $25,640 during its first year. This magnanimous gesture provided for a staff of 15 to formulate the basic goals and start a program of research. Fortunately, as a result of Lathrop's determination to secure appointments for merit rather than political reward, all 15 of the other staff members were hand picked, committed, and efficient colleagues. Lathrop waged a diplomatic campaign to increase the bureau's financial support. By 1915 the keepers of the purse increased the annual allowance to the original figure, at which time the staff was increased fivefold. Nevertheless, the government's parsimony was to hamper the functioning of the bureau for most of its career.[60]

Various tasks were begun immediately. Recognizing that one object of the agency was "to bring together the existing material relating to children so that we might know what is being done throughout this country and in foreign countries for the welfare of children."[61] the bureau laid the foundations of a specialized library. A librarian-translator was secured whose job, for the first lean years, was to cajole books, pamphlets, and reports from federal agencies and private welfare organizations. The growth of the Library Division (as it became in 1915) allowed the staff to tackle another duty, that of answering the voluminous correspondence that poured into its offices. Requests for information came from all parts of the United States as well as from foreign nations. In 1916, for example, the bureau replied to over 53,000 letters, providing the correspondents with specific data, including printed material where possible, or referring them to specialized organizations that could offer help. One type of information the bureau provided was, of course, statistical. Although the Children's Bureau did not see itself as primarily a statistical agency, it did see the necessity for a solid foundation of factual information. A separate division was thus organized in 1915 to bring together and correlate statistics that had already been collected by the federal government on questions of infant mortality, education, labor, and dependency. When the bureau's field investigations got underway, a new source of statistical information was opened up to bureau analysts.[62]

Although a large part of the material gathered and prepared by the Children's Bureau was directed at professionals in the child welfare field, the general public was not forgotten. The education of the mass of Americans as to the problems confronting the nation's children was high on the bureau's list of priorities. For this reason its members never neglected an opportunity to reach a wider audience. Short stories and bulletins were passed on to daily newspapers; articles were written for magazines; and exhibitions were staged in which photographs, lantern slides, models, and discussions brought home the message of child health and welfare.[63]

INFANT MORTALITY

Collection and redistribution of second-hand information was one important part of the work of the Children's Bureau. Original research was another. The problems of dependent children cried out for attention but had to vie with those of other handicapped and disadvantaged groups. Money was scarce, the staff limited. With only $2,500 and two field investigators, the bureau could not undertake any wide-ranging program of investigation in 1913. In consequence, the study of infant mortality was chosen as a starting point. Given the opposition to the bureau's creation, the infant death rate was thought to be perhaps the least controversial area of child welfare, far less so than child labor or delinquency. Infant mortality investigations were designated as "baby-saving" campaigns to further quell anxiety, and the emphasis was placed on fact finding. Of course, in the Progressive reformer's mind, knowledge and action were closely linked, and exposure of social ills

was taken as leading quite naturally to legislative change. Lathrop
was not alone in believing that "if the Government can 'investigate
and report' upon infant mortality, the conscience and power of
local communities can be depended upon for necessary action."[64]

For two years the topic absorbed almost the entire force of the
bureau. Indeed, prior to 1920 the protection of infancy and maternity largely eclipsed other child welfare issues. The first report was
innovative and, while not attacking poverty directly, established an
incontrovertible connection between poverty and a high infant
death rate. The factual study was made of a small industrial city,
Johnstown, Pennsylvania. Bureau staff, aided by a phalanx of
volunteers from women's organizations, secured birth records of
infants born in 1911 and traced their careers over the next 12
months, if indeed they survived that period. The average death rate
was found to be 134 per 1,000 live births, this figure rising to 171
per 1,000 for children of foreign parents.[65]

This survey and later analyses had many repercussions. They
gave impetus to reform movements seeking better sanitary conditions, minimum wage legislation, and widows' pensions. Within
the bureau they encouraged the dissemination of simple, authoritative literature for parents on the care of their infants. Unfortunately, this literature clearly presumed middle-class incomes and
promoted middle-class, native-born American mores. Advice to
engage a nurse for the month after childbirth and to breast-feed
for one year was only relevant to families with a reasonable standard
of living. Warnings concerning feeding infants certain types of
"ethnic" food demonstrated a lack of sympathy for culturally
diverse methods of child rearing. Despite this, the pamphlets did
provide a vast amount of important material for parents, who were
increasingly convinced that parenthood was a scientific undertaking, to be approached with due seriousness.[66]

By shining a light on infant mortality, bureau staff inadver-
tently illuminated the increasing maternal death rate, a problem
that had been neglected "due to age-long ignorance and fatalism."
A program for new legislation to protect mothers and infants was
outlined. It included availability of public health nurses, hospital
and medical attention for mothers, instruction in hygiene, and
centers for advice. Importantly, the legislation allowed for federal
grants to the states to implement its provisions. Supported by

social workers, women's organizations, and the American Federation of Labor, the Sheppard-Towner Bill was passed in 1921 by large congressional majorities. Unfortunately, this pioneer attempt at federal grants-in-aid was to be crushed seven years later when the specter of paternalism and socialism reappeared.[67]

CHILD LABOR

Although the bureau was expressly designated as an agency to "serve all children," it was still very much concerned with the problems of the handicapped. Investigations were begun into a number of problems of special need. The conditions of working children received attention from 1916 onwards. Treading carefully and insisting that "the role of the Federal Government must play in the training of children is that of an intelligent and interested cooperator, ready to assist but not to control nor hamper,"[68] the bureau nevertheless played an important part in the nation's reassessment of the value of child labor. Its activity was directed along three lines. First, the bureau produced statistics, surveys, and complemented and expanded the invaluable investigations that had inadequate legal safeguards against exploitation. Its work thus complemented and expanded the invaluable investigations already already been conducted by the National Child Labor Committee. Second, the Children's Bureau did much to promote the idea of children as dependent beings, who needed to be excluded from the labor market for a longer period. This involved a rethinking not only of the value of labor for young persons but also of the necessity for compulsory education. As one member of the bureau explained, "we used to think that the care of our children was entirely an affair of the home. It was a great step forward when, after much opposition, the idea that it is the duty of the State to furnish schools for its children and to see that they attend those schools, gradually found expression in our public school system and our compulsory education laws."[69] Finally, for the 273 days between September 1, 1917, and June 3, 1918, during which the Federal Child Labor Law was in force, the bureau was charged with its administration. Grace Abbott, who joined the bureau to supervise its enforcement, fought a difficult battle to ensure that children under 14 years of age were excluded from industries that transported goods interstate and internationally and that children between the ages of 14 and 16 were issued with the appropriate age certificates. During the short period of the law's enforcement, Abbott issued 19,546 certificates in five states. Even after the law was declared unconstitutional, she managed to guarantee that federal standards were adhered to on all government contracts.[70]

DELINQUENTS

Juvenile delinquents and the mentally handicapped also received their share of inquiry. Starting with the juvenile courts in Connecticut and the District of Columbia in 1914, the bureau went on to investigate the working of children's courts in selected areas throughout the country. In 1918 the bureau conducted a study of delinquency in wartime and attempted to piece together an overall picture of the juvenile court movement. As a result of field work undertaken in 1921 on the organization and methods of 10 courts, a two-day conference on juvenile court standards was held in June of that year under the joint auspices of the Children's Bureau and the National Probation Association. Some of the criticisms heard at that conference have already been mentioned in this chapter. Thus during its early years the bureau made a valuable contribution to the nation's assessment of its juvenile legal system, pointing out the flaws and foibles and the considerable diversity in organization, procedure, and jurisdiction. This in turn encouraged the formulation of standards for America's juvenile courts.

THE MENTALLY HANDICAPPED

The mentally handicapped were not overlooked. At the request of a local citizens' committee, the bureau undertook an investigation of the mentally defective children in the District of Columbia and, following this, two studies—one rural, one urban—in Delaware. In 1919 an attempt was made to draw out some of the connections between delinquency and mental retardation. While the problems of this group of children could only claim a small part of the bureau's funds and energy, a start was nevertheless made in improving facilities for children with intellectual deficiencies.[71]

THE DEPENDENT AND NEGLECTED

Finally, there were the dependent and neglected, a group whose numbers were unknown and whose treatment was only vaguely understood. The Children's Bureau did not try to delve into all aspects of the problems of this group. Instead it concentrated its energy in areas that were currently major topics of interest in the child welfare field. The mothers' pension movement was an obvious starting point. The staff of the bureau, like their colleagues in other welfare organizations, felt that "the majority of dependent children are members of families and therefore the question of protecting children must be considered as a question of family structure and support." As advocates of child labor regulation, they also wanted to know what supplementary provisions were necessary to keep children out of the work force. A study of the still-experimental mothers' pension movement seemed timely. In 1914, a brief report on current legislation in the United States, New Zealand, and Denmark was submitted. This was later revised by Laura A. Thompson in 1919. Apart from offering a detailed account of the laws themselves, the later study gave a history of the development of the movement and indicated problems in the operation of the laws. It illuminated the inequalities within the states and between the states. The survey also showed the inadequacy of the welfare machinery used to administer the pensions and the insufficient amounts meted out to the families concerned. By doing so it encouraged a liberalization of the mothers' pension laws and a tightening up of their operation. Interest in this area continued, and the bureau periodically updated its survey of legislation and investigated the administration and casework services involved in the pension program.[72]

ILLEGITIMACY

Illegitimacy was a second major focus of attention. In the third annual report of 1915, Lathrop discussed the bureau's reasons for initiating a study of the conditions of children born out of wedlock. The bureau was interested in the handicap of illegitimacy not only for its effect on the individual child, but also for "the light it should throw upon studies which are now under way or which the bureau is directed to make."[73] Infant mortality, orphanage, adoption, and institutional care were areas that would presumably be clarified by a study of illegitimacy. The United States, it was realized, was far behind many European countries in its knowledge of the relation of illegitimate children to their families and communities. The interest shown by Americans had so far been mainly local.

The bureau was determined to rectify this situation. When the results of its investigations were finally published in 1920 and 1921, social workers had before them the basic dimensions of the illegitimacy problem. For the first time there was an assessment of the prevalence of illegitimacy in America. Social workers were made aware of the high death rate of children born out of wedlock, of these children's vulnerability under the prevailing legal system, and of the existing facilities for the care of unmarried mothers and their infants. An in-depth study of the fate of 782 illegitimate babies in Boston provided further insight into the family backgrounds of the youngsters, the possibilities of parental care, the relationship between illegitimacy and dependency, and the need for new support legislation.

There is no doubt that the bureau was encouraged in its investigations by the outbreak of war in Europe. Although it was realized that the increase in the European rate of illegitimacy was not as dramatic as it had been portrayed and that the rate in the United States was much lower, nevertheless the bureau felt that "in making plans for government allowances, the question of the support of illegitimate children of members of the military must be considered." The fears of social workers that America might be inundated with illegitimate children kept up pressure for a continued examination of the conditions affecting illegitimacy.[74]

A number of publications followed, clarifying the social and legal positions of these children. A 1918 translation of the progressive Norwegian Castberg law demonstrated to reformers the possibilities for improvement. Similarly, a compilation of relevant laws in the United States and other foreign countries enabled reformers to see the inequities in U.S. legislation. Perhaps the most important monograph distributed by the bureau was *Standards of Legal Protection for Children Born out of Wedlock*, an account of the conferences on illegitimacy held in Chicago and New York during February 1920. The Children's Bureau had previously held local conferences with associations dealing with unmarried mothers. In 1920, however, nationally recognized leaders in social welfare met to consider urgently needed reforms. The resolutions of the two conferences were virtually identical. Both called for immediate improvements in the registration of births, in the nature of paternity proceedings, and in the amount of support given to a child. All the delegates advocated greater state participation to protect the interests of children born out of wedlock, in particular the licensing and supervision of hospitals receiving unmarried mothers. They also voiced their approval of the extension of inheritance rights and the child's right to the paternal surname once paternity had been established. The creation of this consensus of opinion among influential welfare figures was an important boost to securing reforms during the 1920s.[75]

INSTITUTIONS AND FOSTER CARE

In comparison with the issues of pensions and illegitimacy, the actual care of dependent and neglected children away from the family home received relatively little attention before 1920. The only institutional study done in the early years, for instance, was the one of defective children in the District of Columbia. In wartime more general welfare considerations, such as child labor, education, and the protection of infants took precedence over institutions and foster care. As the bureau's chief explained in the annual report of 1918, "naturally the emphasis of the year's work has been on the wartime care of children, which is more at hazard as industry and society are increasingly affected by the organization and maintenance of the military forces." Nevertheless, in 1917 the bureau did start drawing up plans for a nationwide survey of state provisions for dependent children. Its aim was "to learn how much such public responsibility is recognized and how expressed." The question of institutional and foster care also received some attention at the White House Conference on Child Welfare Standards, the second White House conference, which was held in 1919.[76]

This conference was a culmination of the Children's Year activities of 1918 and was sponsored by President Woodrow Wilson's emergency fund for the purpose of "bringing together and co-ordinating opinion concerning the welfare of children in the United States."[77] Two hundred social workers, educators, pediatricians, judges, and medical personnel met in Washington in May

1919 to formulate basic standards of health, education, and welfare. Their efforts were supplemented by eight regional conferences. If major themes may be singled out, they were the need for more public activity on behalf of children and the need to recognize the individual characteristics of each child in the solution of welfare problems. With respect to dependent and neglected children, the 1919 conference resolutions reaffirmed all the basic tenets of the 1909 meeting. They stressed the value of home life and the wisdom of preventing the breakup of the family unit where possible. However, more emphasis was laid upon the need for an adequate income and the responsibility of the government to supplement the resources of the family where necessary. Mothers' pensions had by this time been accepted as a vital and valuable part of the welfare system. The commitment to foster care was even stronger in 1919 than it had been ten years earlier. Delegates voiced their overwhelming support for child placing, provided that "adequate consideration... be given to... health, mentality, character and family history and circumstances." The necessity of proper investigation, of the keeping of records, and of state supervision was stressed once again.[78]

It was in the 1920s that bureau activity in the area of institutional and foster care really gained momentum. Studies were made, for example, of children deprived of family care in Delaware and their subsequent placement in foster homes. Among other things, the bureau confirmed the fact that a large percentage of the children had two parents living and might possibly have been saved from the emotional ordeal of separation. A wider study was made in 1922 of the methods of two statewide and ten community organizations. The product was a monograph entitled *Foster Home Care for Dependent Children*, in which 11 child welfare authorities contributed influential articles on subjects ranging from state supervision to standards of case work. Further surveys were made of the development of adoption legislation, of the continued use of indenture in Wisconsin, and of the current status of interstate placement laws. Finally, at the request of a number of states the bureau undertook a series of studies to evaluate the methods and results of state activities on behalf of dependent, neglected, and delinquent children.[79]

ACCOMPLISHMENTS

The development of the Children's Bureau along the lines envisaged by its creators was not an easy task. The budget allotted to the agency remained small. Lathrop, addressing the National Conference of Social Work in 1921, expressed her disappointment that the bureau's share of the funds for educational, social, and industrial research was still less than one-half of one percent.[80] Finances and expertise had to be distributed in a highly discriminating manner. The problems of dependent and neglected children had to compete with those of other, equally handicapped groups of youngsters. Despite this, certain areas were investigated, information was collected and disseminated, and compilations of the laws were made. These activities clarified issues for members of the social work profession; they encouraged the formulation of standards of treatment; and they provided the factual basis for changes in legislation and improvement of its administration. The tentative steps taken before 1920 in the study of mothers' pension, illegitimacy, and foster care prepared the way for larger studies in the following decades.

NOTES

1. Julia Lathrop, "The Background of the Juvenile Court in Illinois," in Jane Addams, ed., *The Child, the Clinic and the Court* (New York: New Republic, 1925), pp. 291-92. Robert H. Bremner, ed., *Children and Youth in America: A Documentary History* (Cambridge, Mass.: Harvard University Press, 1971), vol. 2, pp. 494-95.

2. Robert Mennel, *Thorns and Thistles: Juvenile Delinquency in the United States 1825-1940* (Hanover, N.H.: University Press of New England, 1973), pp. 80-99, William A. White quoted p. 88.

3. Julian Mack, "Juvenile Courts as Part of the School System of the Country," *Proceedings of the 35th NCCC*, 1908, p. 373.

4. Anthony M. Platt, *The Child Savers: The Invention of Delinquency* (Chicago: University of Chicago Press, 1969). Joseph M. Hawes, *Children in Urban Society: Juvenile Delinquency in Nineteenth Century America* (New York: Oxford University Press, 1971).

5. Letter of Lucy L. Flower to Louise de Koven Bowen, May 1917 (papers of the Juvenile Protective Association, University of Illinois, Chicago Circle, Ill.), p. 1.

6. Hawes, *Children in Urban Society*, pp. 163-67.

7. Julia Lathrop, "Memorandum," 1902 (papers of the Juvenile

Protective Association), p. 2. As shown in Chapter 2 of this book, Lathrop was president of the Juvenile Court Committee of the Illinois Board of Public Charities.

8. Rev. Lloyd Jenkins Jones, "Who are the Children of the State?," *Proceedings of the Third Illinois Conference of Charities and Correction*, 1898, p. 281. Frederick Wines, closing speech, *Proceedings of the Third Illinois Conference of Charities and Correction*, 1898, p. 336.

9. Timothy Hurley, *Origin of the Juvenile Court Law* (Chicago: Visitation and Aid Society, 1907), pp. 18-24.

10. Helen Jeter and Sophonisba P. Breckinridge, *A Summary of Juvenile Court Legislation in the United States*, U.S. Children's Bureau Publication no. 70 (Washington, D.C.: Government Printing Office, 1920), pp. 10-11. Benjamin Barr Lindsey, "Colorado's Contribution to the Juvenile Court," in Addams, *The Child, the Clinic and the Court*, pp. 275-89.

11. Hurley, *Origin of the Juvenile Court Law*, p. 79.

12 .Jeter and Breckinridge, *A Summary of Juvenile Court Legislation*, pp. 19-21.

13. Hastings Hornell Hart, statement, *Proceedings of the 14th Illinois Conference of Charities and Correction*, 1909, p. 634.

14. *Annual Report of the Cook County Juvenile Court*, in Cook County, Ill., Board of Commissioners, *Charity Service Report*, 1905, pp. 100-4.

15. Helen Jeter, *The Chicago Juvenile Court* (Chicago: University of Chicago Press, 1922), pp. 11-12.

16. "Report of the Sub-Committee on Juvenile Courts," *Proceedings of the 32nd NCCC*, 1905, p. 151.

17. Theodore Roosevelt, quoted ibid.

18. Henry Thurston, "The Relation of the Juvenile Court to Public Schools and other Social Agencies," *Proceedings of the 14th Illinois Conference of Charities and Correction*, 1909, p. 657.

19. Hurley, *Origin of the Juvenile Court Law*, p. 62.

20. Bernard Flexner, "A Decade of the Juvenile Court," *Proceedings of the 37th NCCC*, 1910, p. 17.

21. Richard Tuthill, quoted in Commercial Club of Chicago, *How Can Juvenile Offenders be Cared for and Reformed?* (Chicago, 1900), p. 60.

22. Frank T. Flynn, "Judge Merritt W. Pinckney and the Early Days of the Juvenile Court in Chicago," *Social Service Review* 28 (1954): 20-30. Peter G. Slater, "Ben Lindsey and the Denver Juvenile Court: A Progressive Looks at Human Nature," *American Quarterly* 20 (1968): 211-23. Benjamin Barr Lindsey to Charles R. Henderson, August 29, 1904, quoted in *Thorns and Thistles: Juvenile Delinquency in the United States 1825-1940*, Robert Mennel (Hanover, N.H.: University Press of New England, 1973), p. 137.

23. Julian Mack, "Chancery Procedure in the Juvenile Court," in Addams, *The Child, the Clinic and the Court*, p. 313.

24. Homer Folks, "Juvenile Probation," *Proceedings of the 35th NCCC*, 1906, pp. 117-22. Louise de Koven Bowen, "The Early Days of the Juvenile Court," in Addams, *The Child, the Clinic and the Court*, p. 300. Hurley, *Origin of the Juvenile Court Law*, quoted p. 62.

25. Jeter, *The Chicago Juvenile Court*, pp. 36-37. *Annual Reports of the Cook County Juvenile Court*, in *Charity Service Reports*, 1914, pp. 3-4, 7; 1918, p. 216.

26. Jeter, *The Chicago Juvenile Court*, p. 58. Merritt W. Pinckney, "The Juvenile Court," in Addams, *The Child, the Clinic and the Court*, p. 318.

27. Jeter, *The Chicago Juvenile Court*, p. 84. *Annual Report of the Cook County Juvenile Court*, in *Charity Service Report*, 1905, p. 100.

28. Jeter, *The Chicago Juvenile Court*, p. 65.

29. Hastings Hornell Hart, statement, *Proceedings of the 14th Illinois Conference of Charities and Correction*, 1909, p. 635.

30. Hurley, *Origin of the Juvenile Court Law*, p. 63.

31. U.S. Children's Bureau, *Proceedings of the Conference on Juvenile Court Standards*, held in June 1921, Publication no. 97 (Washington, D.C.: Government Printing Office, 1921), Julia Lathrop quoted p. 8; Edward Schoen quoted p. 33.

32. Evelina Belden, *Courts in the United States Hearing Children's Cases*, U.S. Children's Bureau Publication no. 65 (Washington, D.C.: Government Printing Office, 1920), pp. 11-12.

32. Grace Abbott, "A History of the Juvenile Court Movement throughout the World," in Addams, *The Child, the Clinic and the Court*, p. 268.

34. Katharine Lenroot and Emma O. Lundberg, *Juvenile Courts at Work*, U.S. Children's Bureau Publication no. 141 (Washington, D.C.: Government Printing Office, 1925), pp. 30, 99. J. Prentice Murphy, "The Juvenile Court at the Bar," *AAAPSS*, 145 (1920), pp. 80-97. Lilburn Merrill, "Diagnostic Methods as an Aid in Juvenile Court Administration," *Proceedings of the 40th NCCC*, 1913, p. 325.

35. Samuel Murphy, "The Aims and Methods of the Juvenile Court as Distinguished from Criminal Procedure in General," *Proceedings of the 47th NCSW*, 1920, p. 170.

36. Carl Christian Carstens, statement, *Proceedings of the Conference on Juvenile Court Standards*, pp. 9-10.

37. U.S. Children's Bureau, *Standards of Child Welfare: A Report of the Children's Bureau Conference, 1919*, Publication no. 60 (Washington, D.C.: Government Printing Office, 1919), p. 15.

38. Bernard Flexner and Roger N. Baldwin, *Juvenile Courts and Probation* (New York: Century, 1912), pp. x, xi, xvii, quoted p. x.

39. Alfred F. Whitman, "Keeping Neglected Children out of Court," *Proceedings of the 47th NCSW*, 1920, p. 87.

40. Edith Abbott and Sophonisba P. Breckinridge, *The Delinquent Child and the Home* (New York: Russell Sage, 1912), quoted pp. 11-12, 174.

41. Platt, *The Child Savers*, pp. 3-4, 10-11, 134-35, 137-45, quoted p. 4.

42. Margaret K. Rosenheim, "Wards of Court: A Perspective on Justice for Children," in Alvin Schorr, *Children and Decent People* (New York: Basic Books, 1974), pp. 165-72.

43. U.S. Bureau of the Census, *Benevolent Institutions, 1904* and *Benevolent Institutions, 1910* (Washington, D.C.: Government Printing Office, 1905 and 1913).

44. Lillian Wald, *The House on Henry Street* (New York: H. Holt & Co., 1915), p. 163.

45. Florence Kelley, *Some Ethical Gains through Legislation* (New York: Macmillan, 1905), pp. 99-104, quoted p. 99.

46. Nancy Weiss, "Save the Children: A History of the United States Children's Bureau 1912-1918" (Ph.D. diss., UCLA, 1974), p. 48. Weiss's dissertation is particularly valuable for its discussion of the changing concept of childhood and for its profile of the women involved in the creation of the Children's Bureau. A more recent, more administrative account has been given by Louis Covotsos, "Child Welfare and Social Progress: A History of the United States Children's Bureau, 1912-1935" (Ph.D. diss., University of Chicago, 1976).

47. Covotsos, "Child Welfare and Social Progress," pp. 20-23. Owen Lovejoy, statement, *Proceedings of the [1909] Conference on the Care of Dependent Children*, p. 178. Florence Kelley, "The Federal Government and Working Children," *AAAPSS* 27 (1906), quoted p. 289.

48. Minutes of the Executive Committee meeting, Oct. 12, 1905, quoted in Walter I. Trattner, *Crusade for the Children* (Chicago: Quadrangle Books, 1970), p. 96.

49. Weiss, "Save the Children," pp. 59-70.

50. Theodore Roosevelt, *Proceedings of the [1909] Conference on the Care of Dependent Children*, p. 7.

51. Arguments before the Committee on Expenditures in the Interior Department, U.S. House of Representatives, Jan. 27, 1909 (Grace Abbott Papers, University of Chicago Library), Homer Folks and William S. Bennett quoted, pp. 2, 4.

52. Letter from John W. Lindsay to Davis Lewis, Feb. 13, 1912 (Grace Abbott papers).

53. Elbridge Gerry, *New York Times*, Jan. 28, 1912, p. 14.

54. *Majority and Minority Report on the Children's Bureau Bill, 1909*, in Robert H. Bremner, *Children and Youth in America: A Documentary History* (Cambridge, Mass.: Harvard University Press, 1971), vol. 2, pp. 762-64.

55. *Congressional Record*, 62nd Cong., 2nd Sess. (1911-12), pp. 764-69, Senator Heyburn quoted p. 765.

56. Covotsos, "Child Welfare and Social Progress," pp. 27-37. Philander P. Claxton, letter to the Secretary of the Interior, Jan. 3, 1912, p. 2 (Grace Abbott papers).

57. Covotsos, "Child Welfare and Social Progress," pp. 40-42. *United States Statutes*, 62nd Cong., 2nd Sess. (1911-12), Part 1, Chapters 73, 79-80.

58. Weiss, "Save the Children," pp. 120-54, Jane Addams quoted p. 120.

59. Walter I. Trattner, *From Poor Law to Welfare State* (New York: Free Press, 1974), pp. 48, 68-62, 76, Pierce quoted p. 62.

60. *Annual Report of the United States Children's Bureau*, 1915, p. 5. Weiss, "Save the Children," pp. 178-84.

61. Lewis Merriam, "The Aim and Objects of the Federal Children's Bureau," *Proceedings of the 40th NCCC*, 1913, p. 318.

62. Ibid., pp. 318-19. *Annual Report of the United States Children's Bureau*, 1917, p. 28.

63. *Annual Report of the United States Children's Bureau*, 1921, p. 30.

64. Weiss, "Save the Children," pp. 185-88. U.S. Children's Bureau, *Infant Mortality: Results of a Field Study in Johnstown, Pa., Based on Births in One Calendar Year* (Washington, D.C.: Government Printing Office, 1915), Julia Lathrop quoted p. 9.

65. Weiss, "Save the Children," pp. 188-93.

66. Ibid., pp. 197-209.

67. Julia Lathrop, "State Care for Mothers and Infants," *Proceedings of the 45th NCSW*, 1918, pp. 389-92. Dorothy E. Bradbury, *Five Decades of Action: A Short History of the Children's Bureau*, U.S. Children's Bureau Publication (Washington, D.C.: Government Printing Office, 1964), pp. 6-11, 13-14.

68. Grace Abbott, "Children's Bureau," *Childhood Education 5* (March 1929): 363.

69. Eva Merritt, "What the Government is Doing to Conserve Child Life," *The Kindergarten and First Grade 4* (May 1919): 174.

70. Weiss, "Save the Children," pp. 255-63.

71. Bradbury, *Five Decades of Action*, pp. 18-20.

72. *Annual Report of the United States Children's Bureau*, 1916, quoted

p. 22. *Laws Relating to Mothers' Pensions in the United States, Denmark and New Zealand*, U.S. Children's Bureau Publication no. 63 (1919). *The Administration of the Aid to Mothers Law in Illinois*, U.S. Children's Bureau Publication no. 82 (1921). *Public Aid to Mothers with Dependent Children*, U.S. Children's Bureau Publication no. 162 (Washington, D.C.: Government Printing Office, 1926).

73. *Annual Report of the United States Children's Bureau*, 1915, p. 15.

74. *Annual Report of the United States Children's Bureau*, 1917, quoted p. 39. Emma O. Lundberg, "Illegitimacy in Europe as Affected by the War," in Emma O. Lundberg and Katharine Lenroot, *Illegitimacy as a Child Welfare Problem*, Parts I and II, U.S. Children's Bureau Publication no. 66 (Washington, D.C.: Government Printing Office, 1920), pp. 299-304.

75. *Norwegian Laws Concerning Illegitimate Children*, U.S. Children's Bureau Publication no. 31 (Washington, D.C.: Government Printing Office, 1918). Ernst Freund, *Illegitimacy Laws in the United States and Foreign Countries*, U.S. Children's Bureau Publication no. 42 (Washington, D.C., Government Printing Office, 1919). *Standards of Legal Protection for Children Born out of Wedlock*, U.S. Children's Bureau Publication no. 77 (Washington, D.C.: Government Printing Office, 1921).

76. *Annual Reports of the United States Children's Bureau*, 1918, quoted p. 5; 1917, p. 25.

77. Julia Lathrop, quoted in *The Story of the White House Conferences on Children and Youth*, U.S. Children's Bureau (Washington, D.C.: Government Printing Office, 1967), p. 6.

78. U.S. Children's Bureau, *Standards of Child Welfare*, pp. 440-42.

79. U.S. Children's Bureau, *Children Deprived of Parental Care: A Study of Children Taken under Care by Delaware Agencies and Institutions*, Publication no. 81 (Washington, D.C.: Government Printing Office, 1921); *Foster Home Care for Dependent Children*, Publication no. 136 (Washington, D.C.: Government Printing Office, 1924); *Children Indentured by the Wisconsin State Public School*, publication no. 150 (Washington, D.C.: Government Printing Office, 1925); *Laws Relating to the Interstate Placement of Dependent Children*, Publication no. 139 (Washington, D.C.: Government Printing Office, 1924); *Child Dependency in the District of Columbia*, Publication no. 140 (Washington, D.C.: Government Printing Office, 1924); *Adoption Laws in the United States*, Publication no. 148 (Washington, D.C.: Government Printing Office, 1925).

80. Julia Lathrop, "Our Nation's Obligation to Her Children," *Proceedings of the 48th NCSW*, 1921, p. 69.

10

THE
PROFESSIONAL
UNDERCURRENT

To many contemporaries the U.S. decision to enter World War I rang the death knell for reform. Historians such as Richard Hofstadter also concluded that "participation in the war put an end to the Progressive movement."[1] Hofstadter saw the second and third decades of this century in direct opposition. Before the Great War, he argued, the domestic scene was dominated by various hard-fought campaigns to improve the harsh urban-industrial environment. Victory, however, ushered in a decade of conservatism in which businessmen and their political allies strove to undermine the new regulations while many other Americans succumbed to crass materialism or demonstrated their intolerance in racist, nativist, and anti-Communist outbursts. Reformers retreated to their private domains.

More recent analyses of the period have placed a greater emphasis on the gradual shift from one era to another, on the elements of continuity that lay beneath the changing surface. Clark C. Chambers and Donald Swain are two commentators who have traced the path of reform in the "age of normalcy." Swain's study of the conservation movement in the 1920s demonstrates that solid gains were made, while Chambers's broader survey of social reformers before 1918 and 1933 similarly shows that reform

was not dead but "merely catching its breath." On the welfare
scene, many voluntary associations "continued to play out their
prophetic role, proclaiming the need for remedy and alleviation,
for prevention and for cure." Though many social workers gave
up the task of reconstruction, others remained to agitate for child
labor regulations, for social insurance, and for improved working
and living conditions. If much of this effort was greeted with
hostility and indifference, nevertheless it maintained an awareness
of unsolved problems that would benefit later campaigns.[2]

Just as the course of social reform may be followed into the
1920s, so the social workers' professional concerns of that decade
may be traced back into the Progressive era. Control of the environment and service to the individual went hand in hand, although
the balance between them varied considerably. In the 1920s, social
workers were preoccupied with the search for professional status.
This involved them in the provision of adequate training and the
development of methods and standards of treatment. These same
concerns formed the undercurrent in the previous period of reform
activity. As this chapter will show, gradual changes took place in
child welfare work before 1920 that would determine the predominant interests of the later years.

EARLY LACK OF THEORY

Before 1890 the dominant emphasis in social work was on the
treatment of the individual. The foremost propaganda agents for
this point of view were the newly founded charity organization
societies. Closely patterned on the London Society for Organising
Charitable Relief and Repressing Mendicancy, the American
associations had spread rapidly since their introduction in 1877.
Their members preached a gospel of benevolence based on the
belief that "charitable work in the best sense must be done by the
individual... for the individual." To them each case was special,
"demanding special diagnosis, keenest differentiation of features
and most intense concentration of thought and effort."[3]

Since they assumed that poverty was a moral issue, the aim of
this rigorous investigation and careful diagnosis was to distinguish
the worthy from the unworthy and subsequently to bring to each
the uplifting influence of charity. Charity organization societies

saw the greatest need as being the moral exhortation of one of their "friendly visitors" rather than the dispensing of relief. These superior creatures were to discern the moral failings involved and to provide the guidance necessary to bring the sinner into a right relation with both family and community. While the charity organization society might employ paid agents to carry out the investigations and to perform other administrative duties, their friendly visitors would be mainly volunteers, who would bring warmth, sympathy, spontaneity, and enthusiasm to the task. The relationship was to be that of neighbor, however unlikely that may have seemed, and not the professional relationship between social worker and client. District committees of residents and representatives of charitable organizations were to be the main link between the poor and their saviors.[4]

Organizations for the care and protection of dependent and neglected children were less inclined to theorize about the basic premises of their work. However, they too were largely concerned with the individual. The major duty, for these associations, was to rescue and place a child in a Christian environment, whether the local orphanage or a willing foster home. Like the charity organization societies, these early agencies made a simplistic, moralistic analysis of the problem. Misfortune or immorality were accepted as the basic causes of dependency and neglect. The parents were dead or destitute, insane, immoral, or incapacitated. There seemed to be no other task than to place the child in another situation, where foster parents or institution staff would provide the required moral guidance.

UNPAID AND UNTRAINED WORKERS

Most of the people connected with child-saving in the late nineteenth century were unpaid workers. Placing-out agents who scoured the countryside for homes were frequently remunerated for their services, either by commission or by a regular salary. Institution staff were similarly employed. Apart from the clergy, who devoted themselves to this mission on a full-time basis, however, the majority of helpers gave their services freely. Boards of directors who defined the agencies' purposes and formulated policies were usually respectable, well-meaning citizens. Local philanthropists also comprised the advisory committees or organizations such as the Illinois Children's Home and Aid Society, the function of which was to recommend suitable applicants for foster children.[5]

Very few of the staff members of these agencies had any training in skills relevant to child welfare work. One early superintendent of the Illinois Soldiers' Orphans' Home had previously been employed by the freight department of the Chicago and Northern Railroad. Other workers were college graduates with no specific social work education. The nearest that Homer Folks came to formal instruction in social work was a course in social ethics under Francis G. Peabody at Harvard University. Apprenticeship was the normal mode of entry into child welfare work. Enthusiastic men and women entered the lower echelons of children's agencies and hoped to acquire the skills necessary to succeed in their chosen field.[6]

A LACK OF INVESTIGATION

Unlike the charity organization societies, the child-saving organizations of the 1880s felt they had little need for detailed investigations of their clients' circumstances. Except to ensure that they were not being taken advantage of by lazy parents, they were not concerned with distinguishing the deserving from the unworthy. Sympathy rather than "scientific charity" was their watchword. Consequently, their standards were generally very poor. Admission policies were largely idiosyncratic. Agencies might admit any child if they had room, regardless of the child's need. Alternatively, they might rule out large numbers of children whose religious backgrounds were thought unsuitable.

The decision as to which children should be placed out was equally haphazard. Youngsters were sorted out by ages, almost by sizes, rather than by their suitability or emotional needs. Placing itself, as mentioned in Chapter 4, was a precarious business. The informal methods of the Illinois Soldiers' Orphans' Home give a suggestion of the laxity of many associations. Persons who wanted a child might drive up to the institution, pick out one that attracted them, and drive away. Rarely did the superintendents write down the addresses of the visitors. When the parents were found by a placing agency, often church attendance and a house were sufficient credentials. There was a widespread, unshakable faith in the ability of a Christian home to fulfill any child's needs.[7] As a result of this superficial matching of child and adult, frequent replacements occurred. The callousness and carelessness involved in moving a child from home to home is reflected in the thoughts of the superintendent of the Bloomington section of the Illinois Children's Home and Aid Society. "Sometimes," he wrote, "it is necessary to place children in homes to see what there is in them."[8]

Very seldom were detailed records kept of these transactions. At the Illinois Children's Home and Aid Society in the early years, each child was registered by a number and a record card was kept that contained little information except name, age, sex, and address. Naturally, supervision standards left a lot to be desired. Sometimes there was no contact at all; on other occasions letters were thought to be sufficient. In the more advanced societies visits were arranged, but often these were no more than quick glances at the children's physical condition and the sleeping arrangements. Abuse and acute unhappiness frequently went undetected.[9]

CHANGES IN ATTITUDE DURING THE PROGRESSIVE ERA

Thus, at the start of the Progressive era, child welfare work was unsystematic and in the hands of people who qualified by their good intentions rather than by their expertise. Concern for morality took precedence over a desire for accurate diagnosis. Societies and institutions were concerned with the individual rather than the environment, but they were light years away from understanding the makeup and emotional needs of each child they received. In the ensuing decades many of their members would turn their attention to legislative campaigns for the improvement of the child's environment and the amelioration of the worst features of urban-industrial America. Folks, Judge Benjamin Barr Lindsey, and Florence Kelley joined forces with others to fight against child labor, tuberculosis, and slum housing. They worked untiringly for better working conditions, health, and accident and unemployment insurance, all of which would reduce the incidence of dependency and neglect. However, this change in emphasis did not mean that the treatment of cases of dependency and neglect was left in suspended animation. Far from it. During this same period, child welfare workers

made significant strides toward treating each child as an individual
human being, with distinct problems that might be known in depth
and hopefully solved. They also began to demand that their colleagues be trained in relevant skills and paid accordingly.

TRAINING

Despite their insistence that paid workers lacked the humanity
and sympathy necessary for effective social work, charity organizations were gradually forced to recruit an increasing number of paid
personnel. Adequate treatment and organizational efficiency forced
agencies to reverse the balance of nineteenth-century philanthropy.
An embryonic concern for professional status similarly encouraged
the demotion of volunteer help. Societies did not want to eliminate
the amateurs altogether, because their contacts with the local community and their ability to raise funds made them essential to the
welfare system. However, their role in the treatment of cases was
increasingly seen as a subordinate one. Hastings Hornell Hart, who
was the superintendent of the Illinois Children's Home and Aid
Society, expressed a common belief when he wrote in his annual
report in 1904 that "we have had much valuable service from
volunteer and unpaid workers but experience proves that
volunteers cannot be depended upon for continuous service.
Volunteers do not have the training and cannot be held to the strict
accountability which is necessary for the detailed work."[10]

Not only did children's agencies and other welfare organizations
want trained agents, but they began to insist that this training be
standardized. Mary Richmond's address to the 1897 meeting of the
National Conference of Charities and Correction was among the
first forceful arguments in favor of a school of social work. Recognizing her era as one of specialization, the General Secretary of the
Baltimore Charity Organization Society criticized her colleagues
for their tardiness in producing a steady flow of social work expertise. "The question now," she said, "is how to get educated young
men and women to make a life vocation of organizing work." Her
proposal was a training school in applied philanthropy. She refused
to accept the objection that a school of social work was infeasible
until social work itself had achieved a professional standard. On
the contrary, she felt that the school was necessary in order to

achieve such a standard. There was, Richmond claimed, a common fund of knowledge that could be passed on to various types of social workers and certain principles that might be developed.[11]

As a result of Richmond's agitation and the wholehearted support of the president of the New York Charity Organization Society, a six-week summer school was set up in 1898 for graduate students and social workers with experience. For the princely sum of $10 they could hear Peabody, Edward T. Devine, Folks, and other experts explain the problems of needy families and the opportunities for constructive action. It was a small but important step in the development of social work education. In the next six years 208 students would attend lectures, and after 1900 they would visit agencies and carry out practical work under the direction of New York social workers. The welfare of children was not forgotten. One week of the six was devoted to the care of dependent, neglected, and delinquent children. Students such as Carl Christian Carstens who took this brief Cook's tour heard six addresses on the subject and visited seven of New York's children's institutions.[12]

Naturally there was continued criticism of the meagerness of this amount of training. Jeffrey Brackett, president of the Department of Charities and Correction in Baltimore, while praising New York's efforts, complained in 1901 that there was "as yet no training school for charity workers to which any properly qualified person may readily turn for a sufficiently long term of instruction combined with real training." He himself was to be a decisive influence in the founding of the Boston School of Social Work in 1903.[13] Meanwhile, similar conclusions were being reached at the New York Summer School. In a report of the Committee on Philanthropic Education produced in 1901, it was recommended that a full-time course be established in affiliation with Columbia University. Despite disputes over whether the course should reflect university or social agency policies and values, agreement was reached and both one-year and two-year courses were set up.[14]

In Chicago there was a parallel process. A series of lectures given by settlement house workers was expanded in 1903 into the Chicago Institute of Social Sciences. This organization, led by an indefatigable minister and social worker, Graham Taylor, offered part-time courses until 1907, when with welcome funds from the

Russell Sage Foundation, it was transformed into the Chicago School of Civics and Philanthropy and admitted students to a full-time social work program. Philadelphia, St. Louis, and Boston followed suit before 1910.[15] College graduates and experienced social workers were admitted. Attitude rather than academic achievement was stressed as the key to success. The schools were not recruiting impractical scholars. Instead they looked, perhaps overoptimistically, for "evidence of open-mindedness, of teachableness, of humility of spirit . . . evidence of originality, of personal independence, of sheer mental ability, the power to judge honestly, to think straight, to pierce the heart of things and to brush aside unimportant details."[16]

The curricula and methods of instruction of the new schools were strikingly similar. In the early years the courses revolved around the problem of poverty and methods of treating the handicapped and dependent. Eminent guest speakers such as Kelley, Folks, and Julia Lathrop complemented the lectures of the regular staff. They touched on broad issues of social improvement as well as providing a historical perspective to current relief policies and institutional methods. The importance of these survey courses waxed and waned over the years. Complaints that there was too much of everything and too little of a technical nature alternated with objections to specialists who could not relate their expertise to the wider field of social work. Despite these fluctuations, casework remained of supreme importance. In response to the practical demands of welfare agencies, the schools provided courses in methods of investigation. In addition to being given lecture material, students also participated in case discussions, this later becoming the favored form of instruction. Finally, budding social workers were required to undertake 10 to 15 hours of practical work with a variety of local social agencies, both general charity organizations and specialized welfare institutions. At the end of their one or two years of study, it was hoped that they would be well equipped to tackle the personal crises and social problems of those who came to them for help.[17]

Many of the graduates of these pioneer training schools would later take up positions in public and private child care agencies. Apart from ingesting general information on welfare problems and diagnostic methods, they also gained some insight into the particular needs of handicapped children. The work of the Boston School of Social Work illustrates the scope of the education for workers in this area. The school first opened its doors in 1904, at which time it admitted 16 full-time and 11 part-time students. It was the brainchild of Brackett; Alice Higgins, secretary of the Boston Associated Charities; and other enthusiatic representatives of Boston's agencies. Financially supported by Simmons College and, until 1916, Harvard University, the new school aimed to be "wholly practical, to increase the number of available and efficient persons paid and volunteer, who in facing problems of need shall stand for earnest efforts of cure and prevention."[18]

In the early years new students were exposed to a number of general courses, including "The Aims of Social Service," "Leading Principles Underlying All Social Effort," and "Improvement of Conditions of Living." They were also offered a course entitled "Persons out of Their Families," which dealt with the law concerning family separation and the care of children in institutions and foster homes.[19] In 1909 special emphasis was given to various family problems, such as desertion, widowhood, and the neglected child. As the school matured, its curriculum expanded. Under pressure from welfare agencies for an increase in specialized courses and instruction in casework techniques, it offered a second-year program from which students might choose "Organized Charity Work with Children," "Medical Social Service," or "Neighborhood and Community Work" as their field of interest.[20]

The course on child welfare was intended "to prepare persons for effective service as executive officers, visitors or agents of societies for both the care and protection of children."[21] It involved lectures on the principles and practices of certain children's organizations and on methods of social inquiry given by Carstens whose reputation in children's work was widening rapidly year by year. It also required students to examine case records and problems, participate in a detailed study of a particular subject, and undertake practical work with agencies such as the Boston Children's Aid Society. Changes were continually made, however, and in 1917 a broader course of child welfare was offered that included a brief discussion of the physiology and psychology of childhood with special emphasis on the care of dependent, neglected, and delinquent children. It also touched on hitherto ignored problems, such as illegitimacy.[22]

A steady flow of trained child welfare workers left the classroom for the agency office; yet to some it seemed an inadequate trickle. Carstens himself, in 1927, could still bemoan the fact that "the greatest need at the present time is training in children's case work." There were, he wrote, "but few schools in the United States where courses in child welfare are supplemented with supervised training in children's case work."[23] There were too few graduates and too many instances in which child welfare work suffered from such a degree of inefficiency and malpractice that legal action was almost justified. The education of child welfare workers did, however, have a significant effect on those agencies lucky enough to attract graduates. The days of the superannuated clergyman, worn-out schoolmaster, and enthusiastic matron were numbered.

ANALYSIS

Acceptance of the need for formal education of social workers naturally implied that there was a base of scientific knowledge, as well as a special skill and function that set them apart from laymen and members of other professions. Increasingly, social workers were reluctant to agree with opinions given by such as Abraham Flexner, assistant secretary of the General Education Board of New York, that social work was "not so much a separate profession as an endeavor to supplement certain existing professions pending their complete development."[24] Acknowledging that they had only imperfectly grasped the investigative techniques, diagnostic skills, and treatment methods necessary to cope with the problems of their clients, social workers nevertheless felt that they were making significant progress in the acquisition of a relevant body of facts and the formulation of certain basic principles. Having gradually shed much of the moralism that had paralyzed their earlier attempts to understand the causes of destitution and distress, case workers could now develop a truly differential approach.

The most well-known and sophisticated analyses of casework techniques were Richmond's studies, *Social Diagnosis* (1917) and *What is Social Case Work?* (1922). She herself had for many years been involved in charity organization work, starting her career as assistant treasurer and general secretary of the Baltimore Charity Organization Society and moving on to direct the Philadelphia Society in 1900. Nine years later the Russell Sage Foundation wisely offered her the directorship of its Charity Organization Department. During this time, Richmond devoted herself to raising the standards of casework practice, supporting training programs and social work conferences, and publishing case histories. The accumulated experience of these years was sifted and translated into a theory of casework. Her allegiance to diagnostic techniques did not rule out a belief in the necessity for social reform. On the contrary, in her eyes "man's betterment and individual betterment are . . . interdependent, . . . social reform and social case-work of necessity progressing together." However, it was the individual that assumed greater importance for Richmond. The field of casework was "the development of personality through the conscious and comprehensive adjustment of social relationships." While every human being came into the world with certain innate qualities, his or her "individuality," that person also acquired unique traits and behavior from the social environment. This constituted the "personality." It was this part of an individual's being and the problem involved therein that could be beneficially affected by careful diagnosis and treatment.[25]

Certain skills were essential; an insight into individuality and personal characteristics and an insight into the resources, dangers, and influences of the social environment. Successful treatment involved the "direct action of mind on mind," in which a program of participation by the client was worked out and indirect action on the environment. Thus treatment would range from personal services guided by affection, patience, and sympathy to changes in working and living conditions.[26]

An elaborate account of the methodology to be used in isolating a client's problems was given in Richmond's earlier book, *Social Diagnosis*. Regardless of the type of casework, certain techniques were seen as being universally applicable to an understanding of an individual's social situation. The first step was the collection of evidence, that is, "any or all facts as to personal or family history which, taken together indicate the nature of a given client's social difficulties and the means to their solution.'' Each type of evidence, whether gleaned from interviews with the client, from observations of the family, or from contacts with social agencies and neighbors, was to be considered in minute detail as to its relevance and value. Once the pertinent data had been gathered, they might then be subjected to critical comparison and examination to produce an interpretation of the client's particular difficulty.[27]

An essential part of this efficient diagnosis and treatment was cooperation with other agencies. According to Richmond, "whenever the processes of co-operation and investigation have progressed far enough to have genuine social betterment for their aims, they might almost be described as one piece of goods.''[28] Looking backwards at the development of charity organizations, she distinguished a number of phases, the first competitive stage being one of chaos, of a race to create a demand for inmates. A society's esteem depended on its numbers. This period was followed by a second, in which approaches were made in a vacuum. A few facts were gathered; plans were drawn up; and societies later appealed to their colleagues for support. A third phase ensued, in which routine division of cases was made on the basis of territory and need. A systematic interchange of information was begun through registration and confidential exchanges, which eliminated a fair amount of duplication and wasted effort. At the time *Social Diagnosis* was published, Mary Richmond was looking forward to a fourth era in cooperation, when social workers would combine forces with good will, supplying to each other useful data and the results of inquiries as well as supporting programs of treatment.[29]

The care of dependent and neglected children reflected this larger trend toward improved casework and cooperation. Progress was slow before 1920. However, among many advanced agencies it is possible to observe that there was a growing awareness of the social, physiological, and psychological problems of children, gleaned through more rigorous investigation, and to see this new understanding applied to both institutions and foster care.

Charles W. Birtwell, guiding light of the Boston Children's Aid Society from 1886 to 1911, was a major spokesman for the new differential casework. A graduate of Harvard, Birtwell took over from the society's ailing founder, Rufus Cook, and through his enthusiasm, energy, flexibility, and broad insight into human problems, made the Children's Aid Society the foremost exponent of progressive casework ideals. Birtwell was an unusual man. When most of his colleagues were committed to one particular method of treatment for stereotyped groups of children, Birtwell was preaching diversification in order to cater to each child's unique needs. In 1902, at the National Conference of Charities and Correction, he expounded his long-held view that "the study and service of the individual case" was the foundation of child-saving. Charities for children were, in his opinion, "under the same obligation of knowledge, or investigation as is recognized for instance, by the charity organization societies." Investigation was "the natural first step in the effort to individualize each child."[30] By studying the facts, without making rigid assumptions, social workers could develop a method of treatment that would suit the particular problem of every needy child. By 1902 the Boston Children's Aid Society had already begun to apply the casework method and to steadily improve and refine its techniques of diagnosis and treatment.[31]

Other agencies for destitute and neglected children also made tentative moves toward a differential casework approach. Their new skills were displayed in a number of areas: in their admission policies, in their examination of the children received, in placement methods, and in their supervision of children after discharge.

ADMISSION POLICIES

Among caseworkers there was a growing recognition that large numbers of children were unnecessarily admitted to institutions and children's agencies, that the societies' need rather than the clients' dictated the intake. Increasingly it was felt that "children should not be accepted by institutions until a sufficiently intensive investigation has been made to determine whether or not admission to an institution is the proper treatment for the case in hand."[32] Caseworkers sought scientific criteria on the basis of which a child might be separated from the natural parents. They questioned the definition of an inadequate home and debated the relative rights of child, mother, and father. Certain guidelines were offered to caseworkers who were responsible for making the initial survey. They were to discover in detail the family background, the occupation and income of its members, their characters and habits and their physical and mental condition, education record, disabilities, and so on. Separate interviews with the individuals concerned, with neighbors, and with community agencies would provide supplementary information. Very importantly, social workers were advised "to get the child's point of view, to weigh what it will mean to him to be separated even for a short period from parents and brothers and sisters."[33] This was indeed a change in attitude.

Even at this early stage in the treatment of a case, the necessity of an efficient record system was stressed. Practical experience, it was thought, would indicate which system should be adapted to fit the exact needs of each particular children's agency. Agencies produced standardized application forms and report cards to make the accumulation of knowledge regarding each child more simple and effective. They argued that not only would detailed office records assist the organizations themselves to carry out work and assess results but that they would also provide the data from which statisticians and other social agencies might draw important conclusions.[34]

If at all possible, problems involving dependent and neglected children were to be adjusted without separation. The children's agency itself might try to effect an improvement in the family's educational, employment, or recreational opportunities, while hopefully reducing any internal friction. Alternatively, more suitable relief agencies, legal aid services, or community organizations might be commandeered. If the family situation was beyond immediate redemption, however, the children were removed, either temporarily or permanently.

EXAMINATIONS

Once admitted to an institution, the dependent or neglected child was then subjected to an examination to determine his or her suitability for the various types of care available. Among the more progressive children's agencies, this amounted to a rigorous physical, mental, and character study. Unless children were "known," unless their individual habits, strengths, weaknesses, hopes, and fears were discovered, then placing them in a new environment would be, it was thought, as hazardous as it always had been. Medical examinations of new inmates were carried out by most organizations, large and small. From 1894, when Samuel Durgin instituted medical examinations in Boston schools, educational authorities has become increasingly insistent on health and physical hygiene. Children's charities followed suit. They recognized that many of the difficulties suffered by children in their social relationships were traceable to such physical problems as infected tonsils, hearing problems, and spinal defects. Consequently they searched for diseases and disabilities and provided corrective treatment or surgery if possible.[35]

Vastly more important to the individualization of the dependent and neglected child than physical assessment was the gradual application of psychological and psychiatric concepts. Looking backwards to the early years of the century, Jessie Taft, mental hygienist with the Seybert Foundation in Philadelphia, rued the fact that children had only been understood in behavioristic terms. "We only saw what the child did," she wrote. "Good children were never conceivably in need of understanding; . . . if [a child] was actively disturbing and anti-social we joined forces with the foster parents in devising punishments and correctives or got him a new home."[36] By 1916 a leading Illinois public welfare official could declare that "the study of the child from the standpoint of the scientific interpretation of mind and its making is a new science—but it is here to stay."[37] While widespread application of psychiatry did not occur until the 1920s, in the previous decade important lines of communication were opened between psychiatry and social work.

As Roy Lubove demonstrated in *The Professional Altruist*, the major influence before World War I was not Sigmund Freud but rather a "social psychiatry" associated with such men as William A. White, Adolf Meyer, August Hoch, and William Healy. Rejecting the archaic and futile institutional methods of treating the mentally ill, which had persevered to the end of the nineteenth century, this group of psychologists and psychiatrists tried to discover causes of mental illness and offer beneficial therapy. Mental activity, according to Meyer, was not the outcome of a "peculiar form of mind stuff" but rather "the adaptation and adjustment of the individual as a whole."[38] It was firmly believed that mental being could not be extracted from social interaction. Thus, by studying people in their social environments it was felt that, in many instances, mental illness could be prevented and many disturbed individuals could be reeducated so as to successfully adapt themselves to their social milieus. Like their fellow Progressives, leading psychologists and psychiatrists felt that the malleability of human beings offered limitless possibilities for the construction of a better society.[39]

Slowly psychiatry tore itself loose from the insane asylum. Beginning in 1906, psychopathic hospitals were set up, in association with either universities or mental institutions. Following Clifford Beers's autobiographical account of mental illness, *A Mind That Found Itself*, published in 1909, a nationally organized movement for mental hygiene got under way.[40] Independent psychopathic clinics were set up, the Psychopathic Institute of Chicago being opened in 1909 and the Judge Baker Foundation in Boston in 1917, both in affiliation with juvenile courts. It was the Psychopathic Institute that, more than any other institution, was responsible for the introduction of the principles of social psychiatry to the growing body of social workers.

At the head of this inspirational organization was William Healy, a former physician at the Wisconsin State Hospital and associate professor of nervous and mental disorders at Chicago Polyclinic. Interested in the causes of behavioral difficulties among children and adolescents, Healy wanted the opportunity to study children using medical, social, psychiatric, and psychometric techniques. His wish was fulfilled when, in 1909, Chicago philanthropist Ethel Sturges Dummer was persuaded by Lathrop, Addams, and others to finance the Juvenile Psychopathic Institute for five years. Through his work in Chicago and his books, Healy disseminated a multicausal approach to delinquency. In order to understand and thus treat behavior problems, it was, he thought, necessary to consider the unique confluence of mental, physical, and social factors involved. Social workers who were struggling toward differential casework saw their new approach substantiated by Healy's research. They slowly came to agree with him that "the one science that has most to contribute now or ultimately to social casework is unquestionably the science of mind."[41] Subsequently they sought to apply the kinds of psychiatrc insights that Healy had uncovered to their own particular fields of work. Some were sufficiently involved in the new science to consider themselves part of a separate category, psychiatric social workers. With the commencement of a training school for psychiatric social workers established at Smith College in 1918 and the later introduction of mental hygiene and psychiatric material to the curricula of schools of social work, the alliance was firmly cemented.[42]

Psychiatry did not yet dominate social casework, as it would in later decades. Historians Lubove and Kathleen Woodroofe have shown that after 1920 the acceptance of Freudian doctrines and the benefits of psychoanalysis helped to direct attention further from the social environment to the mental process. Caseworkers, whether involved in psychotherapy or not, came to believe that the psychiatric thread constituted "the entire warp of the fabric of social work." Before that time, however, the new science had a deepening impact on social work. With respect to child welfare where sensitively used it offered greater insights into individuality and behavior.[43]

The initial interest of children's agencies in the mental makeup of their children was not a broad psychological concern but rather an obsession with mental defect. In the early twentieth century there was a fairly widespread fear that the feeble-minded constituted a large proportion of all groups of dependents and delinquents and that they would, if unchecked, flood America with their idiotic offspring. Somewhat uncritically, American educationalists, penologists, and philanthropists accepted the intelligence tests devised by Sydney Simon and Alfred Binet in 1905 and refined three years later. Healy at the Juvenile Psychopathic Institute was among the first to use and develop this sort of psychological test. The peak of popularity for mental testing came with World War I, when statisticians claimed that almost one-half of white male draftees were mentally deficient. A more balanced approach was achieved in the 1920s. Despite the overemphasis on the Binet test as a means of determining mental capacity, intelligence testing of dependent and neglected children did allow agencies to isolate those with specific deficiencies and hence provide particular treatment. It guarded against a child being rejected by foster parents because his progress was disappointing.[44]

While children's agencies might see the mental test as "a short cut to a more thorough acquaintance with the individual," they soon realized that it did little to help them understand the child's personality in its emotional and impulsive aspects.[45] Further observation and study were necessary, preferably by qualified psychiatric personnel. The efforts of the New England Home for Little Wanderers in Boston illustrate the gradual change in attitude. In 1915 the agency set up a diagnostic study home for 40 children who might be observed 24 hours a day before their placement. A pediatrician, a psychologist, and a psychiatrist were employed, and the service was opened to other agencies in the area. Of course, even this advance was a far cry from studying the emotional needs of all children. Although the study home did not cater to the subnormal, it was largely for "unusual" children, those with behavior difficulties that would make foster care a risk. Nevertheless, the New England Home for Little Wanderers looked forward to the day when it could offer "careful attention to understanding the mental life of all children committed to our care, just as we now endeavor to give an adequate physical examination."[46] Other agencies were similarly seeking a psychological understanding of their children. Boston's Children's Aid Society benefited from its connection with the Judge Baker Foundation, while the Illinois Children's Home and Aid Society was closely associated with the Juvenile Psychopathic Institute in Chicago. Psychopathic hospitals offered services to children's organizations, and individual psychiatrists were recruited for full-time or part-time help.[47]

One outcome of this new insight into dependent and neglected children was a realization of the effects of dependency upon them. In a report to the board of managers of the Boston Church Home Society in 1917, the society's psychiatrist, Alberta S. Guibord, the society's psychiatrist, outlined the "emotional states arising from injury to the instinctive tendency of self-regard or self-esteem as a result of the break-down of family integrity." She recognized that for the child the family circle was a crucial medium of security; when broken it left the child with a feeling of helplessness and difference. The child desperately needed to achieve self-approval. Failure to do so would lead to depression, a sense of inadequacy, and possibly to troublesome behavior. "The psychology of the dependent child is potentially a psychopathology and as a result it must be met if the dependent child is to have a fair chance," she wrote. Sympathetic talks were beneficial, but most important was the securing of conditions, particularly home conditions, that would make the child feel on a par with children in unbroken families.[48]

PLACEMENT

The aim of all this social diagnosis and mental and physical investigation was the construction of a plan that would suit the child's needs. Naturally, if the child were to be understood and treated as an individual, no rigid program would suffice. The Illinois Children's Home and Aid Society was one agency that had come to recognize that "there must be more elasticity of treatment in order to do justice by all the individual cases." Under the guidance of Hart, its staff came to understand that in the past there had often been a "tendency to twist the child to fit the plan rather than to mold the plan to meet the needs of the child." They now attempted to reverse the process.[49]

This new attitude was most visible with regard to placing children in foster homes. Whereas previously any family that was neither immoral nor in debt was considered suitable, in the later years much greater care was taken in matching parent and child. Progressive agencies rejected the notion that a child should be placed "without regard to temperament or suitability just because physical conditions in a home may be good."[50] To guarantee that an individual child was suited to an applicant, it was necessary that the prospective parents be investigated as thoroughly as the child had been. Annual reports of placing agencies and studies such as *The Selection of Foster Homes for Children*, produced by the New York School of Social Work in 1919, gave caseworkers and placing agents a detailed list of the questions to be asked and features to be observed. A comprehensive application form was the usual first step. It required information on the family's economic status, educational level, religious beliefs, object in taking the child, attitude toward children's discipline, and so on. If this picture seemed promising, the organization would rigorously check references, not only those supplied by the applicants but also doctors, clergymen, bankers, school teachers, and neigbors who might be able to throw light on the family's situation.[51] Finally, and most importantly, there was the inspection of the home. Through careful questioning and keen observation, the training agent would attempt to determine more clearly the motives of the parents in taking a foster child, their capability of looking after the child, and the relationships between members of the family. Agencies were looking for adults who "should show a wholesome attitude of appreciation of the needs of the young in matters of companionship, recreation and reasonable freedom from restraint."[52] It was considered important that the parents should not harbor any illusions about the child they would receive. Associations realized that it was impossible "to transplant a boy or girl from a home life of neglect into a well-regulated family and expect an immediate natural relationship."[53] By preparing prospective parents for the likelihood of bad manners, difficult behavior, resentment, and initial anxiety, they hoped to smooth the way to a mutual acceptance.

SUPERVISION

The task was by no means completed once the child was transferred to the new environment. Supervision was necessary. This, however, was no longer the occasional correspondence or the flying visit to ensure that the child was not being beaten or overworked. Instead agencies were gradually coming to see supervision as a continuing function "demanding vigilance, sympathy with both the family and the child, the ability to interpret the one to the other, and a capacity for practical assistance."[54] Frequent visits were essential, not just to check whether things were going well, but also to anticipate future problems. Recognizing the feelings of rejection and loneliness that dependent youngsters suffered from, the social worker could provide encouragement to the children while explaining their problems to the parents. Likewise, for the first time child welfare workers showed an awareness of the frustrations, disappointments, and fears that foster parents felt. By reassuring them that these feelings were not abnormal, they guarded against an unwarranted sense of failure.[55]

This new sensitivity and improved supervision was by no means a common phenomenon by 1920. Carstens, reviewing child caring work since the White House Conference on the Care of Dependent Children, could still complain in 1927 that "not much headway has been made in this country as a whole for providing an intelligent discharge service."[56] The heavy case load that most agency staff members carried prohibited them from giving the type of support they wished. Nevertheless, they had before them improved supervision standards to strive for in future years.

The after-care of dependent and neglected children was important not only for their successful adjustment in their new families, but also as a means of assessing the value of the methods applied by child care agencies. Results had to be analyzed if knowledge in this area was to increase. Addressing the National Conference of Charities and Correction in 1915, Ruth Lawton of the Boston Children's Aid Society emphasized the fact that "if social work is ever to develop into a profession, searching analysis and criticism of methods and results, no matter what the consequences may be, become prime essentials."[57] She complained that in areas of child welfare work such as illegitimacy, literally millions of dollars had been spent without there being a scientific statement of what had been done about the problem.

The Boston Childrens' Aid Society had been one of the few children's organizations to subject itself to a critical examination. In October 1913 it added a research worker to its staff to measure the value of its own work and to isolate areas of failure. Its first survey followed the careers of 129 children and found an inordinate amount of replacement, excessive case loads, and inadequate supervision by too many different visitors.[58]

RESEARCH

In general, however, the period before 1920 produced virtually nothing in the way of research. A few agencies investigated what became of their children, but they only touched on the economic status of these youngsters and their characters, whether "good" or "bad." The vast majority, of course, were found to be "good" and a credit to the society involved.[59] As was indicated in Chapter 4, no comparative study of foster care and institutional care was made during this period. Foster care was accepted as the superior method without any scientific, empirical evidence in its favor. Even in the 1920s, substantial research projects in this area were rare. The investigations by Sophie Van Senden Theis of 910 New York foster children and by Elias Trotzkey of the working of several Chicago institutions and placing agencies stood alone. It would be many years before research would be of common concern to child welfare workers throughout the nation.[60]

COOPERATION

If little headway was made in this area, more advances were made toward regular cooperation of children's agencies. Richmond had pointed out the close interconnection between good casework and efficient cooperation. Those men and women involved in the care of dependent and neglected children had also come to the conclusion that "no agency in the country is sufficiently well equipped to meet adequately all the needs of all the children whom it serves." They condemned the competitive atmosphere among societies, which produced stagnation and ignorance. "A knowledge of existing resources would," it was thought, "result in the abolition of the foolish, shameful and extravagant duplication of effort. It would lead to a program of treatment that could take into account the needs of every child.[61]

Sporadic attempts at joining forces with agencies in similar fields had been made early in the period. In 1891, for example, the Illinois Children's Home and Aid Society called a meeting to discuss cooperative effort "upon the part of the several institutions of this city having for their objects the care of homeless and dependent children."[62] Subsequently it offered its services as a placing agency to many other associations without such facilities. Other local groups of children's agencies organized conferences to exchange information and ideas or used confidential exchanges set up by general charity organizations. Individuals assisted their colleagues in the solution of particular problems. Information and assistance began to be offered on a statewide and sometimes a national basis. Perhaps the best example of the latter form of cooperation was the Bureau of Exchange of Information, later the Child Welfare League of America.

The bureau had its beginnings at an informal dinner conference of child care workers in Baltimore in 1915. The National Conference of Charities and Correction was being held in that city during May, allowing experts in various fields of social work to thrash out the most urgent problems. Representatives of 14 children's organizations, among them Carstens, Wilfred S. Reynolds of the Illinois Children's Home and Aid Society and Cheyney Jones of the Cleveland Humane Society, agreed on the need for a national association, like the American Association of Societies for Organizing Charity, to raise standards and guide children's agencies in making requests for rendering interagency service. As a result, a Committee on Cooperation for Child-helping Organizations was established to put the plan into action. With the help of the Russell Sage Foundation, the founder members of the Bureau of Exchange of Information formulated ideas for standardizing cooperation and collecting and distributing material. During the first year, in which the bureau operated informally, it attracted 43 member societies, mainly children's aid societies, SPCCs, humane societies, and juvenile protective associations. Each was requested to agree "to co-operate heartily with other members of the Bureau, . . . to send to the Bureau copies of all literature published, . . . to furnish such other information regarding its work as the Bureau may request from time to time." The executive committee also drew up a set of articles of agreement concerning the types of services agencies should render to each other and the conditions of such service.[63]

The bureau's usefulness was increasingly recognized. In 1918 the bureau started to make itself self-supporting when it was decided to levy a $10 fee from each constituent association. Plans were made to extend its activities even further to make it "an organization which will devote itself to assisting children's agencies in putting programs into operation and in working out details, such an agency to concern itself definitely with questions of technique."[64] The problem was the extra financing needed to support such an ambitious program. Salvation came in the guise of the Commonwealth Fund, which after much dithering agreed to appropriate $25,000 per annum for five years. The bureau was subsequently transformed, in late 1920, into the Child Welfare League of America under the able direction of Carstens. In later years this important center of information encouraged higher standards of casework, uniform terminology and methods, and a rigorous, efficient interchange of data and services among its member organizations.[65]

The professional undercurrent of the Progressive era would become the mainstream of the following decade. Before 1920, as we have seen, social workers, child-care personnel among them, had begun a self-conscious movement toward professional status. They advanced and refined new techniques and demanded and provided standards of investigation and treatment. They established educational facilities and promoted cooperation among a wide variety of welfare and community agencies. They expressed an increasing interest in the individual. All these developments influenced the treatment of dependent and neglected children. When new insights and techniques were sensitively applied they led to an increasing understanding of each particular problem, a more flexible program of care and more satisfactory supervision. Social workers concerned with the successful socialization of these groups of children hoped that improved casework would complement legislative reforms and institutional changes. In the next decade professional concerns overshadowed reform activities.

NOTES

1. Richard Hofstadter, *The Age of Reform* (London: Jonathan Cape, 1962), p. 273.

2. Clark C. Chambers, *Seedtime of Reform: American Social Service and Social Action 1918-1933* (Minneapolis, Minn.: University of Minnesota Press, 1963), pp. 87-106, quoted pp. xi, 87. Donald Swain, *Federal Conservation Policy* (Berkeley, Calif.: University of California Press, 1963). See also Allen Davis, "Welfare Reform and World War I," *American Quarterly* 19 (1967): 516-33.

3. George B. Buzel, "Individuality in the Work of Charity," *Proceedings of the 13th NCCC*, 1886, p. 187.

4. Kathleen Woodroofe, *From Charity to Social Work in England and the United States* (London: Routledge & Kegan Paul, 1962), pp. 25-55, 88-93.

5. Elizabeth White, "The History of the Illinois Children's Home and Aid Society" (master's thesis, University of Chicago, 1934), pp. 14, 31.

6. Alice Channing, "The Illinois Soldiers' Orphans' Home" (master's

thesis, University of Chicago, 1926), p. 24. Nathan Huggins, *Protestants Against Poverty: Boston's Charities, 1870-1900* (Westport, Conn.: Greenwood Press, 1971), pp. 124, 131-32.

7. Mamie Ruth Davis, "A History of the Policies and Methods of Social Work in the Chicago Orphan Asylum" (master's thesis, University of Chicago, 1927), p. 31. Nathan Berman, "A Study of the Development of the Care of Dependent and Neglected Jewish Children in the Chicago Area" (master's thesis, University of Chicago, 1933), p. 34. Channing, "The Illinois Soldiers' Orphans' Home," p. 10.

8. J. E. Field, quoted in the *Children's Home Finder* 6, no. 11 (July 1899), p. 8.

9. White, "The History of the Illinois Children's Home and Aid Society," p. 52.

10. Roy Lubove, *The Professional Altruist: The Emergence of Social Work as a Career, 1880-1930* (Cambridge, Mass.: Harvard University Press, 1965), pp. 18-19, 49-52. Hastings Hornell Hart, *Annual Report of the Illinois Children's Home and Aid Society*, 1904, p. 15.

11. Mary Richmond, "The Need for a Training School in Applied Philanthropy," *Proceedings of the 24th NCCC*, 1897, pp. 181-88, quoted p. 181.

12. Elizabeth Meir, *A History of the New York School of Social Work* (New York: Columbia University Press, 1954), pp. 5-13.

13. Jeffrey Brackett, "Present Opportunities for Training in Charitable Work," *Proceedings of the 28th NCCC*, 1901, p. 290.

14. Meir, *New York School of Social Work*, pp. 20-22.

15. Ernest V. Hollis and Alice T. Taylor, *Social Work Education in the United States* (New York: Columbia University Press, 1951), pp. 9-11. Jesse Steiner, *Education for Social Work* (Chicago: University of Chicago Press, 1921), pp. 12-17.

16. Edward T. Devine, "Education for Social Work," *Proceedings of the 42nd NCCC*, 1915, p. 607.

17. Chicago School of Civics and Philanthropy, *Bulletin*, 1911, p. 369; 1912, p. 7. Roswell McCrea, "The Professional School for Social Work, Its Aims and Methods," *Proceedings of the 38th NCCC*, 1911, p. 381. Edith Abbott, "Field Work and the Training of the Social Worker," *Proceedings of the 42nd NCCC*, 1915, pp. 615-22. George B. Mangold, "The Curricula of Schools of Social Service," ibid., pp. 612-15. Jeffrey Brackett, "The Curriculum of the Professional School of Social Work," ibid., pp. 610-12.

18. "Historical Sketch," Boston School of Social Work, *Bulletin*, 1914, pp. 3-5; 1906, quoted p. 6.

19. Ibid., p. 8.

20. Boston School of Social Work, *Bulletin*, 1909, p. 6; 1914, p. 15.

21. Ibid., p. 18.

22. Ibid.; Boston School of Social Work, *Bulletin*, 1917, p. 7.

23. Carl Christian Carstens, "Child Welfare Work Since the White House Conference," *Proceedings of the 54th NCSW*, 1927, p. 131. Carl Christian Carstens, "Present Provisions for the Training of Children's Workers" (Carstens papers, Social Welfare Archives, Minneapolis, Minn.), pp. 1-2.

24. Abraham Flexner, "Is Social Work a Profession?" *Proceedings of the 42nd NCCC*, 1915, p. 586.

25. Mary Richmond, *Social Diagnosis* (New York: Russell Sage, 1917), p. 25. Mary Richmond, *What is Social Case Work?* (New York: Russell Sage, 1922), p. 92, quoted p. 98. Woodroofe, *From Charity to Social Work, pp. 101-17.*

26. Richmond, *What is Social Case Work?* p. 102.

27. Richmond, *Social Diagnosis*, p. 43.

28. Ibid., p. 292.

29. Ibid., pp. 292-96.

30. Charles W. Birtwell, "Introduction to the Discussion on Children," *Proceedings of the 29th NCCC*, 1902, p. 398.

31. Huggins, *Protestants Against Poverty*, pp. 131-33.

32. Carl Christian Carstens, "Minimum Standards of Child Caring Institutions" (Carstens papers), p. 1.

33. Edwin Solenberger, "Record of Child Placing Agencies," *Proceedings of the 37th NCCC*, 1910, pp. 123-24. J. Prentice Murphy, "Conserving the Child's Parental Home," in U.S. Children's Bureau, *Foster Home Care for Dependent Children*, Publication no. 136 (Washington, D.C.: Government Printing Office, 1924), p. 25.

34. Solenberger, "Record of Child Placing Agencies," p. 131. Georgia Ralph, *Elements of Record Keeping for Child Helping Organisations* (New York: Russell Sage, 1915), p. 125.

35. Robert H. Bremner, ed., *Children and Youth in America: A Documentary History* (Cambridge, Mass.: Harvard University Press, 1971), vol. 2, pp. 895-930. *Annual Report of the Masschusetts Society for the Prevention of Cruelty to Children*, 1912, p. 17.

36. Jessie Taft, "A Changing Psychology of Child Welfare," *AAAPSSS* 151 (1930): 122.

37. Frank Norbury, "The Function of the Psychological Clinic," *Illinois Quarterly* 7, no. 2 (June 1916), p. 141.

38. Lubove, *The Professional Altruist*, pp. 55-63, Adolph Meyer quoted pp. 58-59.

39. John C. Burnham, "Psychiatry, Psychology and the Progressive Movement," *American Quarterly* 12 (1960): 457-65.

40. Clifford Beers, *A Mind That Found Itself* (New York: Longmans, 1909).

41. William Healy, "Some Bearing of Psychology on Social Casework," *Proceedings of the 44th NCSW*, 1917, p. 105.

42. Virginia P. Robinson, *A Changing Psychology of Social Case Work* (Chapel Hill, N.C.: University of North Carolina, 1930), pp. 22-31.

43. Lubove, *The Professional Altruist*, pp. 85-117. Woodroofe, *From Charity to Social Work*, pp. 118-36. Mary Jarrett, "The Psychiatric Thread Running through All Social Case Work," *Proceedings of the 46th NCSW*, 1919, quoted p. 587.

44. *Annual Report of the Boston Church Home Society*, 1917, p. 6. "The Binet Test," *Illinois Quarterly* 2 (1911): 7. Statistics on the percentage of defectives among the armed forces given in Lubove, *The Professional Altruist*, p. 69.

45. Rose Hardwick, "The Mental Examination and Child Welfare," *Little Wanderers Advocate* 51 (1915): 17.

46. Frederick H. Knight, "The Problem of Social Adjustment," ibid., quoted p. 10. *Little Wanderers Advocate* 50 (1914): 19; 51 (1915): 1-10; 57 (1920): 13-19.

47. See Anna C. Haskins, "Progress in Social Case Work in Child Welfare," *Proceedings of the 50th NCSW*, 1923, pp. 339-41. Jessie Taft, "The Relation of Personality Study to Child Placing," *Proceedings of the 46th NCSW*, 1919, pp. 63-67.

48. Alberta S. Guibord, "The Handicap of the Dependent Child" (Boston: Boston Church Home Society, 1917), quoted pp. 3, 5.

49. *Annual Reports of the Illinois Children's Home and Aid Society*, 1909, p. 8; 1915, p. 5.

50. Ibid., 1917, p. 6.

51. Mary S. Doran and Bertha C. Reynolds, *The Selection of Foster Homes for Children* (New York: School of Social Work, 1919), pp. 13-34.

52. Amos Butler, "The Essentials of Placement in Free Family Homes," in U.S. Children's Bureau, *Foster Home Care for Dependent Children*, p. 34.

53. Wilfred S. Reynolds, "Adjusting Children and Foster Parents," *Home Life for Childhood* 5 (Nov. 1916): 6.

54. Sophie Van Sender Theis, *The Child in the Foster Home* (New York: School of Social Work, 1921), p. 79.

55. Ibid., pp. 88-94. Murphy, "Conserving the Child's Parental Home," p. 24.

56. Carstens, "Child Saving Work Since the White House Conference," p. 26.

57. Lawton, "A Study of the Results of a Child Placing Agency," p. 164.

58. Ibid., pp. 164-74.

59. For example, see Elizabeth White, "The History and Development of the Illinois Children's Home and Aid Society" (master's thesis, University of Chicago, 1934), p. 76. Rudolph Coffee, "What Becomes of our Graduates?" *Proceedings of the 2nd National Conference of Jewish Charities*, 1904, pp. 82-87.

60. Sophie Van Senden Theis, *How Foster Children Turn Out* (New York: State Charities Aid Association, 1924). Elias Trotzkey, *Institutional Care and Placing Out: The Place of Each in the Care of Dependent Children* (Chicago: Marks Nathan Jewish Orphans' Home, 1930).

61. C. V. Williams, "Cooperation between the Children's Agency and Other Community Resources," in U.S. Children's Bureau, *Foster Home Care for Dependent Children*, pp. 153-55, quoted p. 144.

62. Davis, "A History of . . . the Chicago Orphans' Asylum," p. 89.

63. "A Sketch of the Origin and Development of the Child Welfare League of America" (papers of the Child Welfare League of America, Social Welfare Archives, Minneapolis, Minn.), pp. 1-2. Undated document on the conference in Baltimore, May 17, 1915. Memorandum of June 1916, quoted.

64. "A Sketch of the Origin," p. 4.

65. Letter to the Commonwealth Fund, Nov. 26, 1919. Report of the Director, June 23, 1921 (papers of the Child Welfare League of America, Social Welfare Archives, Minneapolis, Minn.)

CONCLUSION

PROGRESSIVE-ERA REFORMS

In 1912 Ida Tarbell declared that "Youth, its nurturing and developing, has become the passion of the day. This is the meaning of our bureau of Child Labor, of our Children's Courts, our Houses of Correction, our Fresh Air Funds and Vacation Homes, our laws regulating hours and conditions, our Social Settlements."[1] Certainly, the child was central to the Progressive vision of a stable, capitalist democracy where poverty, vice, and crime were minimal and where class antagonisms, racial tensions, and ethnic divisions were no longer substantial threats to the nation's development. To ensure a sound citizenry in an increasingly complex society, reformers extended the idea of the child as a dependent being whose transition to adulthood necessitated a longer period of care and protection than hitherto. They acted to bolster and solidify the bourgeois family and simultaneously, to extend the role of the state in the socialization process.

Their activities covered a broad spectrum. Many concerned themselves with the promotion of middle-class child-rearing practices. Through educative literature and associations, voluntary groups and agencies such as the U.S. Children's Bureau advocated a scientific view of mothering and spelled out the then current dogma on feeding, play, discipline, and parent-child interaction. This also involved and encouraged a concern with infant and maternal health and an attempt to lower the frighteningly high death rate. The climax of years of research, publicity, and political campaigning came in 1921 when the Sheppard-Towner Act was passed, whereby federal funds were provided for the creation of relevant health care facilities.

Child labor regulation and compulsory education were other, complementary, goals pursued for most of this period. Although the struggle to achieve federal regulation of the age of entry to the work force was largely frustrated—the Federal Child Labor Law of 1917 was allowed to remain in existence for a mere 273 days—at the state level new and amended legislation raised the minimum working age, usually to 14, demanded proof of age and a suitable level of education, and frequently insisted on adequate health and physical development.

Simultaneously, to reinforce this control on child labor, laws to compel school attendance were expanded and tightened so that by 1918, with the enactment of the Mississippi law, compulsory education was universal. Educational reform, of course, went far beyond the question of attendance to an expansion and diversification of facilities, a revision of curricula, and changes in the methods of teaching, all of which were designed to produce the desired industrious, cooperative citizens of the future.

The area of education is an obvious example of the increasing entry of the state into the socialization of children. This same trend may be observed in the Progressive reformers' interest in child abuse. Although physical abuse of children was a particularly sensitive issue, since the right to discipline children was a correlative of a parent's duty to support them, only gradual gains were made in the regulation of parental force. Between 1890 and 1920 a significant number of states passed legislation making it illegal for parents to endanger the health or life of their child, by physical force or by failure to provide necessary food, clothing, and shelter. In addition to punishing the parents, the state increasingly intervened to remove children from "unsuitable" homes.

The reform impulse relating to American children flowed into many channels. Certain groups of children were singled out as being in need of special attention. The problems of the mentally and physically handicapped made their claims on reformers' energy, although their problems were clearly eclipsed by the issues relating to juvenile delinquency. Potentially antisocial adults were a more numerous and obvious threat to the social order; consequently, a broad coalition of professionals and voluntary groups joined to support a redefinition of deliquency in a flexible and expanded form, to create new children's courts characterized by procedural informality, and to provide alternatives to institutionalization through a probation system.

A third major group of children were the dependent and neglected. The position of this group underwent significant changes between 1890 and 1920. As this study has argued, much of this change was beneficial. By 1920 facilities for the care of these children was more comprehensive: the quality of the services they offered had improved. Children outside their own homes were cared for in foster homes and a wide variety of institutions. The latter were less and less open to criticism for their unhealthy, routinized, monotonous conditions. In both placing agencies and institutions, the quality of diagnosis and treatment services had risen substantially. Child welfare was becoming professionalized; more social workers were formally trained in casework techniques. Aided by new investigative methods and psychological insights, they were better able to offer an individualized solution to a child's problems.

In addition to improving facilities, reformers of the Progressive era also made moves toward the prevention of dependency and neglect. Public pensions for mothers with dependent children were intended to keep children in their own homes. Further attempts to reduce dependency and neglect involved an alteration in the legal relationship between parent and child. Tighter desertion laws discouraged parents from abandoning their families, while provisions for maintenance, even if the father was in jail, prevented children from being surrendered by their mothers. Similarly, new legislation updated the archaic illegitimacy laws. It became harder for a father to escape his responsibilities; unmarried mothers were encouraged to start paternity proceedings, and more generous support provisions were introduced.

Public child welfare was another area in which important innovations were made. In the post-Civil War period, the inability of
private charity to cope with the increasing number of applicants
for aid led to increased government participation. More local and
state authorities established their own institutions and placing
agencies. State supervisory bodies introduced a number of
measures designed to obliterate abuses in the charity system.
Private organiztions were no longer left to go their own way
regardless of whether they catered to a genuine need or not. By
1920 many states demanded that private children's agencies be properly incorporated, and annual licenses were granted that might be
revoked in cases of abuse. Regular reports were required, and
periodic visitation by a government agent was considered essential. These changes brought a certain amount of order and accountability to a somewhat chaotic and unregulated system. New
government agencies sprang up. The juvenile court, although
predominantly concerned with delinquents, heard cases of
dependency and neglect that had previously been dealt with
through a multitude of adult courts.

The Children's Bureau, founded in 1912, embodied much of the
nation's concern for the rearing of its young and the delineation of
children's role in society. As the first federal agency concerned with
children, it provided a number of invaluable services. It collected
and disseminated information on child welfare, organized conferences, compiled statistical surveys, and conducted research into,
among other things, illegitimacy, mothers' pensions, and foster
care. The Children's Bureau gave a necessary national perspective
to developments in child welfare, and it helped to break down the
detrimental isolation of agencies dealing with dependent and
neglected children.

There were benefits in all these legislative and institutional innovations. However, in 1920 the emphasis was still on overcoming
separate and specific handicaps rather than on providing all
children with their full, human, individual chance. Child welfare
reformers did, however, support wider campaigns that would
benefit all the nation's youth. As has been briefly mentioned, there
was a slow acceptance of the fact that the power to maintain a decent family living standard was essential to the welfare of every

child. Many of those concerned with children did advocate an adequate working wage, although less for working men than for working women. They were frequently bound by the nineteenth-century belief that all earnest, industrious men could find adequately paid work and by a reluctance to acknowledge the necessity of collective bargaining. Protection of working mothers and future mothers could elicit a less complex response. Likewise, a guaranteed income by some form of social insurance was necessary for all children's welfare. While there was support for workmen's compensation in the event of accident, unemployment insurance was greeted with less enthusiasm. Other areas in which the needs of children were recognized were health and housing reform. The larger Progressive battles to eliminate diseases such as tuberculosis, to improve sanitation, to ensure healthy food and milk supplies, and to construct decent, well-ventilated housing were intimately linked with the future well-being of all the nation's youth. However, the broader vision of some child welfare reformers and the attempts by the Children's Bureau to direct its work toward questions affecting every child do not erase the fact that, in general, only special needs of special groups received significant attention.

If much of the activity on behalf of dependent and neglected children had beneficial results, it is also clear that much was undermined by the ambivalent position of social workers and philanthropists. The men and women who agitated for child welfare reform were mainly middle-class, native-born, urban-based professionals. The stable society they wished to ensure was one that was conducive to their own social and career aspirations. They did not wish a radical redistribution of wealth nor a basic restructuring of social relationships. Their intervention in the lives of children would theoretically guarantee that American society would suffer no such upheaval. At the same time they were also genuinely concerned about the plight of an unfortunate group of children.

The inherent contradictions in this position are visible in a number of instances. One example is the mothers' pension scheme. These funds were ostensibly granted to the mother for her services in bringing up her children. They were not to be charitable offerings. Their application contradicted this idea. Pensions were only granted to mothers who were morally "proper"; unmarried mothers and deserted wives were more suspect and were often denied aid. In addition, pensions were conditional on the assumption of middle-class behavioral norms. If women demurred, their financial aid might be cut off. This same concern with the safety of society also encouraged the treatment of dependent children as predeliquent. Many children brought to court as delinquent had been accused of purely juvenile offenses such as truancy. Children from poor family backgrounds were often treated for what they *might* do rather than for any wrong they had committed.

A preoccupation with social stability may also be seen in the precipitant acceptance of foster care. Anxious for the survival of the apparently crumbling family unit, social workers promoted foster care despite the fact there was no factual evidence to support its superiority over the institution. The needs of illegitimate children received little attention because illegitimacy seemed a threat to the family unit. Only when World War I threw up the specter of increasing numbers of soldiers' "bastards" did social workers really become concerned. Finally, fears of social instability led to the continuation of somewhat punitive attitudes in the desertion laws. Not many of the laws passed before 1920 allowed for suspension of sentence or for the earnings of the father in jail to be passed on to his family. The desire to discourage antisocial behavior led to overemphasis on punishment at the expense of the child's well-being. Likewise, most desertion laws stipulated that a child must be in destitute circumstances before the laws were applicable. Lawmakers were more concerned with avoiding the support of dependents than with the right of the child to be supported by both parents.

In many areas of reform, legislative changes were also undermined by administrative inertia or conflicts between state agencies. Where financial aid was involved, bureaucratic caution and a fear of encouraging dependency led authorities to dispense meager amounts. Aid was frequently insufficient to solve the problem. Many mothers with large families, who were eligible for pensions, found it impossible to secure the maximum amount. Often they needed to supplement the pensions with other income but were handicapped by poor health or young infants. In such instances they were forced to apply for ordinary relief, thus making a mockery of the idea that economic security was their right. Similarly, a lack of understanding and sympathy on the part of judges led to an inadequate application of the illegitimacy laws. In only a negligible proportion of cases was the unmarried mother awarded reasonable support. The illegitimate child continued to find its way to the children's agency.

CONTEMPORARY PARALLELS

Many of the concerns of this study are ongoing issues. As critics reevaluate the American child welfare system, as they become aware that children's rights and needs have frequently been ignored by statutes, courts, and agencies, they are faced with problems that were familiar in the Progressive era. The virtues and failings of noninstitutional and institutional care of children continue to be debated; the adequacy of the Aid to Families with Dependent Children program remains in question; the need to tighten the support laws for legitimate and illegitimate children has resurged as a crucial issue, and the dangers of vague legal definitions of neglect and delinquency are still being exposed. Voices can be heard regretting the failure of child welfare agencies to promote the interests of all American children and berating them for their provision of poor services for those, largely economically disadvantaged, children who come under their care. It is clear from current analyses that class interests continue to undermine measures for the care and protection of young people, that the contradiction between social order and social justice is an ever-present welfare dilemma.

Contemporary literature attests to a consistent flow of criticism of the care of children outside their own homes. Despite claims that foster care is the optimum short-term solution to certain family problems, the reality of the situation is that the majority of children remain in foster homes for over two years and that, for many, the placement is permanent, if not recognized as such by the people involved. Promises, reminiscent of the early twentieth century, to help families secure the return of their children as soon as possible seem unfulfilled today. Acccording to a recent article by Martin Rein, Thomas E. Nutt, and Heather Weiss, parent-child contact and parent-agency contact tend to decrease once a child is placed and often ceases to exist altogether.[2] Services such as day care or home help that might prevent the removal of children are frequently not offered. A further complaint reinforces the argument put forward in this study that much support for foster care has emanated from a faith in the value of the nuclear family rather than from an empirically verified knowledge of the value of substitute homes. In the opinion of Rein, Nutt, and Weiss, few agencies currently undertake studies "to evaluate the adjustment of children during and after foster care," and those studies undertaken tend to be basically descriptive.[3] Rarely is it known what eventually happens to these children. While noninstitutional care is by far the preferred means of caring for children outside their own families, thousands of children still experience institutional life. Criticisms of present-day institutions often echo those heard eighty or ninety years ago. Even those who stress the potential of the institution to provide a positive and creative environment are forced to admit that, in effect, present institutional care tends to deteriorate into an emphasis on routine, discipline, and chores and is based on an expectation of mediocrity from the inmates. The fact that the clients are poor often leads to poor service by inadequately trained staff.[4]

The introduction of the mothers' pension scheme in the second decade of the twentieth century was heralded as the means of preventing a great deal of dependency and neglect. The scheme has since expanded phenomenally, to become one of the country's most important welfare programs and, to some, one of the nation's largest welfare headaches. The limitations of the scheme in terms of eligibility requirements and behavioral conditions are as evident today as they were at its inception. Many people fail to receive the aid they desperately need. Frances Fox Piven and Richard A. Cloward estimated that in the mid 1960s, for "every family on the A.F.D.C. rolls, at least one other was eligible but unaided."[5] Despite activities by welfare rights organizations demanding the extension of these benefits, many thousands of families remain without help. Vague "suitability of the home" clauses continue to keep the undesirable, often blacks and unwed mothers, off the rolls.[6] Wives may be forced to wait a stipulated period after being deserted before they are considered eligible, while funds may be denied to any mother who has a lover in her household, however, casual that relationship may be. Relief, when obtained, rarely provides a reasonable standard of living. In times of recession and inflation like those experienced in the 1970s, the meager funds become even more inadequate.

A further area in which there has been a resurgence of interest in issues central to Progressive child welfare reform is the protection of children against the irresponsibilities of their parents. In the mid-1960s the "battered child syndrome" became a subject of much controversy. Welfare personnel analyzed the socioeconomic and psychological factors contributing to the excessive use of force against children and advocated counselling and rehabilitative facilities for parents. They also gave their support to the enactment of mandatory reporting laws, the establishment of a central clearing house for all reported cases, and greater state intervention to remove children when necessary.[7]

Child support and the rights of illegitimates are also current subjects of debate and statutory reform. Given the sensitivity of government agencies to the skyrocketing relief rolls, it is not surprising that, as in the late nineteenth century, the question of enforcing parental support of children should be resurrected as an urgent issue. The trend toward stricter accountability may be seen in legislation passed in August 1975 providing assistance to the states through a new enforcement unit in the Department of Health, Education and Welfare and for a federal parent location service. The bill places responsibility on the states to bring suits against parents and increases the supervision of state enforcement programs. Recipients of welfare funds unfortunately seem to come under new pressures, being expected to identify the fathers of their children if they are absent and to cooperate in any support proceedings the state might initiate.[8] Similar pressure is presently being brought to bear on unmarried mothers to name the fathers of their children so that the children may claim support.

Since 1968, when the Supreme Court held that the illegitimate child had "constitutional rights," the legal status of the child born out of wedlock has received much attention. Prior to that time each state could enact its own legislation and could deny the illegitimate child the right to support and inheritance from his or her father. While recent court decisions have not consistently followed the 1968 ruling, the tendency has been to include illegitimate children in the benefits of welfare legislation where they provide for children in general.

The states are also clearly concerned with removing illegitimate children from the relief rolls. In a recent federal court decision a Connecticut statute compelling an unwed mother to reveal the identity of her child's father was upheld. She was threatened with the withdrawal of government funds if she refused to comply. Now, as at the turn of the century, the extent to which the state may advance the rights of the child against those of the parent is a question of much controversy.[9]

A final continuity worth mentioning is the current debate on the dangers inherent in the vague legal definitions of the terms "neglect" and "delinquency." While some argue, as the originators of the juvenile court did, that general definitions and standards are essential to allow a maximum of judicial flexibility, others strongly disagree. They point, I think rightly, to the fact that vague terminology and a lack of formal procedure create a perilous dependence on the judge's discretion. As one critic claims, they "call for individualized determinations based on discretionary assessments of the best interests of the child and these determinations cannot be made consistently or fairly."[10] Imprecise terminology has allowed, and still allows, children to be judged according to the possibility of future wrongdoing rather than acts already committed. Undue dependence on judicial discretion permits state intervention in cases, for example, where parental habits are not in line with dominant mores but have had no demonstrably harmful effects on the child. Informal hearings, involving such practices as the admission of hearsay evidence, do not necessarily guarantee that the child's interests will be best represented. Flaws pinpointed in the legal treatment of neglected children before 1920 are being restated and hopefully repaired at the present time.

In much of this discussion of the links between the reforms of the early twentieth century and current problems in the welfare system, it is clear that the ancient tension between charitable instincts and social order remains to plague America's treatment of its youth. In general it may be said that those largely middle-class professionals who design welfare policy and staff welfare facilities have an ambivalent reaction to the poor and dependent. While they may empathize with the sufferings of those who come to them in need of support, they are unable to shed a basic fear and resentment of the dependent. The fear is that, left to their own devices, the poor and dependent might destroy the present social system; the resentment is based on a deep-seated belief that the dependents are "abnormal" and may somehow be responsible for their own condition. The aid given, therefore, tends to be of poor quality, and financial relief is kept to a minimum lest it encourage irresponsibility and further dependency. Aid and protection also tend to be conditional upon the recipient conforming to acceptable behavioral patterns and cooperating unquestioningly with the authorities. Privacy is still less secure for those in need of state care.

In view of the threads running through twentieth-century welfare provisions for children, the foregoing study may be useful. An understanding of activity on behalf of the dependent and neglected at the turn of the century makes these developments more intelligible.

NOTES

1. Ida Tarbell, *The Business of Being a Woman* (New York: Macmillan, 1921), p. 198.

2. Martin Rein, Thomas E. Nutt, and Heather Weiss, "Foster Family Care: Myth and Reality," in Alvin Schorr, ed., *Children and Decent People* (New York: Basic Books, 1974), pp. 24-52.

3. Ibid., p. 41.

4. David G. Gil, "Institutions for Children," ibid., pp. 53-87.

5. Frances Fox Piven and Richard A. Cloward, *Regulating the Poor: The Functions of Public Welfare* (New York: Vintage Books, 1971), p. 303.

6. See also Winifred Bell, *Aid to Dependent Children* (New York: Columbia University Press, 1965).

7. David Bakan, *Slaughter of the Innocents* (San Francisco: Jossey Bass, Inc., 1971).

8. Sanford Katz, *The Youngest Minority: Lawyers in Defense of Children* (Chicago: American Bar Association, 1977), vol. 2, pp. 6-8.

9. Robert L. Stenger, "The Supreme Court and Illegitimacy: 1968-1977," *Family Law Quarterly* 11 (1978): 365-401. Harry D. Krause, "Child Welfare, Parental Responsibility and the State," *Family Law Quarterly* 6 (1972): 379-88.

10. Robert H. Mnookin, "Foster Care—In Whose Best Interest?" *Harvard Educational Review* 13 (1973): 599-638, quoted p. 602.

BIBLIOGRAPHICAL ESSAY

As the text of this study has been extensively documented, it is perhaps unnecessary to list each item consulted. Instead a more general, selective survey of relevant primary and secondary sources may be more helpful to the reader interested in pursuing the topic further.

Given that the history of childhood and youth in America has only recently begun to receive serious attention, it is not surprising that dependent and neglected children have virtually been ignored. For many years the most comprehensive narrative on the subject was Henry Thurston's study, *The Dependent Child: A Story of Changing Aims and Methods in the Care of Dependent Children* (New York: Columbia University Press, 1930). He traced the evolutionary progress of the care of dependent children from the early poor laws through the almshouse and asylum to foster care and, as he saw it, a better, more individualized treatment of the child in the early twentieth century. Thurston's history was complemented by the documentary material compiled by Grace Abbott for her invaluable reference work, *The Child and the State*, 2 vols. (Chicago: University of Chicago Press, 1938). This collection was, and is still, useful not only for its documentary coverage of public policy relating to child welfare, apprenticeship, child labor, delinquency, and the legal status of children, but also for the illuminating introductory sections in which Abbott traces the development of legal, judicial, and administrative activity in the various areas.

Since the 1930s there have been few texts that offer a history of child welfare, particularly as it relates to dependent and neglected children.

Dorothy Zietz's *Child Welfare: Service and Perspective* (New York: John Wiley, 1969) and Alfred Kadushin's *Child Welfare Services* (New York: Macmillan, 1967) give a historical perspective to their accounts of child welfare services but approach the subject from a social work rather than historical perspective. One aspect that has been studied in some depth is the Aid to Families with Dependent Children program. Winifred Bell's study, *Aid to Dependent Children* (New York: Columbia University Press, 1965), is a critical account of the development of the scheme and the eligibility requirements that, from its inception, have been used to keep undesirable applicants, largely blacks and unwed mothers, from receiving aid.

The most important contribution to this field in recent years has been the three-volume *Children and Youth in America: A Documentary History*, edited by Robert H. Bremner (Cambridge, Mass.: Harvard University Press, 1970-1974). This work, sponsored by the American Public Health Association, was undertaken to update Grace Abbott's reference work. It has consequently extended her area of interest to include such topics as child health, education, and minority groups while adding a large amount of valuable source material to subjects already covered by *The Child and the State*.

The aim of this book has been to give more substance to and throw further light upon specific areas of child welfare that Bremner's history touched upon relating to dependent and neglected children. An exhaustive analysis of changes in legislation, institutional structure, and social work techniques was obviously an infeasible task. However, widely influential debates and developments were accessible through such primary material as the proceedings of major conferences, professional journals, and agency reports.

One of the most valuable sources was the *Proceedings of the National Conference of Charities and Correction*. First held in 1874, the annual conference was for many years the main forum for social workers and philanthropists to discuss major problems. Particularly before 1917, when the conference changed its name to the National Conference of Social Work and became more involved in intraprofessional concerns, it also served as the base for much reform agitation. The problems of children were regular items on the agenda. The conference also produced a special report on the history of child-saving, presented at the 20th annual meeting, held in Chicago in June 1893. This was later printed as *A History of Child Saving in the United States* and reprinted by Patterson Smith (Montclair, N.J., 1971).

The national conference naturally reflected a wide diversity of opinions. Variations along religious lines were visible at the larger gathering. These were more clearly elaborated at the National Conference of Catholic

Charities, begun in 1910, and the National Conference of Jewish Charities, begun in 1900. The proceedings of these biennial meetings offer a fascinating picture of the particular concerns of these religious minority groups, such as the Catholic fear of Protestant proselytization, which retarded Catholic acceptance of foster care: Catholic resistance to state regulation of Catholic activities; and Jewish anxiety about the desertion of children by Jews.

Other national conferences that were central to child welfare were the decennial White House conferences on children and youth. The first of these was held in Washington in 1909. *The Proceedings of the Conference on the Care of Dependent Children*, printed by the U.S. Government Printing Office and later reprinted by Arno Press (New York, 1971), contain debate on and recommendations concerning foster care, cottage institutions, prevention of dependency, public regulation of children's agencies, and establishment of a federal children's bureau. A second conference was held in 1919, at which 200 social workers, educators, pediatricians, judges, and medical personnel formulated basic standards of health, education, and welfare. This was published as Children's Bureau, *Standards of Child Welfare. A Report of the Children's Bureau Conference, 1919*, Publication no. 60 (Washington, D.C.: Government Printing Office, 1919).

In addition to national conferences, individual states held their own regular conferences of charities and correction to give direction to their welfare activities. The Illinois Conference of Charities and Correction, started in 1896, was a particularly valuable mine of information in all areas of destitution and dependency.

Apart from conference proceedings, the journals of the growing profession of social work reflected changing national trends in child welfare. The major organs of opinion were *Charities Review* (1890-1901); and *Survey*, formerly *Charities* (1897-1905); and *Charities and the Commons* (1905-1909).

A huge amount of primary material was gleaned from the reports and publications of government and private welfare agencies. The two federal bureaus most useful to this study were the Bureau of the Census and the Children's Bureau, which was established in 1912. The Bureau of the Census produced a number of special statistical reports on the inmates of asylums and children's institutions, from which changing trends can be traced. These reports include *Benevolent Institutions, 1904* (Washington, D.C.: Government Printing Office, 1905); *Benevolent Institutions, 1910* (1913); *Paupers in Almshouses, 1910* (1915); *Paupers in Almshouses, 1923* (1924); *Children under Institutional Care, 1923* (1927); and *Children under Institutional Care, 1933* (1935).

The annual reports of the U.S. Children's Bureau detail its slow and painful development as an entity while outlining ongoing investigations, the results of which were later published. Among the most useful Children's Bureau publications for this study were those relating to mothers' pensions legislation and administration, namely *The Administration of the Aid to Mothers Law in Illinois*, Publication no. 82 (Washington, D.C.: Government Printing Office, 1921); *Laws Relating to Mothers; Pensions in the United States, Canada, Denmark and New Zealand*, Publication no. 63 (1919); and *Mothers' Aid, 1933*, Publication no. 220 (1933). An important series of studies attempted to determine the dimensions of the illegitimacy problem in the United States, the number of illegitimates, the extent of their legal protection, and child welfare services for them. The results of the bureau's research were published as *Illegitimacy as a Child Welfare Problem*, Parts I and II, Publication no. 66 and no. 75 (1920-21); *Illegitimacy Laws in the United States and Foreign Countries*, Publication no. 42 (1919); *Norwegian Laws Concerning Illegitimate Children*, Publication no. 31 (1918); *Result of Minnesota's Laws for the Protection of Children Born out of Wedlock*, Publication no. 26 (1924); *Standards of Legal Protection for Children Born out of Wedlock*, Publication no. 77 (1921). A similar summary of juvenile court provisions is contained in *Juvenile Courts at Work*, Publication no. 141 (1925); *Proceedings of the Conference on Juvenile Court Standards*, Publication no. 97 (1921); *A Summary of Juvenile Court Legislation*, Publication no. 70 (1920). In the period 1890 to 1920, little was produced on the value or validity of foster care. One useful later publication, however, was *Foster Home Care for Dependent Children*, Publication no. 136 (1926), in which 11 authorities in the field evaluated the effectiveness of various aspects of foster care.

State and local reports were also a valuable source of information. To document in detail the general trends in child welfare, I decided to focus on Illinois, Massachusetts, and New York. The main justification for this choice was that all three states were in the vanguard of reform relating to children. These states also offered useful contrasts and comparisons in the methods they adopted. Masschusetts, for example, developed much more reliance on government agencies to care for and protect dependent children, while New York relied very heavily on private associations. The annual or biennial reports of the Illinois Board of Public Charities, the New York State Board of Charities, and the Massachusetts State Board of Charities offer a wealth of information on changes in policy and funding and give detailed statistical data on the groups in their care. To supplement this at the local level, I used, for example, the Cook County, Illinois Board of Commissioners, *Charity Service Reports*, which gave general information on the level of dependency in Chicago and the surrounding areas. They also included the annual reports of the Chicago Juvenile Court, established in 1899, which gave statistical information on the children treated by the court as well as outlining its goals and the agency's changes in policy.

Obviously, private organizations were as important to this study as public organizations, given the predominance of voluntary charitable work throughout the nineteenth and early twentieth centuries. I chose a range of charities and children's agencies that reflected different types of care, regions, and religious denominations. The reports of these agencies varied considerably. Some were perfunctory, particularly in the early years, and were more concerned with finances and unusual events than with outlining their goals and methods. Others offered more detailed accounts of the agencies' policies and social work practices. Among the most useful were the Boston Church Home Society; the Chicago Home for Jewish Orphans; the Marks Nathan Jewish Orphans' Home, Chicago; the New England Home for Little Wanderers, Boston; the New York Catholic Protectory; and the Glenwood Industrial Training School, Illinois. Agencies that were based on foster care rather than institutional care were the New York Children's Aid Society, the Boston Children's Aid Society, and the Illinois Children's Home and Aid Society.

Another type of organization was the protective association, which came into existence in the late nineteenth century to deal with child abuse and neglect. The New York SPCC is particularly interesting because of its consistent opposition to public welfare and regulation. Other such organizations looked at were the Massachusetts SPCC and the Juvenile Protective Association of Chicago. The latter, comprised largely of lawyers, social workers, and members of women's clubs, was instrumental in the creation of the first juvenile court and the first juvenile psychopathic institute as well as in the rescue of neglected children. The papers of this association are kept in the library of the University of Illinois, Chicago Circle, Chicago.

The majority of these organizations were citywide or statewide in scope. An agency of national importance was the Child Welfare League of America, established in 1920. The papers, situated in the Social Welfare Archives, Minneapolis, Minnesota, contain important letters and memoranda relating to its establishment and annual reports outlining the development of policy.

Personal papers did not provide much material for this analysis. However, some useful information was obtained from the Grace Abbott papers, particularly relating to the creation of the Children's Bureau. These are housed in the library of the University of Chicago, as are the James Tufts papers and the Ernst Freund papers, both of which provide some material relating to changes in social legislation in Illinois. The Carl Christian Carstens papers at the Social Welfare Archives, Minneapolis, Minnesota, are unfortunately mostly published articles and reports but nevertheless useful. More information on Carstens is obtainable from the papers of the Child Welfare League of America, of which he was the first director.

Finally, the research for this study naturally included contemporary monographs. For the purpose of this bibliography, I shall not consider them separately but combine them with secondary material according to subject area.

CHILDREN AND YOUTH IN AMERICAN HISTORY

The history of childhood in America is a new and relatively unexplored field. Before 1960 little information was available. Alice Earle's study *Child Life in Colonial Days* (New York: Macmillan, 1899) was a typical collection of factual detail with no substantial analysis. The best works produced on this subject were Bernard Bailyn, *Education in the Forming of American Society* (Chapel Hill, N.C.: University of North Carolina Press, 1960); Arthur W. Calhoun, *A Social History of the American Family from Colonial Times to the Present*, 3 vols. (New York: Barnes & Noble, 1960); and Edmund S. Morgan, *The Puritan Family: Essays on Religion and Domestic Relations in Seventeenth Century New England* (Boston: Trustees of the Public Library, 1944). Grace Abbott's documentary history, *The Child and the State*, has already been mentioned.

Fortunately, historians have begun to fill this void. Recent publications in this area include John Demos, *A Little Commonwealth: Family Life in Plymouth Colony* (New York: Oxford University Press, 1970); John Demos and Virginia Demos, "Adolescence in Historical Perspective," *Journal of Marriage and the Family* 31 (1969): 632-38; Joseph F. Kett, "Adolescence and Youth in Nineteenth Century America," *Journal of Interdisciplinary History* 1 (1971): 283-88; and Richard L. Rapson, "The American Child as Seen by British Travellers, 1845-1935," *American Quarterly* 17 (1965): 520-34. For comparative purposes see Phillippe Aries, *Centuries of Childhood* (London: Jonathan Cape, 1962), and Ivy Pinchbeck, *Children in English Society*, 2 vols. (London: Routledge & Kegan Paul, 1969-73).

THE GENERAL HISTORY OF SOCIAL WELFARE
AND SOCIAL WORK

A number of broad accounts of American welfare were valuable in placing child welfare activity in perspective. Among the early discussions of charity were Boris D. Bogen, *Jewish Philanthropy* (New York: Macmillan, 1917); Edward T. Devine, *Misery and Its Causes* (New York: Macmillan, 1918); and Amos Warner, *American Charities* (New York: Thomas Crowell, 1894). More recent analyses include Robert H. Bremner, *American Philanthropy* (Chicago: University of Chicago Press, 1960) and *From the Depths: The Discovery of Poverty in the United States* (New York: New York University Press, 1967); Frank J. Bruno, *Trends in Social Work, 1874-1956: A History Based on the Proceedings of the National Conference of Social Work* (New York: Columbia University Press, 1957); Clarke C. Chambers, *Seedtime of Reform: American Social Service and Social Action 1918-1933* (Minneapolis, Minn.: University of Minnesota Press, 1963); Nathan Huggins, *Protestants Against Poverty: Boston's Charities, 1870-1900* (Westport, Conn.: Greenwood Press, 1971); George Jacoby, *Catholic Charities in Nineteenth Century New York* (Washington, D.C.: Catholic University of America, 1941); Francis E. Lane, *American Charities and the Child of the Immigrant* (Washington, D.C.: Catholic University of America, 1932); and Walter I. Trattner, *From Poor Law to Welfare State* (New York: Free Press, 1974).

To trace the development of social work as a profession, I used Roy Lubove, *The Professional Altruist: The Emergence of Social Work as a Career, 1880-1930* (Cambridge, Mass.: Harvard University Press, 1965), the best detailed account of the emergence of the profession, and Kathleen Woodroofe, *From Charity to Social Work in England and the United States* (London: Routledge & Kegan Paul, 1962), an extremely useful comparative study. Further information on social work education I drew from Ernest V. Hollis and Alice T. Taylor, *Social Work Education in the United States* (New York: Columbia University Press, 1951), and Elizabeth Meir, *A History of the New York School of Social Work* (New York: Columbia University Press, 1954).

There are few biographies of individuals relevant to this area of research. There is, for example, no biography of Hastings Hornell Hart or Carstens, although Trattner's *Homer Folks: Pioneer in Social Welfare* (New York: Columbia University Press, 1968) is a welcome addition to the field. Jane Addams's attempt to rescue Julia Lathrop from obscurity in *My Friend, Julia Lathrop* (New York: Macmillan, 1935) is a valuable biography, but a more distanced analysis of this remarkable woman is much needed. Florence Kelley has been more fortunate, in having two biographies, Josephine Goldmark's *Impatient Crusader: Florence Kelley's Life Story* (Urbana, Ill.: University of Illinois, 1953) and Dorothy Blumberg's *Florence Kelley: The Making of a Social Pioneer* (New York: August M. Kelley, 1960).

FOSTER CARE AND THE INSTITUTION

A significant part of this research has involved the debate between foster care and the institution as the best means of caring for children outside their own homes. Apart from the conference papers and journal articles, the following contemporary accounts were of key importance: Charles Loring Brace, *The Dangerous Classes of New York and Twenty Years Work among Them* (New York: Winkoop & Hallenbeck, 1872), an account of the destitute youth of New York and Brace's programs for their salvation; Homer Folks, *Care of Destitute, Neglected and Delinquent Children* (New York: J. B. Lyon, 1900), a survey of the full range of child-saving activities; Hastings Hornell Hart, *Preventive Treatment of Neglected Children* (New York: Charities Publication Committee, 1910); and Anna Garlin Spencer and Charles W. Birtwell, eds., *The Care of Dependent, Wayward and Neglected Children* (Baltimore: Johns Hopkins Press, 1894), a collection of papers on child care. Two early evaluations of the relative types of care can be found in Sophie Van Senden Theis, *How Foster Children Turn Out* (New York: State Charities Aid Association, 1924), and Elias Trotzkey, *Institutional Care and Placing Out: The Place of Each in the Care of Dependent Children* (Chicago: Marks Nathan Jewish Orphans' Home, 1930).

A valuable source of information on this subject proved to be dissertations written in the 1920s and 1930s by graduates of social work. The work done by the graduate students at the University of Chicago permitted a much more detailed picture of institutional life to be made than would otherwise have been possible. Among the more useful sources for this study were Nathan Berman, "A Study of the Development of the Care of Dependent Jewish Children in the Chicago Area" (master's thesis, 1933); Alice Channing, "The Illinois Soldiers' Orphans' Home" (master's thesis, 1926); Benjamin Hayenga, "The Glenwood Industrial Training School: Its Development and Present Program" (master's thesis, 1935); Bertha Hosford, "Protestant Institutions for Dependent Children in Illinois" (master's thesis, 1927); and Elizabeth White, "The History and Development of the Illinois Children's Home and Aid Society" (master's thesis, 1934).

More recently, historians have given some attention to this area. Joseph M. Hawes's *Children in Urban Society: Juvenile Delinquency in Nineteenth Century America* has a useful chapter on Charles Loring Brace and the New York Children's Aid Society. A more extended treatment can be found in Miriam Langsam, *Children West: A History of the Placing Out System of the New York Children's Aid Society* (Madison, Wis.: State Historical Society of Wisconsin, 1964). The best account of the debate among philanthropists and social workers on this issue is Martin Wolins and Irving Piliavin, *Institution or Foster Family: A Century of Debate* (New York: Child Welfare League of America, 1964). Wolins has also made a defense of the institution in "The Benevolent Asylum: Some Theoretical Observations on Institutional Care," in Donnel M. Pappenfort, Dee M. Kilpatrick, and Robert W. Roberts, eds., *Child Caring: Social Policy and the Institution* (Chicago: Aldine Publishing Co., 1973). pp. 68-106. In the same volume is a useful overview of nineteenth-century institutions by Rachel B. Marks entitled "Institutions for Dependent and Delinquent Children: Histories, Nineteenth Century Statistics and Recurrent Goals," pp. 9-67. David Rothman's *The Discovery of the Asylum: Social Order and Disorder in the New Republic* (Boston: Little Brown, 1971) places the creation of children's institutions in the context of the wider spate of asylum buildings that took place in the Jacksonian period. A detailed account and analysis of an unusual form of care can be found in Jack M. Holl, *Juvenile Reform in the Progressive Era: William R. George and the Junior Republic Movement* (Ithaca, N.Y.: Cornell University Press, 1971), which deals with communities of juveniles set up along republican lines.

MOTHERS' PENSIONS

Mothers' pensions were introduced from 1911 onwards as a means of preventing dependency and neglect. Apart from conference debates and journal articles, the most useful contemporary sources are Edna E. Bullock, *Selected Articles on Mothers' Pensions* (New York: H. W. Wilson, 1915); Commonwealth of Massachusetts, *Report of the Commission on the Support of Dependent Minor Children of Widowed Mothers* (Boston, 1913); New York State, *Report of the Commission on Relief of Widowed Mothers* (Albany, 1914); and Mary Richmond, *A Study of 985 Widows Known to Certain Charity Organization Societies in 1910* (New York: Russell Sage, 1913). Of the later historical analyses, the most useful are Winifred Bell's *Aid to Dependent Children*, already noted; Mark Leff, "Consensus for Reform: The Mothers' Pension Movement in the Progressive Era," *Social Service Review* 47 (1973): 397-417; and a chapter in Roy Lubove's *The Struggle for Social Security* (Cambridge, Mass.: Harvard University Press, 1968).

PUBLIC CHILD WELFARE

The mothers' pension movement was part of a broader movement toward public welfare. Some of the useful general histories that outline this development are Edith Abbott, *Public Assistance: American Principles and Policies* (Chicago: University of Chicago Press, 1940); Sophonisba P. Breckinridge, *Public Welfare Administration in the United States* (Chicago: University of Chicago Press, 1927); Bruno, *Trends in Social Work, 1874-1956*, already mentioned; Arlien Johnson, *Public Policy and Private Charity* (Chicago: University of Chicago Press, 1931); and David M. Schneider and Albert Deutsch, *The History of Public Welfare in New York State 1867-1940* (Chicago: University of Chicago Press, 1941). Arthur Rosenberg has analyzed municipal reform in New York City at a critical period in the development toward public welfare, in his Ph.D. dissertation, "John Adams Kingsbury and the Struggle for Social Justice in New York, 1914-1918" (New York University, 1968).

One of the most significant new public child welfare agencies created in the Progressive period was the federal Children's Bureau. An early account of its creation is given by James Tobey, *The Children's Bureau: Its History, Activities and Organization* (Baltimore: Johns Hopkins Press, 1925). A later, though still brief, survey is Dorothy E. Bradbury's *Five Decades of Action: A Short History of the Children's Bureau* (Washington, D.C.: Government Printing Office, 1964). Two welcome additions to the field have been recent Ph.D. dissertations by Nancy Weiss, "Save the Children: A History of the United States Children's Bureau 1912-1918" (UCLA, 1974), and Louis Covotsos, "Child Welfare and Social Progress: A History of the United States Children's Bureau, 1912-1935" (University of Chicago, 1976).

The other major innovation of the period was the juvenile court, which dealt with dependent as well as delinquent children. The most useful contemporary accounts are Jane Addams, ed., *The Child, the Clinic and the Court* (New York: New Republic, 1925), a collection of seminal articles on the subject; Edith Abbott and Sophonisba P. Breckinridge, *The Delinquent Child and the Home* (New York: Russell Sage, 1912); Bernard Flexner and Roger N. Baldwin, *Juvenile Courts and Probation* (New York: Century, 1912); Timothy Hurley, *Origin of the Juvenile Court Law* (Chicago: Visitation and Aid Society, 1907); Helen Jeter, *The Chicago Juvenile Court* (Chicago: University of Chicago Press, 1922). Delinquency and the juvenile court system have recently received considerable attention from historians. Among the most useful analyses is Hawes, *Children in Urban Society*, already mentioned, which takes a favorable view of the creation of juvenile courts. More critical assessments can be found in Robert Mennel, *Thorns and Thistles: Juvenile Delinquency in the United States 1825-1940* (Hanover, N.H.: University Press of New England, 1973), and Anthony M. Platt, *The Child Savers: The Invention of Delinquency* (Chicago: University of Chicago Press, 1969).

THE LEGAL STATUS OF CHILDREN

Very little has been written on the development of the legal status of the child in relation to the parents and the state. Florence Kelley outlined some of the issues in her article "On Some Changes in the Legal Status of the Child Since Blackstone," *International Review* 13 (1882): 83-98. More recent surveys of legislation have largely been made from a legal rather than an historical perspective, for example, Helen Clarke, *Social Legislation: American Laws Dealing with Family, Child and Dependent* (New York: Appleton-Century Co., 1940), and Chester S. Vernier, *American Family Law*, 8 vols. (Westport, Conn.: Greenwood Press, 1936).

The three main areas of legal rights dealt with in this study are child abuse, desertion, and the rights of illegitimates. The issue of physical force against children has hardly been touched by historians. The only accounts of the early societies to protect children from parental abuse are Roswell C. McCrea's *The Humane Movement: A Descriptive Survey* (New York: Columbia University Press, 1910), and William J. Schultz's "The Humane Movement in the United States 1910-1922," *Columbia University Studies in History, Economics and Public Law*, Study no. 1 (New York: Columbia University Press, 1924), pp. 1-320. Hopefully it is a situation that will soon be rectified. With respect to desertion and nonsupport, the most important contemporary monographs are Lillian Brandt, *574 Deserters and their Families* (New York: Charity Organization Society, 1905); Joanna Colcord, *Broken Homes: A Study of Family Desertion and its Social Treatment* (New York: Russell Sage, 1919), and Earl E. Eubank, *A Study of Family Desertion* (Chicago: City of Chicago Department of Public Welfare, 1916). Similarly there is a dearth of information on the problems that were faced by unwed mothers and illegitimate children in the past. Useful sources for this topic are Kate Walker Barrett, "Motherhood as a means of Regeneration" (Washington, D.C.: National Florence Crittendon Mission, 1910); Louise de Koven Bowen, *A Study of Bastardy Cases* (Chicago: Juvenile Protective Association, 1914); Juvenile Protective Association of Chicago, *The Care of Illegitimate Children in Chicago* (Chicago, the Association, 1913); Percy Kammerer, *The Unmarried Mother* (Montclair, N.J.: Patterson Smith, 1969, first printed Boston: Little, Brown, 1918) and George Mangold, *Children Born out of Wedlock*, (Columbia, Mo.: University of Missouri Press, 1921). Publications of the U.S. Children's Bureau have been cited earlier.

CURRENT WELFARE PROBLEMS

Finally, this study has benefited considerably from the use of recent material debating the adequacy of the present American welfare system, particularly as it involves children. This material has highlighted the continuities in the welfare system and has provided a greater understanding of the flaws present at the inception of many of the welfare programs for dependent and neglected children. Those I have found most illuminating are David Bakan, *Slaughter of the Innocents* (San Francisco: Jossey Bass, Inc., 1971), on the physical abuse of children; Joseph Goldstein, Anna Freud, and Albert J. Soluit, *Beyond the Best Interests of the Child* (New York: Free Press, 1973), a critique of child placement decisions; Joel Handler and Ellen Hollingsworth, *The Deserving Poor: A Study of Welfare Administration* (Chicago: Markham, 1971), and Joel Handler, *Reforming the Poor* (New York: Basic Books, 1973), both critical of the discriminatory treatment of the poor; Sanford Katz, ed., *The Youngest Minority: Lawyers in Defense of Children* (Chicago: American Bar Association, 1974 and 1977), Vols. 1 and 2, collections of critical articles previously published in the *Family Law Quarterly* on all aspects of the law and children; Frances Fox Piven and Richard A. Cloward, *Regulating the Poor: The Functions of Public Welfare* (New York: Vintage Books, 1971), on the use of relief in regulating the political and economic behavior of the poor; Alvin Schorr, ed., *Children and Decent People* (New York: Basic Books, 1974), a critical evaluation of services to children.

INDEX

About the Author

SUSAN TIFFIN teaches American History at the University of New South Wales in Australia. She specializes in the study of reform movements and women's history.